Thinking between the Lines

Thinking between the Lines
Computers and the Comprehension of Causal Descriptions

Gary C. Borchardt

The MIT Press
Cambridge, Massachusetts
London, England

This book was printed and bound in the United States of America.

Library of Congress Cataloging-in-Publication Data

Borchardt, Gary C.
  Thinking between the lines : computers and the comprehension of causal descriptions / Gary C. Borchardt.
      p.   cm. — (Artificial intelligence)
  Based on the author's thesis (doctoral—MIT Artificial Intelligence Laboratory), 1992.
  Includes bibliographical references and index.
  ISBN 0-262-02374-1
  1. Natural language processing (Computer science) 2. Artificial intelligence.
3. Machine learning. I. Title. II. Series: Artificial intelligence (Cambridge, Mass.)
QA76.9.N38B67   1994
006.3'5—dc20   93-36770
                                                            CIP

*To my wife Sandy,
my parents, Howard and Amy Borchardt,
and my brother Don and sister Paula*

Contents

Series Foreword   ix

Acknowledgments   xi

1   Introduction   1

1.1   What This Book Is About   1

1.2   The Causal Reconstruction Task   5

1.3   The Transition Space Representation   9

1.4   The PATHFINDER Program   22

1.5   A Note to the Reader   33

2   Causal Reconstruction   35

2.1   A Closer Look at the Problem   35

2.2   Task Restrictions for PATHFINDER   39

3   Transition Space   49

3.1   Guidelines from Perceptual Psychology   49

3.2   Representing Transitions and Events   52

3.3   Using Language to Generate Representations   62

4   Matching in Transition Space   69

4.1   Overview   69

4.2   Direct Matches between Referenced Events   73

4.3   Matches Involving Precedent Events   91

5   Inference, Background Statements and Assumptions   99

5.1   Overview   99

5.2   Employing Inference   106

5.3   Making Use of Background Statements   117

5.4   Identifying Supporting Assumptions   123

6   Exploratory Transformations   127

6.1   Overview   127

6.2   Information-Preserving Transformations   136

6.3   Non-Information-Preserving Transformations   147

7   Making Use of Connecting Statements   169

7.1   Overview   169

7.2   Temporal Ordering Statements   174

7.3   Other Specifications of Association   178

8   An Extended Example   185

8.1   Phase 1: Parsing and Encoding the Input   185

8.2   Phase 2: Applying Exploratory Transformations   196

8.3   Phase 3: Associating the Events   198

8.4   Phase 4: Answering Questions   204

9   Related Literature   213

9.1   Research in Artificial Intelligence   213

9.2   Research in Psychology   224

9.3   Research in Linguistics and Philosophy   228

10   Conclusions   233

10.1 Contributions of the Research   233

10.2 Extending the Approach   237

10.3 New Horizons   241

A   PATHFINDER Implementation   251

B   PATHFINDER Test Examples   259

Glossary   275

Bibliography   283

Index   295

Series Foreword

Artificial intelligence is the study of intelligence using the ideas and methods of computation. Unfortunately a definition of intelligence seems impossible at the moment because intelligence appears to be an amalgam of so many information-processing and information-representation abilities.

Of course psychology, philosophy, linguistics, and related disciplines offer various perspectives and methodologies for studying intelligence. For the most part, however, the theories proposed in these fields are too incomplete and too vaguely stated to be realized in computational terms. Something more is needed, even though valuable ideas, relationships, and constraints can be gleaned from traditional studies of what are, after all, impressive existence proofs that intelligence is in fact possible.

Artificial intelligence offers a new perspective and a new methodology. Its central goal is to make computers intelligent, both to make them more useful and to understand the principles that make intelligence possible. That intelligent computers will be extremely useful is obvious. The more profound point is that artificial intelligence aims to understand intelligence using the ideas and methods of computation, thus offering a radically new and different basis for theory formation. Most of the people doing work in artificial intelligence believe that these theories will apply to any intelligent information processor, whether biological or solid state.

There are side effects that deserve attention, too. Any program that will successfully model even a small part of intelligence will be inherently massive and complex. Consequently artificial intelligence continually confronts the limits of computer-science technology. The problems encountered have been hard enough and interesting enough to seduce artificial intelligence people into working on them with enthusiasm. It is natural, then, that there has been a steady flow of ideas from artificial intelligence to computer science, and the flow shows no signs of abating.

The purpose of this series in artificial intelligence is to provide people in many areas, both professionals and students, with timely, detailed information about what is happening on the frontiers in research centers all over the world.

J. Michael Brady
Daniel G. Bobrow
Randall Davis

Acknowledgments

This book grew out of my doctoral dissertation, which was completed at the MIT Artificial Intelligence Laboratory in 1992.

First and foremost, I thank my dissertation supervisor, Patrick Winston, for helping me to see the larger issues pertaining to this work and key ideas embodied in the approach. Patrick's unfailing encouragement was a great inspiration to me in carrying out this research.

I also heartily thank Randall Davis, David Waltz and Susan Carey for serving on my dissertation committee. Randy helped me to sort through a maze of initial intuitions and taught me the importance of stating ideas clearly and evaluating them from all angles. David provided an initial inspiration for this work by serving as my master's thesis supervisor at the University of Illinois. Then and now, I have relied on his keen intuitions regarding the interaction between intelligent reasoning, language and perception. Susan introduced me to a wealth of related literature in psychology and other areas of cognitive science, and helped me to pose the ideas of this research in a manner consistent with this broader context.

Particularly helpful to me were the weekly meetings of the Learning Group at the MIT AI Laboratory. Under Patrick's guidance, our discussions covered a range of topics from machine learning to knowledge representation, reasoning, and perception. This research owes much to the comments and suggestions of many members of this group, including Rick Lathrop, Jintae Lee, Lukas Ruecker, Sajit Rao, Michael de la Maza, Zakia Zerhouni, Marty Hiller, Carl Manning, Deniz Yuret, Sigrid Unseld, Michael Sassin, Jonathan Amsterdam and David Kirsh.

Several other members of the AI Laboratory and other institutions provided important feedback—sometimes unknowingly—on segments of this work, including Jeff Siskind, Boris Katz, Michael Brent, John Mallery, Jeremy Wertheimer, Howard Shrobe, Lynn Stein, Michael Caine, Tom Stahovich, Bob Berwick, Ramesh Patil, Peter Szolovits, Ira Haimowitz, Yeona Jang, Rich Doyle, Steve Chien, Eric Biefeld, Usama Fayyad, Meemong Lee, Tom Gruber, Richard Fikes, Edward Feigenbaum, Robert Engelmore, Yumi Iwasaki, Pandu Nayak, Nils Nilsson, B. Chandrasekaran, Barbara Grosz, Candy Sidner, Cecile Balkanski, Chuck Rich, Ben Kuipers, Brian Williams, Ken Forbus, Daniel Bobrow, Johan de Kleer, James Allen, Lenhart Schubert, David Traum, Dana Ballard, and others whom I will later regret not having mentioned.

I thank the Advanced Research Projects Agency for supporting a substantial portion of this work through Office of Naval Research contract number N00014-85-K-0124.

In addition, I thank my officemates over the past several years—Mike Kashket, Bob Givan, Masahide Konishi, Yasuo Kagawa, Michael Coen and Masaki Yamamoto—for many enjoyable discussions and diversions. And I thank the Vile Servers for getting me addicted to volleyball.

I am grateful to Zamir Bavel of the University of Kansas for introducing me to the world of research, and to Jerry Solomon of the Jet Propulsion Laboratory for encouragement and professional guidance.

To my parents, brother and sister, I extend a deep appreciation for everything that is part of growing up in a wonderful family.

Finally, I thank my wife Sandy for all of the love, companionship and support she has provided, in spite of my having spent the first five years of our marriage in graduate school.

Thinking between the Lines

1 Introduction

1.1 What This Book Is About

We are witnessing the dawn of a new age in which computers will play an increasingly important role in the dissemination of technical knowledge: from experts to students, among scientists and engineers, and from manufacturers to consumers. In this book, we focus on how computers may deal effectively with a particular form of technical knowledge—written causal descriptions of the sort commonly found in encyclopedias, reports and user manuals.

The importance of written causal descriptions can hardly be overstated. Not only are such descriptions extremely abundant, but humans find this form easy to produce and consume. Furthermore, written descriptions cover a wide range of phenomena humans find difficult to describe by other means: complex interactions such as combustion and phase changes; activity involving intuitive concepts such as beams of light, paths and collections; and metaphorically-modeled behavior such as radio signals "spreading" in space.

In dealing effectively with written causal descriptions, computers must treat them not as opaque sequences of characters to be retrieved on cue and sent here or there; rather, computers must be able to understand the descriptions to the extent that they can perform non-trivial tasks such as answering detailed questions about the described physical activities, comparing alternate descriptions of an activity, and summarizing or elaborating descriptions in order to meet the needs of particular recipients. These functions require computers to mimic key aspects of human reading comprehension—in essence, "thinking between the lines" to supply missing objects and events, draw new assertions by inference, and, of critical importance, to determine how the various events in a description fit together to form causal chains and overlapping accounts of activity, as often these relationships are left implicit by a description.

There are three key components to the research presented in this book. Briefly, these are:

The causal reconstruction task. This task codifies the problem of understanding written causal descriptions and involves a sequence of three steps: reading a description, forming an internal model of the described behavior, and demonstrating comprehension through question answering.

The transition space representation. This representation depicts physical events as path fragments in a space of *transitions*—combinations of changes expressible in everyday language. Partial matches between the transition space renderings of events are used as a basis for identifying inter-event relationships in causal descriptions.

The PATHFINDER program. This program demonstrates the use of the transition space representation in performing causal reconstruction on short causal descriptions presented in simplified English. All of the examples in this book have been processed by PATHFINDER.

An Example

To illustrate the problem of understanding written causal descriptions—the causal reconstruction problem—consider the following sentences appearing in the opening paragraph of the entry for "camera" in the *Encyclopedia Americana* ([Grolier Inc., 1989], v. 5, p. 265). PATHFINDER's processing of a slightly simplified version of this description is discussed in section 1.4 and more extensively in chapter 8.

> **CAMERA.** The basic function of a camera is to record a permanent image on a piece of film. When light enters a camera, it passes through a lens and converges on the film. It forms a latent image on the film by chemically altering the silver halides contained in the film emulsion.

Suppose this description is given to a human who is previously unfamiliar with the operation of a camera. We might then reasonably expect that after reading the description, the human would be able to answer non-trivial questions such as the following:

"What happens to the distance between the light and the film?" (... This distance decreases, then disappears as the light converges on the film.)

"How does the light 'converging on the film' relate to the light 'forming the image on the film?'" (...The former causes the chemical alteration of the silver halides, which change appearance, thus constituting the latter.)

"How could a building reflecting light into the camera cause the light to converge on the film?" (...This event ends with light entering the camera, from which it passes through the lens and converges on the film.)

"Does the light come into contact with the film emulsion?" (...Yes. The light contacts the silver halides while chemically altering them, and as these are a part of the emulsion, the light must contact the emulsion.)

To answer these questions, the reader must identify precise relationships between the various events listed in the description and use this knowledge to form a unified account of the described activity. The first question requires knowledge of the temporal sequencing and overlapping of events, so that the progression of changes in a particular attribute can be recounted. The second question requires a summarization of the indirect relationship between two events in the description. The third and fourth questions introduce new events to be associated causally with existing events or as a redescription of part of the activity.

Target Applications

As illustrated above, causal reconstruction involves a combination of language comprehension, language generation, and reasoning capabilities. This combination of capabilities is important to the construction of a range of artificial intelligence applications, six of which are listed in Figure 1.1. Toward the top of the figure, the applications require a somewhat smaller range of capabilities as concerns language comprehension, language generation and reasoning. Toward the bottom, they require a greater range of capabilities. In particular, we might expect that an occasional communication failure would be tolerated for the first and third applications, knowledge acquisition facilities and intelligent technical manuals, because both involve interaction between a teacher and a learner. The other four applications involve interaction more in the spirit of professional consultation, where communication failures would

Knowledge acquisition facilities (c)

By accepting causal knowledge in the form of written descriptions, knowledge acquisition facilities will better accommodate the verbal skills of human teachers. Also, the comprehension process can help uncover hidden gaps in a target knowledge base.

Intelligent service directories (C)

Supplied with a collection of written descriptions outlining services offered by various corporations, government entities and individuals, these programs will assist users in locating particular services relevant to their needs.

Intelligent technical manuals (C,g)

These programs will provide explanations and answer questions about the operation of specific physical systems (e.g., an air-conditioning system for a building). The programs will be prepared in part through the input of written causal descriptions.

Technical design documentation systems (C,G)

These programs will help facilitate communication among engineers working on the design of complex physical systems: comparing required behaviors to modeled or observed behaviors, identifying design precedents, preparing reports, and so forth.

Speculative causal reasoning systems (C,G,r)

By drawing upon an accumulation of written causal descriptions concerning events in a complex environment (e.g., a corporation), these programs will allow users to enumerate possible consequences and side-effects for proposed actions.

Collaborative diagnosis/prediction systems (C,G,R)

These programs will maintain specific areas of expertise and work as a team with other programs and humans in performing difficult reasoning tasks. Each program must be able to rephrase explanations and questions to meet the needs of particular recipients.

Figure 1.1
Target applications involving causal reconstruction (c = comprehension allowing retries, C = comprehension without retries, g = generation allowing retries, G = generation without retries, r = speculative causal reasoning, R = expert-level causal reasoning).

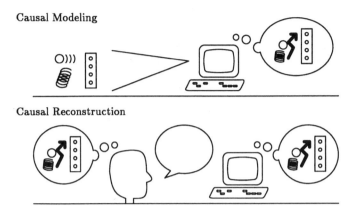

Figure 1.2
Causal modeling versus causal reconstruction.

presumably be more disruptive. At the end of the book, in section 10.3, these six applications are revisited with an eye toward incorporating the book's techniques into their construction.

1.2   The Causal Reconstruction Task

Causal reconstruction is related to causal modeling ([Doyle, 1988], [Pearl and Verma, 1991]) in that both tasks involve *acquisition* of knowledge needed to perform causal reasoning. The tasks differ with respect to the source of this knowledge. Figure 1.2 illustrates the two tasks schematically. In causal modeling, causal knowledge is obtained from direct observation of the environment. In particular, the input data has not been organized or filtered by an intermediate agent prior to entry into the program. In contrast, causal reconstruction involves input expressly supplied by an intermediate agent already possessing causal knowledge of a situation. While the research presented here concerns textual input only, in general, the input might vary between text, diagrams, animations, numerical data, equations, and other types of information.

The presence of the intermediate agent affects the causal reconstruction task profoundly in two ways. The first of these concerns the input provided to the comprehender. Assuming that the intermediate agent

is committed to efficient communication of the intended causal information, we may characterize that agent as a "cooperative" participant in
the communication process and expect the agent to comply where possible with conversational maxims of the sort outlined by Grice [1975]:[1]

The maxim of quantity. Provide as much information as is required
for the current purposes of the exchange, but do not provide more
information than is required.

The maxim of quality. Try to make your contribution one that is
true.

The maxim of relation. Be relevant.

The maxim of manner. Be perspicuous. (Avoid obscurity of expression, avoid ambiguity, be brief and be orderly.)

As a slight simplification, we raise these maxims to the level of *requirements* for writers of causal descriptions, rather than simply admonitions
allowing for compromise in difficult situations. From the comprehender's perspective, these constraints sanction inferences in certain cases.
For example, from the maxim of relation, the comprehender may assume
that because a particular piece of information has been included in the
input text, it is indeed relevant and must be related to some other piece
of information in the input text.

The above maxims also speak to the nature of input provided specifically for consumption by programs. We may note that Grice's maxims
depend on the intended audience of an utterance; for example, in describing a situation to a child, the writer must include more information.
For automated comprehension of causal descriptions, it is entirely un-
clear what supporting knowledge a program ought to have available to
it for use in comprehension. Thus, for the sake of testability given a
lack of standardized background knowledge, we stipulate an absence of
relevant supporting knowledge on the part of the program. As a result,
we require definitions for events, static properties of objects, rules of inference and so forth to accompany an input description. This simplifies
the task, to be sure, but by no means trivializes it. Given the pieces of
a puzzle, the program must still determine how these pieces fit together.

---

[1] Although these constraints are advanced with respect to spoken interaction, we
would expect writers of causal descriptions to obey such constraints as well.

The second profound effect of the intermediate agent in causal reconstruction concerns the manner in which we must test for successful completion of the task. In causal reconstruction, the task is not necessarily one of modeling an existing causal system in the world: for that matter, the input description could conceivably concern a fictitious system. Rather, the task is one of replicating a causal model known to the intermediate agent (hence, the use of the term "reconstruction"). As a result, a test for successful completion of the task must somehow compare the comprehender's inferred causal model with the writer's original model. Chapter 2 discusses this issue as part of a detailed presentation of the causal reconstruction task and various simplifications adopted for execution of the task by PATHFINDER. Briefly, in testing a program for successful completion of the task, we require the program to answer a range of questions, such that the program's internal model of the described activity is sufficiently revealed to enable us to assess whether or not the original input description could alternatively serve as an account of the program's new model of the activity. This assessment is made using a set of evaluation criteria derived from Grice's maxims.

Difficulty of the Task

Given the general nature of the causal reconstruction task, just how difficult is it? For one thing, various structural aspects of causal descriptions would seem to provide some help to the comprehender. As a starting point, suppose the input descriptions consist solely of explicit statements of event occurrences such as "The hammer strikes the firing pin."—*event references*, as described in chapter 2. Even in this simple case, narrative ordering of the event references can be taken as a clue to chronological or even causal ordering of the indicated events. In the following simple description, narrative ordering correctly indicates a causal relationship between the first and second events.

> The steam rises.
> The steam contacts the metal plate.

Similarly, causal chains of events may be constructed by considering the identities of objects participating in the events and the various roles taken by these objects—"agent," "patient" and so forth as described in the linguistics literature on thematic relations (see, for example, [van

Riemsdijk and Williams, 1986], [Fillmore, 1968]). In the example below, a causal chain from the first event to the second event is suggested by both narrative ordering and the fact that "the staple" appears as the patient in the first event and then as the agent in the second event.

> The metal tab presses against the staple.
> The staple pierces the paper.

On the other hand, there are also many cases where these simple heuristics do not work, as illustrated by the following two examples:

> The hand holds the bolt.
> The bolt remains between the first finger and the second finger.
>
> The metal table melts the ice cube.
> The ice cube lands on the metal table.

In the first example, the events do not form a chain as suggested by both narrative ordering and object role-playing; rather, the events are concurrent, with the second merely restating part of the activity of the first. In the second example, the narrative ordering heuristic would suggest a causal chain from the first event to the second. In this case, however, the only plausible interpretation is that the second event, landing on the metal table, has caused the first event, melting of the ice cube.

Another source of assistance to the reader are explicit indications of inter-event relationships. In chapter 2, special sentences called *connecting statements* are introduced to serve in this capacity, explicitly asserting, for example, that one event causes another, precedes another, or is a part of another (e.g., "The burner heating the pan causes the wax to melt.")

While such declarations do provide assistance in causal reconstruction, they do not help as much as might be expected. For one thing, grammatical constructions taking on the function of connecting statements simply do not appear with enough regularity in written descriptions to provide dependable indications of inter-event relationships. There would seem to be two reasons why this is so. First, it is rather cumbersome to explicitly state all of the inter-event associations for a set of events: in some cases we could require on the order of N^2 such indications for a set of N events, since by knowing that event A is a part of event C and that event B is also a part of event C, we still do not know how events A and B relate to one another. The second reason is that, at least for descriptions employing familiar language, humans are quite accomplished at independently *recognizing* inter-event relationships given simple statements of the occurrence of those events. Thus, not only would connecting statements be unnecessary in many cases, but by Grice's maxim of quantity they would even be undesirable, as the resulting descriptions would then be overinformative.[2]

However, there is an even more fundamental shortcoming of explicit indications of inter-event associations, and this shortcoming applies also to the narrative ordering and object role-playing heuristics in those cases where they provide useful clues. The problem is that all of these devices provide only *general* indications of how particular events are related to one another. In the above situation involving events A, B and C, what we really need to know is which parts of event C correspond to each of the events A and B. Similarly, if we are told that event I causes event J, we still do not know what part of I leads to the initiation of J—is it the middle of I? The end of I? Or does I cause an intermediate event which causes J? The reader must determine these correspondences in order to answer questions about the time sequence of changes for particular attributes, such as the first question listed above for the camera description. As a result, the reader must take recourse in his or her knowledge of *what happens* during particular types of events, using this knowledge to work out specific inter-event relationships consistent with the indications provided by devices like connecting statements and clues like narrative ordering and object role-playing.

1.3   The Transition Space Representation

Transition space specifically targets the issue of representing "what happens" during physical events in such a way as to facilitate causal reconstruction. Two important insights are embodied in this approach. First, by representing events primarily in terms of transitions—or sets of *changes* occurring during the temporal unfolding of events—a wide range of associations between events may be recognized by looking for partial matches, or overlaps, between the representations of individual

---

[2] Of course, for complex descriptions or those involving language less familiar to the reader, a higher number of connecting statements are to be expected, as in advanced technical materials.

events. As detailed in chapters 3 and 9, the representation of physical activity primarily in terms of changes—as opposed to states—draws motivation from two general sources:

- Research in psychology characterizes perceived causality as an association between consecutive changes in a scene—as, for example, when a person observes an ongoing sequence of physical activity [Miller and Johnson-Laird, 1976] [Michotte, 1946].

- When describing activity—especially where qualitative changes are involved—it is often necessary to refer explicitly to changes rather than their component states as causal antecedents and consequents. For example, if two objects come into contact and one breaks, it is not the state of *being* in contact that causes the breakage, but rather a *transition* from non-contact to contact. Similarly, the causal effect is not one of *being* broken, but *becoming* broken.

The second major insight is that the representation of physical activity in terms of transitions is easy to generate from simple, stylized verbal accounts of what happens during particular events. This would seem to be because language inherently stresses information about transitions when used to describe the temporal unfolding of physical events.

Collecting these ideas together, we may conceptualize a large space, *transition space*, whose points—or transitions—correspond to temporally-coordinated combinations of changes in various attributes of various objects. Individual changes occurring within particular transitions are grounded in simple English statements of the sort listed below (attributes appear in boldface, indications of change appear in italics).

> The **contact** between the steam and the metal plate *appears*.
> The **concentration** of the solution *increases*.
> The **appearance** of the film *changes*.
> The pin *becomes* **a part of** the structure.
> The water *remains* **inside** the tank.

Miller and Johnson-Laird [1976] enumerate a large number of such attributes and characterize them as typically unary or binary, and additionally either quantitative (e.g., "length" or "pressure") or qualitative (e.g., "color" or "contact"). Boolean attributes (e.g., "contact," "inside") may be considered a subset of the qualitative attributes.

Assuming the existence of a "false" or "absent" value in the range of each attribute, then if a particular attribute of one or more objects is specified as either present or absent at each of two time points, one of which follows the other, and we include possible information concerning the qualitative relationship between the attribute values at the two time points, then the following ten change characterizations cover the range of alternate circumstances based on this information:

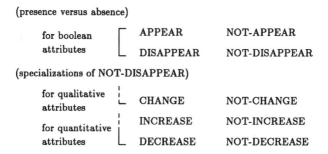

(presence versus absence)

for boolean attributes	APPEAR	NOT-APPEAR
	DISAPPEAR	NOT-DISAPPEAR

(specializations of NOT-DISAPPEAR)

for qualitative attributes	CHANGE	NOT-CHANGE
for quantitative attributes	INCREASE	NOT-INCREASE
	DECREASE	NOT-DECREASE

These ten change characterizations are depicted as predicates taking four arguments: an attribute of concern, an object or tuple of objects, a first time point and a second time point. The assertions below correspond to each of the English statements listed in the above discussion.

```
APPEAR(contact, <the-steam, the-metal-plate>, t1, t2)
INCREASE(concentration, the-solution, t3, t4)
CHANGE(appearance, the-film, t5, t6)
APPEAR(a-part-of, <the-pin, the-structure>, t7, t8)
NOT-DISAPPEAR(inside, <the-water, the-tank>, t9, t10)
```

Two primitive five-argument predicates, EQUAL and GREATER, plus their negations, form a basis for the entire representation. Details of this formulation are provided in chapter 3. From the primitive predicates, six predicates are defined for assertions at a single time point, and the ten predicates listed above are defined for assertions between time points. The higher-level predicates serve as a useful shorthand for commonly-used characterizations, while the underlying primitives provide a substrate for conducting matching and inference.

A *transition* is taken to be a set of assertions at and between two ordered time points. Events are sequences, or more generally, directed acyclic graphs of transitions. The representations for events are called *event traces*, as they correspond to simple paths in transition space.

Throughout this book, we will employ a special graphic format for illustrating transitions and event traces. This format highlights dynamic information, with relevant static information listed simply as assertions beneath the graphic representation. In these diagrams, the ten change characterizations are coded as follows:

A	APPEAR	A̸	NOT-APPEAR
D	DISAPPEAR	D̸	NOT-DISAPPEAR
△	CHANGE	△̸	NOT-CHANGE
+	INCREASE	+̸	NOT-INCREASE
−	DECREASE	−̸	NOT-DECREASE

Below is a graphic representation of an event trace depicting the event "push away." This event has two transitions, each specified as a column of coded assertions between vertical lines depicting time points. The time points are labeled at the bottom, and arguments to each attribute are provided at the left. Also, for expository purposes, a drawing is included above each transition: such drawings are not a part of the actual representation used by PATHFINDER.

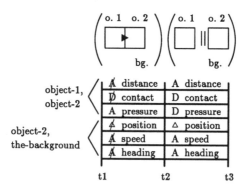

The first transition of this event trace may be read as follows: the distance between "object 1" and "object 2" does not appear, contact between the two objects does not disappear, pressure between the objects appears, the position of "object 2" does not change relative to "the background" (a fixed frame of reference), and the speed and heading of "object 2" with respect to the background do not appear. In the second transition, distance appears between the two objects, contact and pressure disappear, the position of "object 2" changes with respect to the background, and speed and heading appear for "object 2."

In general, a particular event may be represented in a range of ways in transition space, depending on such choices as: (1) the selection and granularity of participating objects for the event, (2) the selection and granularity of particular attributes for describing those objects, and (3) the granularity of time points. The transition space representation explicitly provides this latitude and furthermore explicitly addresses the issue of how such alternate descriptions of events can be related to one another. This is an inherent part of the causal reconstruction task, as the comprehension of causal descriptions inescapably involves a reconciliation of events often described at different levels of abstraction or possibly in terms of different underlying metaphors.

In the other direction, several intuitive guidelines help constrain the use of transition space in representing particular events expressible in language. For instance, in all cases we should be able to say that there exists a causal relationship between two transitions arranged in sequence in an event trace. Regarding temporal granularity, if two adjacent transitions specify equivalent sets of changes, we should merge them, and if a single transition contains a subset of changes that may be said to cause another subset of changes, the transition should be partitioned into a sequenced pair of transitions. Attributes and assertions for those attributes should be included as necessary to distinguish a typical occurrence of a particular type of event from other events. Chapter 3 describes more fully these and other intuitive guidelines for representing events in transition space.

The above event trace involves actual physical objects, and the specified attributes are grounded in perception. Because the representation itself is grounded in verbal *statements* such as listed above, there is no constraint limiting event traces to only physical/perceptual phenomena. Any quantities or attributes which may be referred to in language are available for use in the representation. Thus, we may also depict events involving conceptual phenomena, as in the following example for the event "attach." Here, representing the activity at a rather abstract level, one object engages in an arbitrary event, and a second object becomes "a part of" a third object. Specifically, this representation captures statements of the following forms: "Object 11 becomes (becomes not) engaged in event 12." and "Object 13 remains not (becomes) a part of object 14."

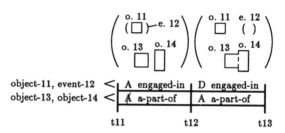

Matching between Event Traces

Given a set of event traces for the events in a causal description, simple inter-event associations may be detected by identifying partial matches between the traces. As an example, suppose that within a causal description, the following two statements appear:

> The steam moves into contact with the metal plate.
> The steam condenses on the metal plate.

Given no indication as to how these two events might be related, at least two plausible possibilities arise: the first event could actually occur first, leading to the second event, or the two could occur simultaneously, with one event possibly forming a part of the other event. A third possibility—although somewhat discouraged by the narrative ordering heuristic—would involve the second event occurring first, leading to the first event.

Suitable event traces depicting the above two events are given below. For the steam moving into contact with the metal plate, the first transition involves the steam approaching the metal plate, and the second transition involves the establishment of contact, with the steam stopping in the process. For the steam condensing on the metal plate, the first transition involves appearance of contact between the steam and the metal plate (independent of which of the two quantities is moving), and the second transition involves a transformation of the steam, such that it becomes a liquid and no longer a vapor.[3]

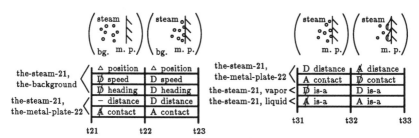

the-steam-21, the-background	△ position	△ position
	Ø speed	D speed
	Ø heading	D heading
the-steam-21, the-metal-plate-22	− distance	D distance
	A contact	A contact
	t21	t22	t23

the-steam-21, the-metal-plate-22	D distance	A distance
the-steam-21, vapor	A contact	Ø contact
the-steam-21, liquid	Ø is-a	D is-a
	A is-a	A is-a
	t31	t32	t33

Here, we will distinguish between two classes of partial matches between event traces. In the first class, *partial chaining* matches, a non-initial transition in one trace partially matches the initial transition in another trace.[4] In the second class, *partial restatement* matches, two traces match in some way other than for partial chaining. For the above two traces, there are two possible partial chaining matches (the final transition of the first trace matching the initial transition of the second trace, or the final transition of the second trace matching the initial transition of the first trace), plus three possible partial restatement matches (involving only the first transitions of both traces, only the second transitions, or both transitions of both traces). In the above case, only one such partial match exists: a partial chaining match from the first trace to the second and involving disappearance of distance and appearance of contact between the steam and the metal plate.

The match identified here is a *partial association,* as the transitions in question do not match completely. The two transitions involved in the match are really distinct points in transition space: they involve distinct time points, and each contains additional specifications not included in the other. By performing simple transformations on the event traces involved in the match, we may bring these transitions into a complete match. Here, we distinguish between two classes of transformations: *information-preserving* and *non-information-preserving.* Transformations of the first type belong to inverse pairs of transformations in transition space; transformations of the second type do not.

---

[3] PATHFINDER typically appends a number (e.g., "...-1") to the symbols for objects in order to individualize them. For the purposes of this example, arbitrary numbers ("...-21," etc.) have been selected.

[4] A slightly refined definition for partial chaining matches appears in chapter 4.

Figure 1.3 illustrates how the partial match between the original event
traces may be elaborated to produce a chain of three transformations
leading to a complete chaining match. Trace A is the original trace
for the steam moving into contact with the metal plate. This trace
is transformed by a *reduction* operation (a non-information-preserving
transformation) which removes all assertions except those involving "distance" and "contact," producing trace C. Trace B is the original trace for
the steam condensing on the metal plate. This trace is transformed first
by an *equivalence* operation (an information-preserving transformation),
replacing time points "t31" and "t32" with their matched equivalents
"t22" and "t23" and producing trace D. Trace D is then transformed by
a reduction operation, removing all assertions except those concerning
"distance" and "contact," producing trace E. Finally, traces C and E
are associated by a complete chaining match, as the second transition
in trace C is identical to the first transition in trace E.

A set of event traces linked by *complete associations*—transformations
and complete chaining or restatement matches—is called an *association
structure*. Association structures are diagramed using a second, more
abstract graphic format corresponding to a stylized three-dimensional
characterization of transition space. Here, transitions appear as points,
with event traces depicted as points, arrows, or simple directed acyclic
graphs. Associations are represented by alignment of the event traces
in three dimensions: horizontal for complete chaining matches, vertical for non-information-preserving transformations, and depthwise for
information-preserving transformations. The following diagram depicts
the sequence of associations illustrated in Figure 1.3. Heavy arrows
represent the original two traces, with lighter arrows depicting the intermediate traces formed in the elaboration of the partial match.

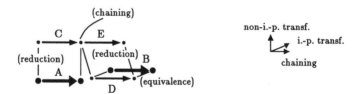

A: The steam moves into contact with the metal plate.
B: The steam condenses on the metal plate.

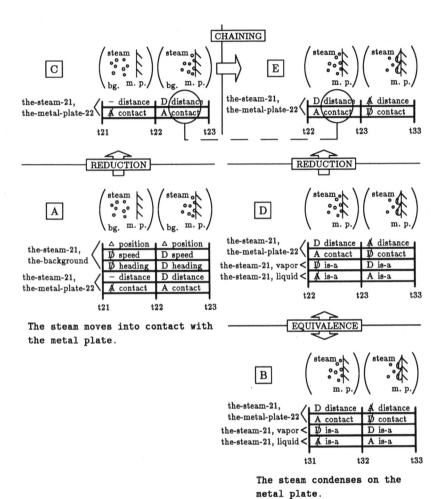

Figure 1.3
Elaboration of a partial match into a chain of complete associations involving three
transformations and a complete chaining match (see text).

Identification and elaboration of partial matches forms the core of the approach presented in this book. Where more than a single partial match exists, heuristics are used to choose an appropriate partial match for elaboration. Section 1.4 outlines the particular heuristics employed in PATHFINDER. In the remainder of this section, three important extensions to the core approach are described.

Inference and Background Statements

The first extension has to do with the incorporation of deductive inference into the approach. Chapter 5 discusses this extension in greater detail. While associations between events are detected and elaborated on the basis of partial matches, inference can be used to augment event traces with relevant new assertions, thereby increasing the likelihood of matching with other traces. Inference may concern symmetric, transitive and other properties of the primitive predicates EQUAL, NOT-EQUAL, GREATER and NOT-GREATER, or it may concern properties of particular attributes or sets of attributes (e.g., symmetry of the attribute "contact," or the fact that being inside an object that is above a second object implies being above the second object too). As part of the inference process, static "background" statements supplied as part of a causal description (e.g., "The water is inside the tank.") may be included, such that implications may be drawn from the combined assertions in individual event traces and the collective set of background statements known to the system.

A second use of inference concerns the checking of partial matches for consistency. Because a partial match between two traces may draw one or more equivalences between quantities (e.g., time points in one trace matched to time points in the other trace), it may be the case that the collective set of assertions of both traces, given the indicated equivalences, is logically inconsistent. When this happens, the partial match in question must be discarded or expanded into reduced partial matches omitting one or more of the indicated equivalences.

Exploratory Transformation of Event Traces

As a second important extension, transformations of both varieties may be applied in an exploratory manner to event traces, forming alternate characterizations of events at different levels of abstraction or in terms of different underlying metaphors. An event trace together with its transformed images forms a small "cluster" of traces, all of which participate in the association process. In this manner, a program may bridge a range of discontinuities arising from the writer's use of analogy or abstraction.

The following traces depict a simple exploratory information-preserving transformation of type *substitution*.[5] If we are told that an object "slides to a stop," it is natural to represent this by the first trace. For a rotating object like a wheel, however, a substitution of attributes taking us into the domain of spinning objects may be more appropriate. By including both traces in the association process, we can determine by matching which interpretation is correct. Beneath the event traces, the association structure fragment produced by the transformation is illustrated. By convention, we distinguish event traces produced by exploratory transformations by diagraming these arrows in outline.

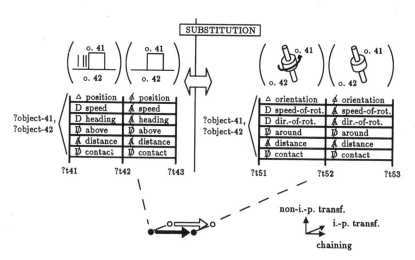

Following is an exploratory non-information-preserving transformation of type *object composition*. Suppose one object is specified as coming into contact with a second object, and the second object is a part of a third object. An alternate, more abstract depiction of the event portrays the first object as simply coming into contact with the third object. Such a situation arises in processing the camera description introduced at the beginning of this chapter: light comes into contact with

---

[5] In this book, variables are notated as symbols beginning with "?".

the silver halides as part of chemically altering them, yet this must be matched with light "converging on the film" which contains the silver halides.

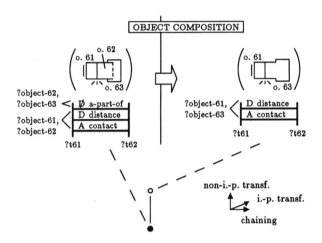

Additional varieties of both information-preserving and non-informa-tion-preserving exploratory transformations are discussed in chapter 6. The following list summarizes the repertoire of exploratory transforma-tions considered in this book.[6]

Information-preserving exploratory transformations:

Equivalence. Replacement of quantities with *synonym* quantities, pro-ducing an alternate specification of the same event.

Substitution. Replacement of quantities with *different, but parallel* quantities, producing a specification of an event distinct from the original event, yet parallel in the types of changes involved.

Non-information-preserving exploratory transformations:

Generalization. Replacement of a reference term (e.g., the object type "container") with a more general term (e.g., "physical-object").

---

[6] The complete set of *association* types employed in this book includes three further varieties: complete chaining associations and reduction transformations—these used only in the elaboration of partial matches—and inference transformations—these considered separately from the exploratory transformations.

Interval composition. Merging of two adjacent time intervals into a single composite interval, with appropriately summarized change characterizations.

Attribute composition. Reexpression of activity originally involving a set of related attributes (e.g., "height," "width" and "depth") with activity involving a single, encompassing attribute (e.g., "size").

Object composition. Reexpression of activity involving the parts of an object with activity involving the whole object.

Attribute-object reification. A transformation replacing activity involving a particular attribute with activity involving a new object representing that attribute applied to its argument (e.g., "the-speed-of-vehicle-51").

Event-attribute reification. A transformation replacing part of an event trace with an assertion involving a new attribute applied to one of the participating objects (e.g., "moving" applied to an object).

Event-object reification. A transformation replacing part of an event trace with assertions involving a new object representing the replaced activity (e.g., an object representing a collision, with other objects "engaged-in" the collision object).

Making Use of Connecting Statements

The third extension, described in chapter 7, has to do with compliance with statements appearing in the causal description and explicitly stating how particular events are to be related; for example, "The device starting to move causes the lever to start to move." As introduced briefly in section 1.2, these statements are referred to as *connecting statements*.

In many cases, it is possible to tell before elaboration of a partial match that it will either: (1) guarantee compliance with a particular connecting statement, or (2) guarantee a failure of compliance with a particular connecting statement. In the heuristics for choosing among competing partial matches, PATHFINDER rewards partial matches in the first case and abandons them in the second case. After a partial match has been elaborated, a more stringent test for compliance with connecting statements is possible. If the constraint imposed by such a statement is violated, the elaborated chain of complete associations can be discarded at that point.

1.4   The PATHFINDER Program

PATHFINDER is a 20,000 line program coded in Common Lisp and run on a Symbolics 3640 Lisp Machine. The primary component of this program is a set of utilities for representing, matching and conducting inference and transformations on events in transition space. Additional components include a parser operating on a simple context-free skeleton of English grammar, a simple language generation capability, and a set of supervisory routines for conducting causal reconstruction. PATHFINDER has been applied to over 60 causal descriptions, most involving 2–4 events, in a wide range of physical domains including: interaction between solid objects and liquids, condensation and melting, combustion, radio signals, light, chemical reactions and electric currents.

All input to PATHFINDER consists of statements in simplified English. (Sample input for the camera description appears later in this section.) First, PATHFINDER is given a causal description, consisting of (1) *event references* (e.g., "The light enters the camera.") (2) *background statements* (e.g., "The head is a part of the nail.") and, in some cases, (3) *connecting statements* (e.g., "The device starting to move causes the lever to start to move.") Next, a set of supplementary information is provided, possibly including (1) additional *background statements*, (2) *event definitions*, describing generic occurrences of events, (3) *precedent events*, which may be of use in reconstructing the activity, (4) *rules of inference,* and (5) *rules of restatement*, including specification of analogical mappings and rules of abstraction.

Given input in this form, PATHFINDER performs causal reconstruction in four phases, as outlined in Figure 1.4 (a). In the first phase, it parses the input text and uses the supplied event definitions to form event traces for all events referenced in the description. In the second phase, it extends the event traces through inference and applies exploratory transformations—these motivated by rules of restatement in the input—producing for each event a cluster of traces describing that activity in different ways. In the third phase, it enumerates a set

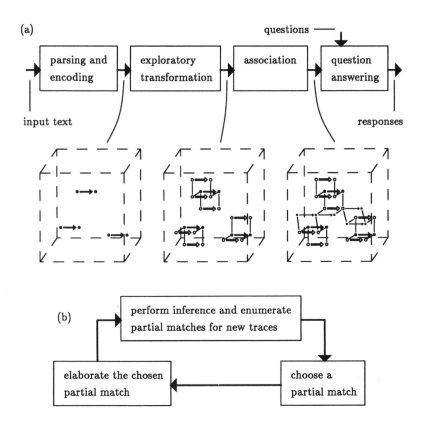

Figure 1.4
(a) Four phases of execution for PATHFINDER when performing causal reconstruction, (b) the association cycle.

of partial matches between event traces in different clusters and constructs an agenda to maintain the set of partial matches in prioritized sequence (e.g., see [Lenat, 1977]). Iteratively choosing the top-ranked partial match and then elaborating it in the manner outlined in the previous section, PATHFINDER associates the clusters together. Inference is used to check each selected partial match for consistency. In the fourth phase, when all of the events have been associated, it answers questions.

Figure 1.4 (b) details the iterative cycle of the third phase. New event traces may be introduced to the association process during each cycle.

For the initial cycle, these are all of the event traces produced in phases one and two; for subsequent cycles, these are new event traces produced during the previous cycle's elaboration of the selected partial match. In any particular cycle, all new traces are extended where possible through the application of inference, and then a matcher is run to identify partial matches between these new traces and other traces previously included in the association process. These partial matches are inserted as new entries in the agenda, and heuristics are used to score all agenda entries. The remaining steps of the association cycle include a selection of the top-ranked partial match in the agenda, and an elaboration of that partial match to produce a sequence of complete associations, possibly generating new event traces in the process of elaboration. Also as part of the elaboration process, inference is used to check the selected partial match for consistency.

Several heuristics are used in choosing the next partial match for elaboration. These heuristics are outlined below and described further in chapters 4 through 7. A detailed account of the heuristic function used in PATHFINDER appears in appendix A. The first heuristic listed below is given strongest influence over the selection process.

Matching between transitions.   Definite changes (APPEAR, DISAPPEAR, CHANGE, INCREASE and DECREASE) are weighted most, other dynamic assertions next and static assertions least.

Proximity to description events.   Penalties are introduced for matches involving precedent events or exploratory transformations of events.

Narrative ordering. Preference is given to chaining matches between events referenced consecutively in the description.

Current status of the association structure. Penalties are introduced for matches providing a second antecedent or consequent for an event, matches between events already connected via associations, and matches involving hypothesized objects (e.g., a conjectured part of a physical object).

Types of associations. Partial restatement matches are penalized slightly relative to partial chaining matches. Also, matches not fulfilling any connecting statements are penalized slightly, and matches violating a connecting statement are penalized heavily.

In addition to the above heuristics, which are applied prior to selection of a partial match for elaboration, several tests are conducted *after* the selection of a partial match. Failure to pass these tests causes the selected agenda entry to be discarded, possibly to be replaced by a set of N reduced matches, where each reduced match omits one of the N equivalence pairings between symbols as generated during the matching process (e.g., equating "t23" in one trace with "t32" in the other trace). These tests are described more fully in chapters 4 through 7 and involve the following constraints:

Equivalences between description objects. Partial matches are not allowed to equate different objects named in the causal description (e.g., "the hammer" and "the nail"). However, such objects may be equated with hypothesized objects (e.g., a finger of a hand).

Logical inconsistency. The combined assertions of two matched traces must not be logically inconsistent, given the object and time point equivalences generated by the matcher.

Violated connecting statements. A partial match may not violate an inter-event relationship specified by a connecting statement in the description or supplementary information. (Some violations can only be detected *after* the elaboration of a partial match.)

In the fourth phase of causal reconstruction, PATHFINDER fields questions of four varieties. An example of each type of question appears at the opening of this chapter, accompanying the camera description introduced there. These questions are answered either by inspecting the association structure completed in the third phase, or by performing one or more additional cycles of association followed by inspection of the resulting association structure. Specific procedures used in question answering are illustrated in the context of the following discussion.

Processing the Camera Description

The remainder of this section outlines the manner in which PATH-FINDER processes the camera description introduced in the opening of this chapter. (Chapter 8 discusses this example in greater detail.) As an overview of PATHFINDER's processing for this example, an abbreviated session transcript is given in Figures 1.5 and 1.6.

(a) *(the causal description in simplified English)*

The camera records the image on the film. The recording of
the image is a function of the camera. The light enters the
camera. The light passes through the lens. The light
converges on the film. The light forms the image on the film.
The light chemically alters the silver halides. The silver
halides are contained in the emulsion. The emulsion is a part
of the film.

(b) *(an event definition for "entering," involving physical objects)*

Object 11 entering object 12 translates to the following
event. Concurrently, object 11 remains a physical object,
object 12 remains a physical object, object 12 remains hollow,
the position of object 11 changes, the speed of object 11 does
not disappear, the heading of object 11 does not disappear,
and object 11 becomes inside object 12.

(c) *(a precedent event: change of appearance during chem. transformation)*

Object 61 changes appearance from chemical transformation.

Object 61 changing appearance from chemical transformation
translates to the following event. Concurrently, object 61
remains a physical object, object 61 becomes not made of
substance 62, object 61 becomes made of substance 63, and the
appearance of object 61 changes.

(d) *(a rule of restatement: light viewed as a physical object w.r.t. "contact")*

Concurrently, quantity 141 is a beam of light, object 142 is a
physical object, and the contact between quantity 141 and
object 142 is present. The following statement parallels the
preceding statement. Concurrently, object 151 is a physical
object, object 152 is a physical object, and the contact
between object 151 and object 152 is present.

(e) *(a rule of restatement: contact w/part summarized as contact w/whole)*

Concurrently, object 201 remains a part of object 202, the
distance between object 203 and object 201 disappears, and the
contact between object 203 and object 201 appears. The
preceding event is summarized by the following event.
Concurrently, the distance between object 203 and object 202
disappears, and the contact between object 203 and object 202
appears.

Figure 1.5
Input text for the camera description (partial).

(a) *(a question of type 1: describing the time-varying status of an attribute)*

What happens to the distance between the light and the film?

First, as the light passes through the lens, the distance between the light and the film decreases. Next, as the light converges on the film, the distance between the light and the film disappears. Next, as the camera records the image on the film, the distance between the light and the film does not appear.

(b) *(a question of type 2: describing the interrelationship between two events)*

How does the light converging on the film relate to the light forming the image on the film?

The light converging on the film causes the light to chemically alter the silver halides, which ends with the silver halides changing appearance from chemical transformation, which occurs at the end of the light forming the image on the film.

(c) *(a question of type 3: identifying a plausible causal connection)*

How could the building reflecting the light into the camera cause the light to converge on the film?

The building reflecting the light into the camera could end with the light entering the camera, which could cause the light to pass through the lens, which could cause the light to converge on the film.

(d) *(a question of type 4: restating a portion of the activity)*

Does the light come into contact with the emulsion?

Yes. The light coming into contact with the emulsion is a part of the light converging on the film.

Figure 1.6
Question answering for the camera description.

The causal description, appearing in Figure 1.5 (a), contains six event references:

```
The camera records the image on the film.
The light enters the camera.
The light passes through the lens.
The light converges on the film.
The light forms the image on the film.
The light chemically alters the silver halides.
```

The remaining statements in the description are background statements motivated by particular constructions in the original version of the text.

Following the causal description, the input file contains several segments of supplementary information, including background information concerning the types of each object (e.g., "The light is a beam of light.") generic definitions for each of the six referenced events (e.g., Figure 1.5 (b)), one precedent event—"Object 61 changes appearance from chemical transformation."—(Figure 1.5 (c)), five rules of inference, three specifications of analogical mappings concerning light viewed metaphorically as a physical object (e.g., Figure 1.5 (d)), and five rules of abstraction (e.g., Figure 1.5 (e)), all stated in terms of generic quantities.

PATHFINDER begins with an empty knowledge base of events, rules of inference and restatement, plus a minimal lexicon containing mostly closed-class lexical items such as prepositions, plus a few built-in verb groups ("change," "not disappear," and so forth). As it parses the input, PATHFINDER must be assisted in determining parts of speech. However, apart from this assistance, PATHFINDER performs its entire causal reconstruction solely on the basis of the information contained in the input file and subsequent question files (these including questions augmented by relevant supplementary information, if necessary).

For this example, PATHFINDER executes six iterations of its association cycle, working out inter-event associations among the six events referenced in the causal description, plus the one precedent event included in the supplementary information. On the first cycle of association, PATHFINDER chooses from 120 candidate partial matches. Following the association process, PATHFINDER is able to answer a range of questions including those listed in Figure 1.6.

Details of processing for this example appear in chapter 8. The following diagram illustrates a part of the association structure generated by PATHFINDER, associating "The light converges on the film." with

"The light chemically alters the silver halides." Additionally, Figure
1.7 illustrates the contents of the traces marked D, F, M, W and Z in
this diagram. Traces M, W and Z (outlined) have been formed by exploratory transformation of the original two traces, D and F. For M and
W, an information-preserving transformation (of type *substitution*) derived from the rule of restatement shown in Figure 1.5 (d) has recast
activity involving a physical object with activity involving a beam of
light.[7] For Z, a non-information-preserving transformation (of type *object composition*) derived from the rule of restatement shown in Figure
1.5 (e) has recast light contacting the silver halides as light contacting
the film. A partial chaining match has been identified between traces M
and Z, both of which specify the light contacting the film. Finally, traces
A1, B1 and C1 have been produced by elaboration of this partial chaining match (involving an equivalence mapping from Z to B1, removal of
assertions from M to A1 and from B1 to C1, and chaining from A1 to
C1).

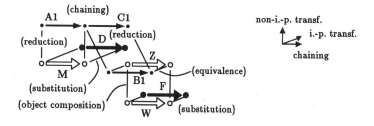

D: The light converges on the film.
F: The light chemically alters the silver halides.

The first type of question answered by PATHFINDER concerns the
time-varying status of particular attributes of objects; e.g., "What happens to the distance between the light and the film?" To answer this,
PATHFINDER forms a *composite trace* of the activity by merging the
traces in the association structure, overlapping where indicated. The
program then extracts the relevant row in the composite trace and ex-

---

[7]Regarding traces M and W in Figure 1.7: in the interest of efficiency, PATH-
FINDER routinely removes assertions from event traces when these assertions are
matched by background (static) assertions known to the system. Such is the case
regarding "the-light-1" being a "beam-of-light," and thus no such assertions appear in traces M and W as might be expected following the indicated substitution
transformation.

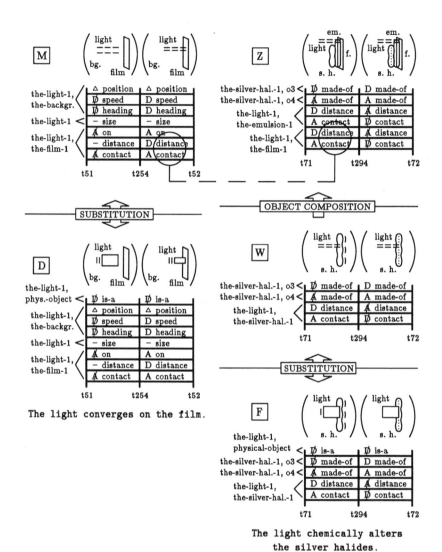

Figure 1.7
Original traces and transformed images for a portion of the camera description (see text). A partial match is identified between traces M and Z.

presses this fragment in simple English. Diagramed below is part of the composite trace for the camera description, indicating the particular row used to answer the above question. PATHFINDER's response is listed in Figure 1.6 (a).

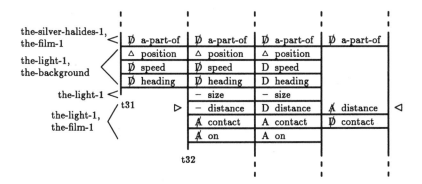

The second type of question concerns inter-event relationships; e.g., "How does the light converging on the film relate to the light forming the image on the film?" To answer this type of question, PATHFINDER extracts the relevant path in the association structure and describes this path in simple English, highlighting important associations along the way. For the above question, the relevant path in the association structure consists of a chain of 14 associations involving the description events "The light converges on the film." and "The light forms the image on the film." plus a transformed image of the description event "The light chemically alters the silver halides." and a transformed image of the precedent event "Object 61 changes appearance from chemical transformation." This chain of associations is summarized below.

> The light converges on the film.
> → SUBSTITUTION → REDUCTION
> → CHAINING → REDUCTION (inverse)
> The light chemically alters the silver halides.
> → REDUCTION → REDUCTION (inverse)
> The silver halides change appearance from chemical transformation.
> → REDUCTION → REDUCTION (inverse)
> → EQUIVALENCE → GENERALIZATION (inverse)
> → INFERENCE (inverse) → COMPOSITION
> → INFERENCE (inverse) → SUBSTITUTION
> The light forms the image on the film.

Priority	Association type	As expressed in English
1.	SUBSTITUTION	"...parallels..."
2.	CHAINING	"...causes..." / "...is caused by..."
3.	REDUCTION	"...is a part of..." / "...involves..."
4.	GENERALIZATION, COMPOSITION, and REIFICATION	"...summarizes..." / "...is summarized by..."
5.	INFERENCE	"...implies..." / "...is implied by..."
6.	EQUIVALENCE	"...is equivalent to..."

Table 1.1
Prioritization and English translations for association types, as used to describe sequences of associations in PATHFINDER.

To summarize sequences of associations, PATHFINDER uses a prioritization of association types. For each pair of description/precedent events represented along the path, a single association of highest priority is used to describe the relationship between those two events. Table 1.1 depicts the prioritization scheme found to be most effective over the set of descriptions processed by PATHFINDER.

If two associations of equal priority but opposite orientations (normal versus inverted) appear along such a path segment, PATHFINDER defaults to a temporal characterization of the inter-event relationship:

"...occurs at the beginning of ..." / "...begins with ..."
"...occurs at the end of ..." / "...ends with ..."

or, if these temporal characterizations do not fit, a catch-all characterization:

"...coincides with ..."

For the above question "How does the light converging on the film relate to the light forming the image on the film?" the answer produced by PATHFINDER is as listed in Figure 1.6 (b).[8]

---

[8] The initial traces representing the two concerned description events are both logically inconsistent, depicting "the light" as a physical object, while it is known from supplementary background statements that "the light" is a beam of light and hence not a physical object. The two substitution associations appearing along the association path recast these events in terms of activity involving a beam of light. In answering the posed question, PATHFINDER excludes mention of the logically inconsistent traces and the substitution associations required to produce consistent traces.

The third and fourth types of questions also ask about inter-event associations, but require PATHFINDER to do further association first. Otherwise, these questions are handled in the same manner as questions of the second type. To assist in the additional association, supplementary information such as event definitions may be provided with these questions. The third type of question involves plausible causal associations, as might be used in making simple predictions or explanations; e.g., "How could the building reflecting the light into the camera cause the light to converge on the film?" Figure 1.6 (c) lists PATHFINDER's response to this question. The fourth type of question asks if a new event may be used to paraphrase a part of the activity; e.g., "Does the light come into contact with the emulsion?" PATHFINDER's response to this question appears in Figure 1.6 (d).

1.5   A Note to the Reader

There are two things you should know about this book. First, some parts of it contain a fair amount of detail, which, while necessary to a clear exposition of the ideas, may also be skimmed if desired. This applies in particular to chapters 4 through 7, which are organized to present a progression of increasingly complex versions of the causal reconstruction problem, from situations involving only matching (chapter 4) to those requiring inference (chapter 5), exploratory transformations (chapter 6) and adherence to accompanying connecting statements (chapter 7). Each of these chapters begins with an overview describing the central ideas of the chapter, and the overview is followed by several sections elaborating upon those ideas with detailed examples. Chapter 8 then combines many of the ideas in chapters 4 through 7 in detailing PATHFINDER's handling of the camera description discussed in section 1.4.

Second, a particularly important component of the book is the Glossary, which contains definitions for approximately fifty terms introduced elsewhere in the book. These terms interact in a number of ways, collectively forming a conceptual framework for viewing the problem of understanding causal descriptions—this perhaps the primary substance of the book itself. As such, the Glossary provides a convenient, centralized listing of interdependencies existing between the various terms, while also serving as a brief synopsis of the conceptual theory they embody.

2 Causal Reconstruction

2.1 A Closer Look at the Problem

In this chapter, a more precise account of the causal reconstruction task is attempted. As a starting point, we take the following specification of the problem:

> Given a causal description, produce an acceptable reconstruction of the described behavior.

This definition provides a three-way fork by which specific aspects of the task may be discussed. In particular, it allows us to focus on the following three questions:

- What is a causal description?
- What is a reconstruction of a causal description?
- When is such a reconstruction to be deemed acceptable?

What Is a Causal Description?

We take a causal description to be a body of text composed by a human for the purpose of conveying knowledge of the causal workings of a particular physical system to another human or to a computer program. Human intuition is used to recognize segments of text qualifying as causal descriptions. Also, as mentioned in chapter 1, we raise Grice's maxims to the level of *requirements* rather than simply admonitions to the writer of a description, so that a causal description is expected to be adequately informative, be truthful, contain only relevant information, and be supplied in a perspicuous manner with respect to the writer's causal model of the situation in question.

As noted in chapter 1, other methods of communicating causal knowledge might be included in a more liberal definition of causal reconstruction. For example, a written description could be accompanied by diagrams, animations, numerical data, equations, or even a physical demonstration. In this book, we consider written descriptions without such additional information.

There are many intricate issues of linguistic analysis related to a discussion of the structure of naturally-occurring causal descriptions.

As our concern is with the *information* conveyed by such descriptions, rather than their precise form, we will adopt a somewhat simplified and stylized notion of what makes up a causal description—at least as far as the operation of PATHFINDER is concerned. The precise form for input text submitted to PATHFINDER is detailed in section 2.2.

What Is a Reconstruction of a Causal Description?

A reconstruction is taken to be an internal model of an activity, understandable to the comprehender, but only indirectly accessible by other agents, as through the asking and answering of questions. In a broader sense, we may take the demonstration of a comprehender's reconstruction of a described situation to include such activities as paraphrasing the input causal description, acting out or constructing an animation of the described scenario. For the purposes of this book, however, we will be concerned solely with demonstration through question answering.

For human comprehenders, it is certainly the case that the results of comprehension are only indirectly accessible in this manner. For programs it is also expedient to specify the result of processing in this way: in contrast, if we were to require a particular type of computational structure to be produced, we would be at the mercy of a trained practitioner of computer science (or worse, the designer of the program) to verify that a correct analysis had been performed. By posing questions to the program, we establish a situation in which the program's responses may be evaluated according to the commonsense intuitions possessed by adults proficient in English (or any other human language, depending on the program) and familiar with the general nature of causal behavior in the world.

Specific question types handled by PATHFINDER are described in section 2.2. While other types of questions might be posed for similar comprehension systems, one general observation may be made regarding the nature of question answering in this context. Causal descriptions as specified above contain information on two levels:

The object level—concerning properties, relationships and other attributes of physical objects and how these entities change over time (e.g., the question "What happens to the distance between the light and the film?"), and

The event level—concerning properties and relationships between events (e.g., the remaining three questions listed for the camera example: "How does the light converging on the film relate to the light forming the image on the film?" "How could the building reflecting the light into the camera cause the light to converge on the film?" and "Does the light come into contact with the emulsion?")

Questions posed to the comprehender of a causal description should address both levels of information/comprehension. On the event level, we might ask the comprehender whether one particular event causes another event. On the object level, we might as the comprehender what happens to a particular attribute of an object (say, its size) during the time-course of the described situation.

When Is a Reconstruction to Be Deemed Acceptable?

Determining whether a human or program has "understood" a piece of text such as a causal description is ultimately an intuitive judgment. There would appear to be no way to escape this reliance, as we have no means of judging the *content* of such texts apart from human comprehension of the material. In spite of this, we may specify the causal reconstruction task somewhat more precisely by decomposing the overall assessment—whether the comprehending agent has understood a supplied piece of text—into a set of assessments that are much more specific and thereby less open to dispute. The following paragraphs outline such a decomposition for the causal reconstruction task.

In advancing questions to a comprehender and evaluating the answers provided by that comprehender, an impartial observer can obtain knowledge of the comprehender's model of a described causal situation. As a first approximation, we might require that the comprehender's model correspond *exactly* to the writer's model of the described situation. But we can easily see that this is too restrictive. For example, if the described system is a mechanical one, the comprehender's model might still be acceptable if it were at a different scale in terms of physical size, or oriented differently in space, or if it were to contain parts having different shapes or composition than corresponding parts in the writer's model. A better criterion is to insist that the comprehender's model be consistent with the writer's causal model only to the extent of the information contained in the causal description. Another way of saying this is that the com-

prehender's model *must also be describable using the input description.*
Viewed in this way, we need not find a way to estimate the exact causal
model held by the writer of the description—an extremely difficult task
at best—rather, we may evaluate the comprehender's model directly by
making a supplementary appeal to Grice's maxims of conversation, this
time in the context of the input description taken as an account of the
comprehender's model as revealed through question answering. Again
raising Grice's maxims to the level of requirements rather than simply
admonitions, then if by these maxims, we find that the input description
is unacceptable as an account of the comprehender's new model, we may
then claim that the new model is faulty and that the comprehender has
failed at the task of causal reconstruction. Specifically, Grice's maxims
motivate use of the following criteria when evaluating the comprehender's understanding of the described activity.

From the maxim of quantity:

1. Does the comprehender's model introduce new objects or events
   not motivated in the causal description? (If so, the comprehender's
   model is unacceptable, because the description is required to be
   adequately informative in motivating such objects or events.)

From the maxim of quality:

2. Does the new model disagree in any way with the description?
   (If so, the new model is unacceptable, because the description is
   required to be truthful.)

3. Is the new model physically unrealizable? (If so, it is unacceptable, because we take the description to provide an account of a
   physically realizable behavior.)

From the maxim of relation:

4. Does the new model fail to incorporate any information supplied
   in the description? (If so, the new model is unacceptable, because
   the description is required to contain only relevant information.)

5. Does the new model fail to associate any pair of events? (If so,
   we may disqualify the new model on the grounds that a causal
   description is expected to relate—causally or otherwise—a set of
   events.)

From the maxim of manner:

6. Does the new model make any component of the description redundant, such that the description could be condensed without
   loss of informativeness? (Suppose the new model interprets two
   referenced events as describing the same identical activity. It may
   then be rejected on the grounds that the description is required to
   be brief and may not contain redundant statements.)

This list is not intended to be exhaustive, merely representative of the
kinds of specific intuitive assessments that may be made in evaluating
the comprehension of causal descriptions. Evaluation according to such
criteria does not require internal knowledge of a program's operation.
Also, it should be noted that in this formulation of the problem, we
do not require the comprehender's reconstruction of the situation to be
deemed "simplest," "most plausible" or otherwise subjectively superior
to another reconstruction satisfying the same criteria: all reconstructions meeting the criteria are simply designated as acceptable. For the
examples appearing in this book, the actual evaluation according to such
criteria is left to the reader.

2.2   Task Restrictions for PATHFINDER

The previous section described the causal reconstruction task in a manner independent of any particular program performing the task. In this
section, the specific task addressed by PATHFINDER is described, focusing on the input and output requirements of the program and the
functionality required of PATHFINDER in order to transform the supplied input into appropriate output.

General Considerations

PATHFINDER addresses only particular aspects of the general causal
reconstruction task. As mentioned previously, the program accepts
only written causal descriptions augmented by supplementary information and does not accept other forms of information such as diagrams,
animations or quantitative measurements. Similarly, PATHFINDER
demonstrates its comprehension only through question answering and

not through other activities such as acting out a scenario, paraphrasing
the description or constructing an animation.

Within the narrower context of text-oriented causal reconstruction,
PATHFINDER also does not address certain aspects of the task, as
listed below.

Advanced aspects of linguistic analysis. PATHFINDER operates
on a simplified, skeleton grammar of English, and thus does not
handle such phenomena as complex grammatical constructions, ellipsis, and the generalized use of adjectives and adverbs. Additionally, PATHFINDER does not address issues such as determination
of parts of speech from grammatical context, lexical and semantic
ambiguity, tense, aspect, mood, metonymy, and discourse issues
such as focus and reference.

Non-simple events. In its current instantiation, PATHFINDER does
not handle descriptions having to do with repetition, hypothetical
events, disjunctions of events, activities specified using modal aux-
iliaries such as "can," "must," and so forth, and situations having
to do with enabling and prevention.

Some types of reasoning. PATHFINDER does not handle situations
involving complex spatial computations (e.g., concerning sizes,
shapes, directions, etc.), classification of objects and situations,
and calculations of likelihood for alternative causal paths.

Intricate causal descriptions. Finally, PATHFINDER does not handle causal descriptions involving multiple paths of association between events (i.e., the graph of inter-event associations must be a
tree) and causal descriptions whose processing may involve modification of previous associations in light of constraints posed by
subsequent associations.

Within the framework of these restrictions, PATHFINDER accepts
input consisting of a stylized causal description followed by zero or more
segments of stylized supplementary information. The causal description
is composed of statements of the following three varieties:

Event references—noting the occurrence of specific events (e.g., "The
rocket pushes away the jet of exhaust." or "The light strikes the
floor.")

Background statements—describing static properties and relationships that hold for the duration of the described activity (e.g.,
"The steel table is hot." or "The lens is a physical object.")

Connecting statements—specifying explicit relationships (causal,
temporal, etc.) between particular events referenced in the description (e.g., "The wood burning causes the wax to melt." or
"The component moving is a part of the structure expanding.")

The supplementary information is generic in nature—not referring to
specific objects or events in the description—and is included to compensate for PATHFINDER's assumed empty knowledge base. In effect, the
inclusion of this information amounts to compliance with Grice's maxim
of quantity relative to PATHFINDER's lack of background knowledge.
Five varieties of supplementary information are accepted:

Additional background statements—supplying object types, properties and relationships of objects that hold for the duration of the
described activity.

Event definitions—describing the temporal unfolding of changes and
momentary attribute values in generic occurrences of events.

Precedent events—additional events described in terms of generic participants and possibly relevant to comprehension of the described
activity.

Rules of inference—specifying deductive inferences permitted for the
transition space representation and relevant to the described activity.

Rules of restatement—specifying acceptable forms for reexpressing
particular physical activities in terms of other physical activities,
possibly at different levels of abstraction or in terms of different
underlying metaphors.

All five varieties of supplementary information are constructed using
the same types of statements as appear in causal descriptions: event
references, background statements and connecting statements.

Input Quantities

Figures 2.1 and 2.2 specify the input syntax accepted by PATHFINDER.
This grammar is a *semantic* grammar in that it includes meaning-based

<*sentence*> ::=
    [<*sequence-continuation*>] [<*relative-time-expression*>]
      <*simple-sentence*>
      [{ , <*simple-sentence*> }* , and <*simple-sentence*>] .

<*question*> ::=
    { What happens to <*attribute-expression*> |
    When { is | are } <*noun-phrase*>
      { { a | an } <*reference-standard*> |
        <*predicate-modifier*> | <*prepositional-phrase*> } |
    How does <*event-expression*> relate to <*event-expression*> |
    How could <*event-expression*> cause <*event-expression*> |
    { Does | Do } <*noun-phrase*> <*bare-infinitive*> <*complements*> |
    { Is | Are } <*noun-phrase*> <*past-participle*>
      {<*prepositional-phrase*>}*
    } ?

<*sequence-continuation*> ::= Also ,

<*relative-time-expression*> ::=
    { First | Next | Concurrently | At the beginning |
    At that point | Immediately after <*event-expression*> } ,

<*simple-sentence*> ::= <*noun-phrase*> <*verb-group*> <*complements*>

<*noun-phrase*> ::=
    <*special-expression*> | <*time-point-expression*> |
    <*attribute-expression*> | <*event-expression*> |
    <*simple-noun-phrase*>

<*complements*> ::=
    { a | an } <*reference-standard*> | <*predicate-modifier*> |
    [<*noun-phrase*>] {<*prepositional-phrase*>}*

Figure 2.1
Input grammar for PATHFINDER (initial portion).

$<predicate\text{-}modifier>$ ::=
  $<attribute>$ [[$<preposition>$] $<noun\text{-}phrase>$
        { { $<preposition>$ | and } $<noun\text{-}phrase>$ }*]

$<prepositional\text{-}phrase>$ ::=
  $<preposition>$ $<noun\text{-}phrase>$ [and $<noun\text{-}phrase>$]

$<attribute\text{-}expression>$ ::=
  the $<attribute>$ $<preposition>$ $<noun\text{-}phrase>$
    { { $<preposition>$ | and } $<noun\text{-}phrase>$ }*

$<event\text{-}expression>$ ::=
  the $<present\text{-}participle>$ {$<prepositional\text{-}phrase>$}* |
  { $<simple\text{-}noun\text{-}phrase>$ | $<attribute\text{-}expression>$ }
    { $<present\text{-}participle>$ | $<infinitive>$ } $<complements>$

$<special\text{-}expression>$ ::=
  the { preceding | following }
    { statement | event | sequence }

$<time\text{-}point\text{-}expression>$ ::=
  the { beginning | end } of $<event\text{-}expression>$

$<simple\text{-}noun\text{-}phrase>$ ::=
  $<object>$ | [a | an] $<reference\text{-}standard>$ | $<attribute>$

$<object>$	::= ...
$<reference\text{-}standard>$	::= ...
$<attribute>$	::= ...
$<verb\text{-}group>$	::= ...
$<infinitive>$	::= ...
$<bare\text{-}infinitive>$	::= ...
$<present\text{-}participle>$	::= ...
$<past\text{-}participle>$	::= ...
$<preposition>$	::= ...

Figure 2.2
Input grammar for PATHFINDER (final portion).

categories such as "attribute," "object," "relative-time-expression" and so forth (see, for example, [Hendrix *et al.*, 1978]). It should be noted that these semantic categories are domain independent in nature. The grammar is context-free and grounds out in a set of five non-terminal categories: object, reference-standard (used for fixed reference terms such as "physical object," "metal," "the forward direction," and so forth—see chapter 3), attribute, verb-group and preposition. The lexicon for PATHFINDER is initialized with a large set of prepositions and attributes related to physical events, plus a range of verb groups providing a foundation for the representation (e.g., "changes," "does not disappear," and so forth). New members of all five categories are inserted into the lexicon following queries to a human operator during the parsing process.

The grammar illustrated in Figures 2.1 and 2.2 supports a range of constructions for composing event references, background statements and connecting statements. Event references may be in active or passive voice (italics added for illustrative purposes):

The nail *deflects* the hammer toward the block of wood.
The iron bar *rusts*.
The wheel *twists* the rod.
The rod *is twisted*.

Additionally, event references may involve either arbitrary verbs and objects, or special verbs and attribute specifications translating directly into assertions in the transition space representation. The following event references are of this second type, translating directly into the transition space representation.

The temperature of the wax *increases*.
The water *remains* inside the tank.

Chapter 3 discusses the mapping between such statements and assertions in transition space.

Background statements always occur in constructions that tie into the transition space representation; these are also discussed in chapter 3. Examples are as follows.

The camera *is* a physical object.
The portion of liquid *is* combustible.

The hub *is* a part of the wheel.

The temperature of the burner *exceeds* the temperature of the
   water.

Finally, connecting statements may specify temporal or other relationships between previously-mentioned events:

The bar pushing on the beam *causes* the beam to move.

The ball moving *occurs after* the hitting of the block.

The wheel turning *involves* the hub turning.

Event references, background statements and connecting statements
are also used to construct the segments of supplementary information
submitted to PATHFINDER. Special qualifiers of either a temporal nature ("First, ..." "Next, ..." "At that point, ...") or non-temporal nature ("Also, ...") are used to group individual statements into sequences
for the purpose of specifying event definitions, rules of inference and so
forth. Additionally, special constructions used in connecting statements
permit reference to a preceding or following statement, event or sequence
of events. Below is an example of an event definition as might be submitted to PATHFINDER. The constructs for grouping of statements and
reference to adjacent information are highlighted in italics.

The unlatching of object 22 by object 21 translates to *the following event. First,* the position of object 21 changes, the speed of
object 21 does not disappear, the heading of object 21 does not
disappear, the distance between object 21 and object 22 does not
appear, the contact between object 21 and object 22 does not
disappear, and the restraint of object 22 by object 21 does not
disappear. *Next,* the position of object 21 changes, the speed of
object 21 does not disappear, the heading of object 21 does not
disappear, the distance between object 21 and object 22 appears,
the contact between object 21 and object 22 disappears, and the
restraint of object 22 by object 21 disappears.

Similarly, such constructs are also used in specifying rules of inference
and restatement, as in the following examples.

Concurrently, object 131 is a part of object 132, and object 132
is a part of object 133. The preceding statement implies the
following statement. Object 131 is a part of object 133.

Concurrently, the amount of solute in liquid 21 does not change, and the amount of solvent in liquid 21 increases. The following event summarizes the preceding event. The concentration of liquid 21 decreases.

One point requires explanation concerning these examples. In "special-expression" constructions (e.g., "the following statement"), PATH-FINDER does not actually distinguish between the tokens "statement," "event" and "sequence," treating all of these as if they refer to the preceding or following sentence or consecutive set of sentences grouped together through the use of either "relative-time-expression" constructions ("First," "Next," and so forth) or the "sequence-continuation" construction ("Also,"—used to connect sets of assertions that are temporally unrelated to one another). For readability, however, the examples appearing in this book are standardized to make use of the token "sequence" when several sentences are grouped using the "sequence-continuation" construction, and otherwise, "event" when the referenced material provides dynamic information and "statement" when it provides static information.

Questions and Answers

Included in Figure 2.1 is a specification of the syntax for the four types of questions handled by PATHFINDER. These question types are illustrated below. The first type concerns object-level information, while the remaining three types concern event-level information.

Type 1. Questions concerning the time-course of changes in particular attributes of objects. For example:

> What happens to the position of the jet of exhaust?
> What happens to the support of the screw by the hand?

An alternate form of this question exists for attributes expressed using a predicate modifier:

> When is the light inside the camera?
> When is the vacuum engaged in the suction?

Type 2. Questions concerning relationships between particular events referenced in the input description. For example:

> How does the light entering the camera relate to the light passing through the lens?
> How does the transmitting of the radio wave into space relate to the strength of the radio wave decreasing?

Type 3. Questions concerning possible causal relationships between events referenced in the description and new events introduced at the time of questioning. Such questions may be used to explore simple predictions or explanations beyond the immediate context of a causal description. For example:

> How could the water boiling cause the steam to condense on the metal plate?
> How could the trigger moving cause the hammer to hit the firing pin?

Type 4. Questions concerning the possible paraphrasing of a portion of the activity in terms of a newly-supplied event. For example:

> Does the steam convert to a liquid?
> Does the hammer start to move?

An alternate form of this question exists for events to be expressed using passive voice (i.e., in order to leave the agent of the event unspecified):

> Is the water heated?
> Is the wheel pushed?

PATHFINDER responds to these questions using approximately the same syntax used for input to the program. However, in the interest of readability a few extensions to this grammar are utilized. Below is a sample segment as might be generated by PATHFINDER in response to a question of type 1.

> First, as the block enters the water, the contact between the block and the water appears. Next, as the water reduces the speed of the block, the contact between the block and the water does not disappear.

Similarly, the following is a sample response for a question of type 2.

> The trigger moving causes the trigger to unlatch the hammer, which causes the releasing of the hammer.

This completes the overview of input and output for PATHFINDER. The functionality PATHFINDER must exhibit in utilizing such input and output is governed by the task framework outlined in section 2.1. Specifically, PATHFINDER is initially supplied with a text file containing a causal description and appropriate supplementary information. Given this information plus grammatical categories for terms not contained in its lexicon, PATHFINDER must form an internal model of the described activity and answer questions of the four types outlined above. PATHFINDER's answers to these questions are then evaluated with respect to criteria such as presented in section 2.1, resulting in an assessment of success or failure at the task of causal reconstruction. As previously noted, in this book the actual evaluation of answers according to such criteria is left to the reader. Additionally, in many cases specific questions and answers are themselves omitted where these are easily ascertained from a detailed presentation of PATHFINDER's internal model of a described activity.

3 Transition Space

The transition space representation was outlined briefly in section 1.3. This chapter elaborates on the discussion presented there, focusing on the overall motivation for the representation, the structure of the representation in terms of primitive and defined quantities, and the grounding of the representation in simple English statements about the physical world.

3.1 Guidelines from Perceptual Psychology

Causal descriptions are created by humans and intended for human consumption. A useful strategy toward attempting automated comprehension of causal descriptions is thus to proceed along the lines of what we know about human cognition regarding events and causality. In doing so, we are not necessarily pursuing a model of *human* comprehension of causal descriptions; rather, we are simply attempting to maximize our chances of success in the computational realm. Ultimately, we will rely on computational performance as the test of this computational model.

The primary thrust in the approach advanced in this book is a representational one. Following Miller and Johnson-Laird [1976], who argue that human use of language and human perception of the world are tightly intertwined, we look to the literature in perceptual psychology for guidance in the construction of an appropriate representation. The list below summarizes several important results from this literature, concerning how humans perceive and describe the world around them.

Representation in terms of objects and attributes. "Objects" may be taken to include any quantities whose properties, relationships or other attributes may be described; e.g., physical objects, spaces, paths, boundaries, events, systems, and so forth. Attributes may be physical (e.g., "distance," "size" and "shape") or conceptual (e.g., an object being a part of another object, or an object being engaged in an event). A good summary of object types and attributes used by humans in describing the world appears in Miller and Johnson-Laird [1976]. These authors characterize attributes as typically unary (e.g, "size") or binary (e.g., "distance"), and also as either qualitative (e.g., "color" or "contact") or quantitative (e.g., "length" or "pressure").

Time as a sequence of moments. A number of studies indicate that
time is perceived—at least at the level of conscious awareness—as
a sequence of discrete moments rather than a continuum of activity
(e.g., see [Miller and Johnson-Laird, 1976]). Further research by
Newtson *et al.* [1976] [1977] indicates that events are delimited by
specific "breakpoints"—time points at which significant changes
are perceived by the observer.

Qualitative comparisons and changes. Following from the superi-
ority of humans at relative—as opposed to absolute—estimation of
attribute values, it is natural to represent both static comparisons
and dynamic changes in a qualitative manner (see, for example,
[Miller and Johnson-Laird, 1976]).

Causation as an association between changes. Experimental evidence characterizes perceived causality as an association between
consecutive changes in a scene [Michotte, 1946]. Concurring accounts appear in the cognitive development literature [Leslie and
.Keeble, 1987] [White, 1988] and elsewhere in psychology (e.g.,
[Miller and Johnson-Laird, 1976]).

Representation in Terms of Changes

The final point above is significant. While a number of representations
in artificial intelligence have permitted the antecedents or consequents of
causality to be *states*, it would seem that *changes* are most appropriate
in the perceptually-oriented realm of physical activity.

Intuition would seem to concur with this characterization of causality.
For causal antecedents, if states do the causing, then we might ask why
a causal effect occurs precisely when it does and not earlier; thus, we
are led to suspect that some additional ingredient has fallen into place
just prior to the causal effect. This final change may then be ascribed
as the antecedent of causality. For causal effects, if there is no change
in a scene, then causation contributes nothing to the reasoning process;
we can reason just as well with what we knew to be true beforehand.

How is it possible, then, to construct representations in which states
serve as antecedents or consequents of causality? It would appear that in
certain circumstances, a level of abstraction exists where this is possible.
One such circumstance involves the presence of ongoing processes supporting an activity: in the human body, a state of having low blood sugar

may lead to various effects, given ongoing circulatory and metabolic processes of the body. Because these processes are presumably always active, they may be left implicit, and we may speak of one state leading to another. In other cases, we may incorporate dynamic information in the specification of states, as when we refer to "moving" objects or characterize instantaneous changes in quantities as "increasing," "decreasing" or "steady," as in the qualitative physics literature (e.g., [Forbus, 1984], [de Kleer and Brown, 1984] and [Kuipers, 1986]).

However, such techniques are not always applicable. In particular, instantaneous directions of change can be specified only for quantitative attributes, like "temperature" or "elevation," which can be differentiated with respect to time, but not for qualitative attributes, like "contact," "support," and "inside," as often appear in verbal accounts of activity. For example, if two objects are specified as coming into contact, with one object breaking as a result, there is no "state of coming into contact" to serve as the causal antecedent. At one instant the objects are not in contact, and this certainly does not cause the breakage, and at a subsequent instant they are in contact—but this cannot be attributed as the antecedent either, because they could have been simply resting, in contact, for a long time. A better characterization identifies the causal antecedent as the change from non-contact to contact between the two objects.[1] Likewise, the causal consequent in this example is more suitably characterized as a change from unbroken to broken for the second object, rather than simply a state of being broken.

Representing causality as an association between changes—where these changes may involve quantitative or qualitative attributes appearing in verbal accounts of activity—we are led to the general notion of transition space. In transition space, individual points—or transitions—correspond to temporally-coordinated combinations of changes in various attributes of various objects, typically within the focus of activity surrounding particular events. Events are short paths in transition space, equating to sequences or simple directed, acyclic graphs of transitions. As such, events correspond to simple causal explanations which may be combined to produce larger causal explanations—larger "paths" in transition space—that serve as models of described activities.

---

[1] Additionally, of course, there are other less articulable factors contributing to the breakage: sufficient momentum on the part of the first object, sufficient brittleness for the second object, sufficient inelasticity of the collision, and so forth.

Important to the construction of this representation is its basis in verbal accounts of activity. Attributes and their changes are taken directly from simple, stylized English statements. Thus, the representation has not only an established semantics (grounded in that of the English statements on which it is based), but as well, individual assertions in the representation may be converted back into their corresponding verbal form when necessary in order to discuss the suitability of representing particular events in particular ways.

Of equal importance, it should be noted that in grounding the representation in verbal accounts of activity, those aspects of human knowledge about events that are less easily expressed verbally are omitted. For instance, the representation is not intended to capture spatial knowledge of a non-propositional nature, as used in estimating shapes, directions, textures and so forth. Also, it is not intended to capture knowledge underlying human ability to classify objects and situations from visual or other sensory perceptions, or knowledge underlying human ability to estimate likelihood of various causal circumstances. These types of knowledge are doubtlessly required for processing some descriptions; however, as illustrated in this book, there is also a range of simple descriptions that can be processed solely on the basis of articulable knowledge about what happens during events.

3.2   Representing Transitions and Events

This section elaborates on the development of transition space presented in chapter 1. Here, we proceed in a bottom-up manner, starting with the primitives of the representation and building up to the representation of transitions and events.

Primitive and Defined Quantities

The following five syntactic categories form a basis for the representation. These are motivated by the representational guidelines extracted from perceptual psychology as listed in the previous section.

Objects—both perceptual and conceptual. For example: solids, quantities of liquid, gas, fire and so forth; spaces, surfaces, paths and edges; events and sequences; collections—ultimately, anything that may participate in an event.

Attributes—both perceptual and conceptual. Some examples include: "length," "width," "depth," "size," "weight" and "color"; "position," "elevation," "orientation," "speed," "heading," "direction" and "distance"; "inside," "pressure," "contact" and "restraint"; "is-a," "a-kind-of," "made-of," "a-part-of," "before" and "after"; "age," "origin," "function" and "value." As in everyday language, a degree of overlap appears in the set of attributes.

Time points—as needed to distinguish particular instants within the time course of events, these instants serving as a basis for the comparison of attribute values.

Reference standards—used as fixed points of reference for comparison. For example: object types ("solid," "event," "collection," etc.), colors, substances, numbers, qualitative directions such as "up" and "forward," a fixed frame of reference for motion ("the-background"), and a quantity "null" representing the "false" or "absent" state for all attributes.

Predicates—used in assertions comparing attribute values. For qualitative attributes, the predicates EQUAL and NOT-EQUAL serve as primitive predicates. For quantitative attributes, these plus GREATER and NOT-GREATER serve as primitives.

Reference standards have two distinct functions: they serve as unchanging points of reference for comparisons, and they span different description discourses. As unchanging points of reference, reference standards support certain types of inference. Suppose the color of an object is specified as matching the color "green" at one time point, and the object's color is also specified as not changing over an interval from that time point to a later time point. We would like to conclude that the object is still green; however, this requires an assumption that the color green has not changed during the course of that same interval: this assumption is provided by classifying "green" as a reference standard. The other aspect, spanning of description discourses, distinguishes reference standards from objects (e.g., "the pin") which must be individualized such that their mention in two different discourses serves to generate two distinct symbols, not one (e.g., "the-pin-1" versus "the-pin-2").

The primitive predicates EQUAL, NOT-EQUAL, GREATER and NOT-GREATER take five arguments: an attribute for comparison, a first object and associated time point, and a second object and associated time point. For binary attributes, tuples of objects are used in the second and fourth positions. Additionally, for unusual attributes such as "between," a nesting of tuples is employed. These predicates may be used in assertions comparing attributes of objects at a single time point or between two time points and serve as a foundation for the entire representation of transitions and events. Three simple assertions involving these predicates are given below.

> GREATER(length, object-1, t1, object-2, t1)
> NOT-EQUAL(position, <object-1, the-background>, t1,
>   <object-1, the-background>, t2)
> EQUAL(distance, <object-1, object-2>, t1, null, t1)

The first assertion states that "object 1" has greater length than "object 2" at time "t1." The second, that the position of "object 1" relative to "the background" is different at time "t1" and time "t2" (i.e., "object 1" has moved). The third, utilizing a comparison to the "null" reference standard, states that there is a (known) absence of distance between "object 1" and "object 2" at time "t1."

While the above predicates are sufficient for the representation of arbitrary, compound transitions, the following definitions provide a useful shorthand. (As before, variables are denoted by symbols beginning with "?".) Note that several of the "NOT-" forms are not strict logical negations: they assume some of the same information as the positive forms, in line with common usage of these terms in language. For comparisons at a single time point:

> PRESENT(?attribute, ?object, ?t1) $\Longleftrightarrow$
>   NOT-EQUAL(?attribute, ?object, ?t1, null, ?t1)
>
> NOT-PRESENT(?attribute, ?object, ?t1) $\Longleftrightarrow$
>   EQUAL(?attribute, ?object, ?t1, null, ?t1)
>
> MATCH(?attribute, ?object-1, ?object-2, ?t1) $\Longleftrightarrow$
>   PRESENT(?attribute, ?object-1, ?t1)   AND
>   PRESENT(?attribute, ?object-2, ?t1)   AND
>   EQUAL(?attribute, ?object-1, ?t1, ?object-2, ?t1)

NOT-MATCH(?attribute, ?object-1, ?object-2, ?t1) ⟺
    PRESENT(?attribute, ?object-1, ?t1)   AND
    PRESENT(?attribute, ?object-2, ?t1)   AND
    NOT-EQUAL(?attribute, ?object-1, ?t1, ?object-2, ?t1)

EXCEED(?attribute, ?object-1, ?object-2, ?t1) ⟺
    PRESENT(?attribute, ?object-1, ?t1)   AND
    PRESENT(?attribute, ?object-2, ?t1)   AND
    GREATER(?attribute, ?object-1, ?t1, ?object-2, ?t1)

NOT-EXCEED(?attribute, ?object-1, ?object-2, ?t1) ⟺
    PRESENT(?attribute, ?object-1, ?t1)   AND
    PRESENT(?attribute, ?object-2, ?t1)   AND
    NOT-GREATER(?attribute, ?object-1, ?t1, ?object-2, ?t1)

For comparisons across time points, the following definitions specify the ten change characterizations introduced in chapter 1. (In these definitions, "null" is also used to designate an irrelevant time point argument.)

APPEAR(?attribute, ?object, ?t1, ?t2) ⟺
    PRESENT(after, <?t2, ?t1>, null)   AND
    NOT-PRESENT(?attribute, ?object, ?t1)   AND
    PRESENT(?attribute, ?object, ?t2)

NOT-APPEAR(?attribute, ?object, ?t1, ?t2) ⟺
    PRESENT(after, <?t2, ?t1>, null)   AND
    NOT-PRESENT(?attribute, ?object, ?t1)   AND
    NOT-PRESENT(?attribute, ?object, ?t2)

DISAPPEAR(?attribute, ?object, ?t1, ?t2) ⟺
    PRESENT(after, <?t2, ?t1>, null)   AND
    PRESENT(?attribute, ?object, ?t1)   AND
    NOT-PRESENT(?attribute, ?object, ?t2)

NOT-DISAPPEAR(?attribute, ?object, ?t1, ?t2) ⟺
    PRESENT(after, <?t2, ?t1>, null)   AND
    PRESENT(?attribute, ?object, ?t1)   AND
    PRESENT(?attribute, ?object, ?t2)

CHANGE(?attribute, ?object, ?t1, ?t2) ⟺
    NOT-DISAPPEAR(?attribute, ?object, ?t1, ?t2)   AND
    NOT-EQUAL(?attribute, ?object, ?t1, ?object, ?t2)

NOT-CHANGE(?attribute, ?object, ?t1, ?t2) ⟺
    NOT-DISAPPEAR(?attribute, ?object, ?t1, ?t2)   AND
    EQUAL(?attribute, ?object, ?t1, ?object, ?t2)

INCREASE(?attribute, ?object, ?t1, ?t2) ⟺
    NOT-DISAPPEAR(?attribute, ?object, ?t1, ?t2)   AND
    GREATER(?attribute, ?object, ?t2, ?object, ?t1)

NOT-INCREASE(?attribute, ?object, ?t1, ?t2) ⟺
    NOT-DISAPPEAR(?attribute, ?object, ?t1, ?t2)   AND
    NOT-GREATER(?attribute, ?object, ?t2, ?object, ?t1)

DECREASE(?attribute, ?object, ?t1, ?t2) ⟺
    NOT-DISAPPEAR(?attribute, ?object, ?t1, ?t2)   AND
    GREATER(?attribute, ?object, ?t1, ?object, ?t2)

NOT-DECREASE(?attribute, ?object, ?t1, ?t2) ⟺
    NOT-DISAPPEAR(?attribute, ?object, ?t1, ?t2)   AND
    NOT-GREATER(?attribute, ?object, ?t1, ?object, ?t2)

The above ten predicates cover the range of alternate circumstances involving presence or absence of a specified attribute at two time points, one of which follows the other, plus a possible inclusion of additional information concerning the qualitative relationship between the attribute values at those two time points. Situations beyond the range of these special circumstances must be described using (NOT-)PRESENT, (NOT-)MATCH, (NOT-)EXCEED, and, where necessary, the primitive predicates (NOT-)EQUAL and (NOT-)GREATER. For qualitative attributes (e.g., "shape," "color," and qualitative "position," "orientation," and "heading"), changes are typically specified in terms of the predicates (NOT-)APPEAR, (NOT-)DISAPPEAR and (NOT-)CHANGE. Boolean attributes (e.g., "contact," "inside," "support" and "a-part-of") are viewed as a subset of the qualitative attributes—namely, those having only a single non-null value. Changes in boolean attributes are specified solely in terms of (NOT-)APPEAR and (NOT-)DISAPPEAR. Finally, changes in quantitative attributes (e.g., "speed," "elevation," "distance" and "pressure") are specified in terms of all ten of the above predicates for comparisons across time points.

Transitions

A *transition* is a set of assertions at and between two ordered time points. For example, the following information (here, consisting of only dynamic assertions) might appear in the specification of a transition involving "object 11" sliding across "surface 12" between the time points "t11" and "t12." (In summary, the physical object "object 11" changes position and decreases in speed with respect to the physical object "object 12," maintains a possibly-changing heading and orientation with respect to "object 12," maintains its relationship above "surface 12," an absence of distance to "surface 12," contact with "surface 12" and support by "surface 12.")

> NOT-DISAPPEAR(is-a, <object-11, physical-object>, t11, t12)
> NOT-DISAPPEAR(is-a, <surface-12, physical-object>, t11, t12)
> CHANGE(position, <object-11, surface-12>, t11, t12)
> DECREASE(speed, <object-11, surface-12>, t11, t12)
> NOT-DISAPPEAR(heading, <object-11, surface-12>, t11, t12)
> NOT-DISAPPEAR(orientation, <object-11 surface-12>, t11, t12)
> NOT-DISAPPEAR(above, <object-11, surface-12>, t11, t12)
> NOT-APPEAR(distance, <object-11, surface-12>, t11, t12)
> NOT-DISAPPEAR(contact, <object-11, surface-12>, t11, t12)
> NOT-DISAPPEAR(support, <object-11, surface-12>, t11, t12)

Because the above form is rather unwieldy from a human perspective, we employ a special graphic representation for transitions and events, as introduced in chapter 1. This graphic form presents only the dynamic information in a transition: changes in attributes are listed as coded entries arranged between vertical lines depicting time points. For the specification of changes, the ten qualitative change characterizations are coded using the following symbols, as presented previously in chapter 1:

A	APPEAR	A̸	NOT-APPEAR
D	DISAPPEAR	D̸	NOT-DISAPPEAR
△	CHANGE	△̸	NOT-CHANGE
+	INCREASE	+̸	NOT-INCREASE
−	DECREASE	−̸	NOT-DECREASE

The graphic representation for the above transition involving sliding is then as follows. The specific objects to which each attribute or group of attributes applies are supplied at the left. Also, for ease of our visualization, a drawing of the activity appears above.

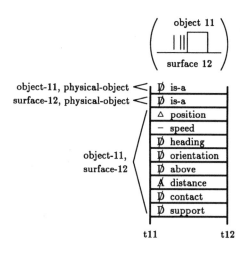

Events

Finally, events are represented as sequences or directed, acyclic graphs of transitions. As noted previously, these representations are called *event traces*, as they correspond to simple paths in transition space. The following diagram portrays an event trace for "hitting." In this event trace, several aspects of the transition space representation are illustrated: sequencing of transitions to indicate causal relationships between sets of changes (approach in the first transition leading to appearance of contact in the second, this leading to an initiation and continuation of movement for "object 22" in the third and fourth transitions), inclusion of attributes and changes necessary to a typical instance of the event, and omission of information where alternative scenarios are to be accommodated (e.g., omitting information concerning possible movement for "object 22" prior to contact and possible movement of "object 21" following contact). These and other aspects of the *usage* of the representation are summarized at the end of this section.

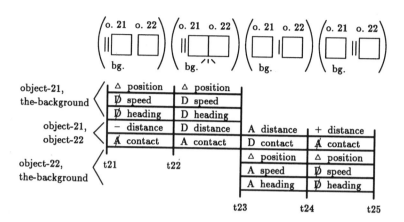

	$\triangle$ position	$\triangle$ position		
object-21, the-background	$\not{D}$ speed	D speed		
	$\not{D}$ heading	D heading		
object-21, object-22	$-$ distance	D distance	A distance	$+$ distance
	$\not{A}$ contact	A contact	D contact	$\not{A}$ contact
object-22, the-background			$\triangle$ position	$\triangle$ position
			A speed	$\not{D}$ speed
	t21	t22	A heading	$\not{D}$ heading

t23   t24   t25

The above event trace is typical of many of the event traces appearing in the examples discussed in chapters 4 through 8. Variations in content and structure are also possible. As noted previously, transition space explicitly addresses the representation of different *descriptions* of what happens during events and how these alternate accounts can be related to one another.

As a second example, the following event trace, extracted from one of the test descriptions processed by PATHFINDER, illustrates the description of an event involving a conceptual object (a radio wave), and a metaphorically-applied attribute ("inside"). In this trace, a radio wave is being transmitted into space, involving an exit from the antenna and an entrance into "space" (represented as a reference standard, as this is a discourse-independent, relatively unchanging quantity).

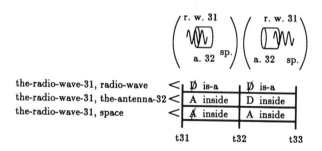

the-radio-wave-31, radio-wave	$\not{D}$ is-a	$\not{D}$ is-a	
the-radio-wave-31, the-antenna-32	A inside	D inside	
the-radio-wave-31, space	$\not{A}$ inside	A inside	

t31   t32   t33

Most of the events processed to date by PATHFINDER are simply sequences of transitions. The following example illustrates a more gen-

eral forking and joining of transitions in an event trace. While PATH-
FINDER can represent and perform matching and transformation operations on such structures, it typically works with event traces that are
at most *trees* of transitions—this because it never attempts to determine
more than a single path of association between any two events involved
in the causal reconstruction process.

The trace below details the activity taking place during one cycle of
vibration for a loudspeaker diaphragm. In this trace, the diaphragm first
pushes on an adjacent quantity of air (from time "t41" to "t43"), then
recoils and pulls on the adjacent quantity of air (from "t43" to "t46").
Meanwhile, the quantity of air moves away from the diaphragm—independently of the initial recoiling of the diaphragm—and is subsequently
pulled back.

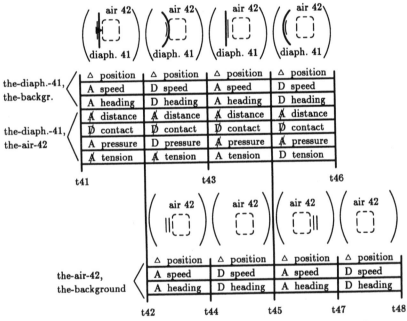

MATCH(heading, <the-diaphragm-41, the-background>, the-forward-direction, t42)
MATCH(heading, <the-diaphragm-41, the-background>, the-backward-direction, t45)
MATCH(heading, <the-air-42, the-background>, the-forward-direction, t44)
MATCH(heading, <the-air-42, the-background>, the-backward-direction, t47)

While there are no explicit size constraints placed on event traces, two factors tend to keep these structures to a manageable size. First, while a large number of possible attributes exist in language, only a relatively small number of these will be relevant to any particular event. In the examples run on PATHFINDER, the event traces produced typically contain no more than about 10 rows of attribute-object applications. Secondly, the subdivision of events into temporal intervals is naturally minimized by the variable temporal resolution employed by humans in thinking about events. Consider three events: carrying, drying out, and decomposing. For carrying, the object doing the carrying moves first, followed by the object being carried (or, so it would appear to occur following introspection on the matter). This comprises a sequence of two transitions, yet the temporal granularity involved in such a subdivision is extremely fine. For drying out, a similar two-transition succession occurs (wind passing by, object becoming dry), yet on a larger time scale. Finally, for decomposing (as by bacteria, etc.), the time scale is even longer.

Using the Transition Space Representation

While the transition space representation inherently offers a degree of flexibility in depicting particular events—indeed, the discussion of exploratory transformations in chapter 6 expressly addresses the issue of how alternate characterizations of an activity can be related to one another—there are also a number of intuitive guidelines constraining typical use of the representation. Several such guidelines have been mentioned in the above paragraphs and previously in chapter 1. The following list elaborates on these guidelines for use of the transition space representation.

- The granularity of temporal intervals is generally not so fine as to produce adjacent, identical transitions (e.g., each attribute specifying something like an INCREASE followed by an INCREASE, with accompanying static assertions also matching between the two transitions).

- On the other hand, intervals are sufficiently subdivided so as to indicate sets of changes that cause other sets of changes, and the temporal granularity may vary within an event trace. Extremely fine temporal granularity may be used to represent situations such as that of appearance of pressure from one object to a second leading to return pressure from the second to the first.

- In all cases, we should be able to say that there exists a causal relationship between the set of changes in one transition and the set of changes in an immediately following transition.

- Unless an event depicts non-activity (e.g., "not moving"), the representation should always include at least one definite change (APPEAR, DISAPPEAR, CHANGE, INCREASE or DECREASE) in its opening transition.

- All attributes and assertions needed to discriminate a *typical* instance of an event from other types of events should be included. For example, the representation for "striking" should include not only an appearance of contact between two objects, but movement for the first object as well. Otherwise, the specification could account for an event in which the second object strikes the first.[2]

- On the other hand, we may choose to omit particular attributes, specifications of changes and static information where we wish to accommodate variations within the set of typical occurrences for an event. For example, in the "hitting" event illustrated above, no information was provided concerning possible movement of the second object prior to contact, or possible movement of the first object following contact.

- "Objects" in the representation need not be physical objects. Any quantities are acceptable whose properties, relationships or other attributes may be characterized using English statements of the sort serving as a basis for the representation. Thus, we may freely include quantities such as spaces, paths, collections, systems, states, events and so forth in the specifications of events.

3.3   Using Language to Generate Representations

Using the grammar outlined in chapter 2, it is possible to form transition space representations in a straightforward manner from stylized English

---

[2] In this book, some liberty has been taken with respect to this guideline—especially concerning object type information, which is often excluded when an event involves only physical objects.

accounts of what happens during particular types of events. This aspect of the representation provides several benefits. First, it minimizes or eliminates the need for a human "representation specialist" to cast particular events in the representation. Second, in the other direction, this ease of translation provides a mechanism by which representational structures produced in the course of program execution may be assessed: by converting these representations to simplified English, their meaning may be comprehended directly, again without recourse to a specialist in the use of the representation. Third, the manner of translation between simplified English and the representation provides a mechanism for including new attributes and types of objects in the representation, based on their use in language. This significantly increases the coverage of the representation in a principled way, permitting description in terms of any quantities or attributes of quantities expressible in language.[3]

Individual Assertions

The grammar listed in chapter 2 provides two syntactic forms for constructing clauses specifying changes. The first form is as follows:

<*attribute-expression*> <*verb-group*>

where

<*attribute-expression*> ::=
    the <*attribute*> <*preposition*> <*noun-phrase*>
    { { <*preposition*> | and } <*noun-phrase*> }*

and the verb group indicates one of the ten change characterizations. This form suffices for the construction of a wide range of clauses specifying changes in quantitative and qualitative attributes of objects, as illustrated by the following examples:

The size of the scratch increases.
The density of the compound decreases.
The shape of the assembly changes.

---

[3] In this regard, the representation need not be restricted to the domain of physical systems as explored in this book, but could also potentially be applied in domains such as political science, law, and management science.

The appearance of the film does not change.
The capacity of the container decreases.
The position of the bolt changes.
The heading of the bolt does not change.
The restraint of the door by the latch disappears.
The confinement of the ball by the box does not disappear.
The pressure between the bar and the plate increases.
The interaction between the wrench and the bolt disappears.
The frequency of the disturbance decreases.
The function of the device changes.
The usefulness of the device for the task disappears.

The second form is applicable only to certain boolean attributes and involves a single object followed by a restricted set of verb groups ("becomes," "becomes not," "remains" and "remains not") and a predicate modifier expression:

$$<object> \quad <verb\text{-}group> \quad <predicate\text{-}modifier>$$

where

$$<predicate\text{-}modifier> ::= \\ <attribute> \; [\; [<preposition>] \; <noun\text{-}phrase> \\ \{ \; \{ \; <preposition> \; | \; \text{and} \; \} \\ <noun\text{-}phrase> \; \}^* \;]$$

Examples employing this second form of specification are as follows:

The surface remains sticky.
The plate becomes fastened to the housing.
The signal becomes at the first circuit junction.
The ball remains inside the basket.
The bolt becomes not supported by the hand.
The structure becomes covered by the extinguishing foam.
The rod remains not bent.
The weather vane becomes directed from the west to the east.
The pin becomes movable.
The liquid remains not frozen.
The sponge becomes dry.

As an alternative for this second form, we also include clauses consisting of an object followed by one of the above verb groups, followed by "a" or "an" and a reference standard naming a class of objects. This construction is taken to concern a special attribute "is-a." For example:

> The water becomes a vapor.
> The solution remains an acid.

All event definitions, rules of restatement and so forth submitted to PATHFINDER specify changes according to the above forms. Each clause translates rather directly to an assertion involving one of the ten change characterizations defined in section 3.1.[4]

In addition to providing a mechanism for specifying information in the representation, the above grammatical templates also provide a mechanism for classifying attributes by noting which of the ten change characterizations are intuitively applicable to each. For instance, the position of an object may change or not change, but may not increase and may not disappear. "Heading" may change or not change, but may appear and disappear as well. All ten characterizations are applicable for the attributes "speed" and "pressure." Boolean attributes like "contact" may only appear, not appear, disappear and not disappear.

Similar to the above constructions for entering dynamic information are two forms for entering static information (producing assertions involving the predicates (NOT-)PRESENT, (NOT-)MATCH and (NOT-)EXCEED). The first form involves an attribute expression followed by "is present" or "is not present," or an attribute expression followed by "matches," "does not match," "exceeds" or "does not exceed" and a second attribute expression (presumably involving the same attribute, but not constrained as such via the grammar). The following are sample specifications utilizing this format:

> The contact between the latch and the door is present.
> The shape of the pin does not match the shape of the hole.
> The temperature of the burner exceeds the temperature of the
>   water.

---

[4] Attributes may also be tagged, if necessary, to indicate the particular form of attribute expression or predicate modifier construction evoking them. This permits a distinction between the two senses of "direction" in "the direction from ... to ..." and "the direction to ... from ..." However, for simplicity, no such distinction is made for the examples in this book. Correspondingly, only one structural variant is employed for each attribute.

The second form parallels the second form for specifications of change, involving the verb groups "is" and "is not" in place of "becomes (not)" and "remains (not)." A similar extension to this form substitutes a reference standard representing a class of objects for the predicate modifier. Examples are as follows:

> The sponge is wet.
> The burner is made of metal.
> The beaker is supported by the burner.
> The water is a liquid.
> The light is not a physical object.

Characterizing Events

Finally, specifications for complete event traces can be entered using the above clause forms plus a few additional grammatical constructions. To specify changes occurring during a single interval, several dynamic specifications may be conjoined into a single sentence begun by "Concurrently," as in the following example concerning an object starting to move:

> Concurrently, the position of the object changes, the speed of the object appears, and the heading of the object appears.

Changes occurring in a sequence of two or more intervals may be specified in a similar manner using the qualifiers "First," and "Next," as in the following example involving a hammer moving into contact with a nail:

> First, the position of the hammer changes, the speed of the hammer does not disappear, the heading of the hammer does not disappear, the distance between the hammer and the nail decreases, and the contact between the hammer and the nail does not appear. Next, the position of the hammer changes, the speed of the hammer disappears, the heading of the hammer disappears, the distance between the hammer and the nail disappears, and the contact between the hammer and the nail appears.

To insert static information before the first interval of such a sequence or between two intervals of a sequence, sentences initiated by "At the beginning," and "At that point," respectively, are inserted at the appropriate places. The following example utilizes these constructs ("the forward direction" is to be parsed as a reference standard):

> At the beginning, the heading of the object matches the heading of the forward direction. First, the position of the object changes, the speed of the object does not disappear, and the heading of the object changes. At that point, the heading of the object matches the heading of the backward direction. Next, the position of the object changes, the speed of the object does not disappear, and the heading of the object does not change.

In addition, a special qualifier "Immediately after <event-expression>" is used to specify changes following a previously-specified portion of an activity. This construct is needed when an event contains two or more independent consequences of some portion of the activity (e.g., when one object applies pressure to a second object and each starts to move).

4 Matching in Transition Space

This chapter and the next three illustrate the use of the transition space representation in performing causal reconstruction in a range of situations, starting with simple situations and progressively adding more complexity. All of the examples appearing in these chapters have been successfully processed by the PATHFINDER program.

This chapter concerns situations involving only the matching of event representations. Specifically, we consider causal descriptions containing only event references, and supplementary information containing only event definitions and precedent events. Background statements and connecting statements are not permitted in the causal descriptions, and background statements, rules of inference and rules of restatement are not allowed within the supplementary information.

4.1 Overview

Enumerating Partial Matches

Chapter 1 introduced the two types of partial matches sought by PATHFINDER in determining relationships among events: *partial chaining* matches and *partial restatement* matches. Intuitively, partial chaining matches identify plausible causal associations between events referenced in a description, with the second event matched in its initial portion and carrying the activity beyond the conclusion of the first event. Given that each event comprises a short path in transition space— a short causal sequence—then by merging two events that overlap in such a manner, we get a *longer* path in transition space—a longer causal sequence. All other partial matches between event traces are classified as partial restatement matches—for example, if two events overlap in their middle portions, or if one event comprises part of another event.[1]

To be more specific, the following definition is used to distinguish partial chaining matches from partial restatement matches:

> A partial chaining match between two event traces is a single-transition partial match involving at least one definite change

---

[1] Additionally, events represented at different temporal granularities may be matched following the application of interval composition transformations, as described in chapter 6.

(APPEAR, DISAPPEAR, CHANGE, INCREASE or DE-
CREASE) and situated such that exactly one of the traces
is begun by the matching transition and continues beyond
that transition.

In this definition, two extra provisions have been added to the intuitive
characterization appearing above. The first is that the match consist of
a single interval. Intuitively, it would seem that events overlapping in
more than one successive complex of changes are more restatements of
one another than causally associated events; however, this rather sub-
jective restriction could alternatively be omitted. The second provision
is that at least one definite change be involved in the match. This restriction is included so that events involving no changes—for example,
continued support of a block by a table—may not be taken as causal
antecedents of other events—for example, the block sliding off the end
of the table.

Given event traces for all events referenced in a causal description,
a matcher may be invoked on all pairs of traces, subsequently divid-
ing the enumerated partial matches into partial chaining matches and
partial restatement matches. The matcher for PATHFINDER treats
time points and objects as variables, such that they may be mapped to
other time points and objects in the service of a match with another
event. However, reference standards, attributes and predicates must
match exactly.[2] This distinction between quantities that must match
exactly and quantities that may be mapped between matching events
is motivated from an analysis of the following sequence of increasingly
disparate types of matches.

No substituted quantities. If two traces match with no substituted
quantities, then the matching portions describe the exact same circumstances. This rarely occurs in causal reconstruction, because
different event references evoke at least different names for time
points.

---

[2] To be precise, predicates must be "covered" rather than matching exactly, which
means that the EQUAL/GREATER-level expansion of the covered predicate must be
a subset of the EQUAL/GREATER-level expansion of the covering predicate, subject
to the object and time point substitutions of the match. For instance, a CHANGE
predicate covers a NOT-DISAPPEAR predicate or a PRESENT predicate applied
to appropriate quantities.

Substituted time points. This is the normal occurrence regarding matching between events referenced in a causal description. Here, two sets of time points originally deemed independent are taken to be equivalent.

Substituted time points and objects. In some circumstances, events may involve hypothesized objects. For example, when a hand grasps a bolt, the generated event trace may include fingers of the hand not explicitly mentioned in the event reference from the causal description. Such hypothesized objects may be freely matched with other objects so long as no two distinct objects mentioned in the description are equated.

Substituted time points, objects and reference standards. Substitutions involving reference standards occur in matches between events involving the same sorts of changes in the same attributes, but regarding different types of objects or changes with respect to different norms (e.g., directions like "the forward direction"). Such matches must be made with caution, or, for example, a solid object moving upward might be reinterpreted as a quantity of liquid moving downward. Explicitly invoked rules of restatement control the use of such substitutions in PATHFINDER, as described in chapter 6.

Substituted time points, objects, reference standards and attributes. Extending such substitutions to the inclusion of attributes covers matches between events involving the same sorts of changes but in different attributes of different types of objects. For instance, a radio signal "spreading out" in space might be equated with a quantity of water spreading out on a table top (substituting "strength" of the signal for "height" of the spreading water). Such mappings are also explicitly controlled through rules of restatement in PATHFINDER.

Ranking the Partial Matches

Once all partial matches between pairs of events in a causal description have been determined, the partial matches must be ranked, such that the strongest matches are used to elaborate complete associations between the events. As described in chapter 1, PATHFINDER uses several

heuristics to rate the overall strength of partial matches. The precise
algorithm employed by PATHFINDER appears in appendix A. As the
weights employed in PATHFINDER have been determined on the basis of a relatively limited set of examples (the 62 examples appearing
in appendix B, plus the extended example described in chapter 8), the
specific numerical values of these weights are of reduced importance relative to the general factors involved in the calculation. The calculation
consists of a raw score based on the degree of overlap between the two
traces, and this raw score is possibly reduced by one or more penalties
incurred by relevant contextual aspects of the match. The following
list of PATHFINDER's heuristics is repeated from chapter 1, excluding
those heuristics relevant only to the more complex causal reconstruction
scenarios described in chapters 5, 6 and 7.

Matching between transitions. Definite changes (APPEAR, DIS-
APPEAR, CHANGE, INCREASE and DECREASE) are weighted
most, other dynamic assertions next and static assertions least.

Proximity to description events. Penalties are introduced for
matches involving precedent events.

Narrative ordering. Preference is given to chaining matches between
events referenced consecutively in the description.

Current status of the association structure. Penalties are introduced for matches providing a second antecedent or consequent for
an event, matches between events already connected via associations, and matches involving hypothesized objects (e.g., a conjectured part of a physical object).

Types of associations. Partial restatement matches are penalized
slightly relative to partial chaining matches.

In addition to the above heuristics, once a partial match has been selected for elaboration, the mapping for that match is checked to see
whether it equates two objects in the description, this in light of current
bindings for hypothesized objects as generated in the course of elaborating previous partial matches. If the selected partial match fails this
test, it may be necessary to replace its agenda entry with one or more
new entries representing reduced partial matches. A similar situation is
described in detail in the next chapter. As the generation of reduced

partial matches is a relatively expensive computation, it is carried out only *after* a partial match has been chosen for elaboration.

As described in chapter 1, once the partial matches between events in a description have been enumerated and ranked, an iterative process of selecting the top-ranked partial match and elaborating it into a sequence of *complete associations* will generate an *association structure*, from which a range of questions may be answered. These operations, as well as the initial translation of event definitions into event traces are described in the following two sections, using specific examples as illustrations.

4.2 Direct Matches between Referenced Events

A Detailed Example

We now proceed with a description of the entire sequence of operations involved in causal reconstruction on a simple example. This initial example is somewhat lengthy due to the inclusion of explanatory material; subsequent examples in this and the next three chapters are presented in a more streamlined manner.

The first example consists of the following two-sentence description:

The board is dented. The wrench is dropped.

Note that while this description is certainly understandable—that is, we as humans can determine how the two referenced events might fit together—it is not as directly stated as it could be. For example, the description could have been presented as "The wrench is dropped. The wrench dents the board." However, supplied in the above-listed form, the description illustrates a simple situation where neither temporal ordering of event references nor identities and roles of objects involved in the events can help in determining how the events fit together. That is, we really need to know what happens during the stated events in order to determine how these two events might be related to one another.

Following is a set of generic definitions for the two events "denting" and "dropping," using the stylized English specification syntax developed in section 3.3. These definitions are supplied to PATHFINDER as supplementary information accompanying the above description. PATHFINDER uses this information to form an initial set of pattern event

traces for "denting" and "dropping," and these traces are subsequently
mapped to the particular circumstances of the input description, producing the traces illustrated in Figure 4.1.[3]

> Object 1 denting object 2 translates to the following
> event. First, the position of object 1 changes, the
> speed of object 1 does not disappear, the heading of
> object 1 does not disappear, the distance between
> object 1 and object 2 decreases, and the contact
> between object 1 and object 2 does not appear. Next,
> the position of object 1 changes, the speed of object 1
> disappears, the heading of object 1 disappears, the
> distance between object 1 and object 2 disappears, and
> the contact between object 1 and object 2 appears.
> Next, space 3 becomes a dent, space 3 becomes a part of
> object 2, and object 1 becomes inside space 3.

> Object 11 dropping object 12 translates to the
> following event. First, the distance between object 11
> and object 12 appears, the contact between object 11
> and object 12 disappears, object 11 becomes not in
> control of object 12, the support of object 12 by
> object 11 disappears, object 12 becomes not supported,
> the position of object 12 does not change, the speed of
> object 12 does not appear, the heading of object 12
> does not appear, and the elevation of object 12 does
> not change. Next, the distance between object 11 and
> object 12 does not disappear, the contact between
> object 11 and object 12 does not appear, object 11
> remains not in control of object 12, the support of
> object 12 by object 11 does not appear, object 12
> remains not supported, the position of object 12
> changes, the speed of object 12 appears, the heading of
> object 12 appears, and the elevation of object 12
> decreases. Next, the distance between object 11 and
> object 12 does not disappear, the contact between
> object 11 and object 12 does not appear, object 11
> remains not in control of object 12, the support of
> object 12 by object 11 does not appear, object 12
> remains not supported, the position of object 12

---

[3] Regarding the event definitions for "denting" and "dropping": for ease in specifying changes in "position," "speed," "heading" and "elevation," PATHFINDER
behaves as if the phrase "with respect to the background" has been included where
no second object has been specified as a frame of reference.

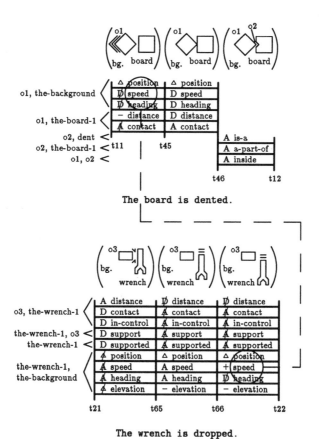

Figure 4.1
Event traces for the description "The board is dented. The wrench is dropped."

changes, the speed of object 12 increases, the heading
of object 12 does not disappear, and the elevation of
object 12 decreases.

In mapping the generic event definition traces to the description-
specific versions appearing in Figure 4.1, hypothesized objects must
be introduced, because both event references in the original description appear in passive voice with no agent specified. (Also, the dent

itself is represented as a hypothesized object "o2.") For the "denting" event, a hypothesized object approaches and then contacts the board, followed by the appearance of a dent in the board. For the "dropping" event, a hypothesized object comes out of contact and relinquishes control of the wrench, followed by the wrench starting and continuing to fall.

The supplied event definitions are intended to be generic in nature, not referring to the specific circumstances of the described situation. In particular, the definition for denting—and thus PATHFINDER's depiction of the event "The board is dented."—leaves open the issue of whether the object causing the denting comes to rest at the completion of the denting or continues its motion, acquiring new speed and heading in the interval from "t46" to "t12." Separately, because the dent does not exist prior to "t46," no information is provided concerning it prior to this point.[4]

Given the event traces depicted in Figure 4.1, six partial matches may be identified. The partial match of highest ranking is illustrated in the figure. Note that with regard the attribute "speed" in this match, an assertion involving the predicate INCREASE in the "dropping" trace has been matched with an assertion involving the predicate NOT-DISAPPEAR in the "denting" trace. This particular matching of assertions relies on the fact that the an INCREASE assertion *covers* a NOT-DISAPPEAR assertion (i.e., its expansion at the level of (NOT-)EQUAL and (NOT-)GREATER assertions is a superset of the corresponding expansion for the NOT-DISAPPEAR assertion).

Of the remaining five partial matches identified by PATHFINDER, three involve only a CHANGE assertion for "position." These are: a partial chaining match from the second transition of "dropping" to the first of "denting," a partial restatement match from the last two transitions of "dropping" to the first two of "denting," and a partial restatement match involving only the second transitions of both traces. PATHFINDER does not explore these partial matches further because

---

[4] The temporal ordering of time points does not always correspond to their numerical ordering in PATHFINDER. Here, for example, an initial allocation of two time points—"t11" and "t12"—to the denting event was subsequently found to be insufficient because the supplied event definition covered three transitions. When the event definition was instantiated to the description objects, new time points "t45" and "t46" were generated and inserted between "t11" and "t12."

they are not ranked highest among the partial matches. However, were PATHFINDER to elaborate any of these three matches, it would discover hidden logical inconsistencies concerning corresponding assertions for "speed" and "heading." Such inconsistencies are detected by performing logical inference on the combined sets of assertions from both traces involved in a match; this procedure is discussed in chapter 5. Finally, there are two partial restatement matches involving NOT-APPEAR assertions for "contact": one matching the second transition of "dropping" with first transition of "denting," and the other matching the third transition of "dropping" with the first transition of "denting." These partial matches would also be deemed unacceptable were they to be chosen for elaboration—in this case due to an equating of description objects "the-wrench-1" and "the-board-1." Again, because a stronger partial match exists, these matches are never fully considered such that the object equivalences would be detected.

The following information is needed to specify the highest ranked partial match, as indicated in Figure 4.1. The three matching assertions are indicated as they appear in the second trace of the chaining match—the "denting" activity—as this is the trace whose assertions are "covered" by assertions in the other trace. The binding list provides a mapping from quantities in the first trace to equivalent quantities in the second trace.

match type: partial chaining
first trace: trace-48 ("The wrench is dropped.")
second trace: trace-17 ("The board is dented.")
matched assertions:
    CHANGE(position, <o1, the-background>, t11, t45)
    NOT-DISAPPEAR(speed, <o1, the-background>, t11, t45)
    NOT-DISAPPEAR(heading, <o1, the-background>, t11, t45)
bindings: { [t66 → t11], [t22 → t45], [the-wrench-1 → o1] }

Given the information describing this match, and in particular, the binding list mapping time points and objects between the two traces, we may construct a sequence of simple transformations to be applied to the original two traces in order to bring them into a *complete match*, whereby the transitions involved in the match contain identical assertions (i.e., they correspond to the same point in transition space). As described in chapter 1, we divide such transformations into two categories: (1) *information-preserving* transformations, belonging to an inverse pair of transformations in transition space, and (2) *non-information-preserving* transformations, not belonging to such an inverse pair.

Figure 4.2 depicts such a sequence of transformations, bringing the "dropping" and "denting" traces into a complete match. In this figure, traces A and B are the original "denting" and "dropping" traces, respectively. Trace B is transformed by a *reduction* operation (a non-information-preserving transformation) which removes all assertions except those involved in the partial match or tracking the same attribute-object combinations—"position," "speed," and "heading" of "o1" with respect to "the-background"—for other intervals. This reduction transformation produces trace C.[5] Trace A is first transformed by an *equivalence* operation (an information-preserving transformation), replacing time points "t11" and "t45" with their matched equivalents "t66" and "t22" and replacing the hypothesized object "o1" with its matched equivalent "the-wrench-1." This transformation produces trace D. Trace E is then produced by a reduction operation on trace D, removing all assertions except those concerning "position," "speed," and "heading" of "the-wrench-1" with respect to "the-background," as involved in the partial match. Finally, traces C and E are linked by a complete chaining association, as the third transition in trace C is identical to the first transition in trace E.

As described in chapter 1, a set of event traces related by complete associations is called an *association structure* and may be diagramed using a special three-dimensional portrayal of transition space. In this graphical characterization, transitions are depicted as points, and event traces are points, arrows or simple directed acyclic graphs. Additionally, complete chaining associations are indicated by shared points between event traces (thereby arranging the event traces in sequence in the horizontal dimension), and associations corresponding to transformations are depicted by alignment of the original and transformed traces in either the vertical dimension—for non-information-preserving transformations—or the depth dimension—for information-preserving transformations. The

---

[5] Note that the reduction operation takes place at the level of EQUAL/GREATER assertions and thereby removes from trace B the extraneous GREATER assertion that is responsible for specification of the speed of "the wrench" as increasing rather than simply not disappearing.

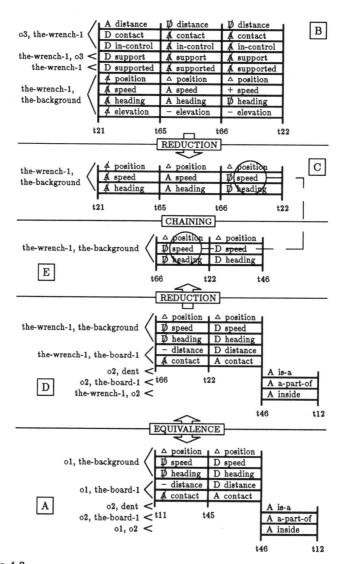

Figure 4.2
Transformations bringing the "denting" and "dropping" traces into a complete chaining match.

association structure below corresponds to the sequence of associations depicted in Figure 4.2. (As in chapter 1, heavy arrows represent events specified in the description, while lighter arrows depict intermediate traces formed in the elaboration of a partial match.)

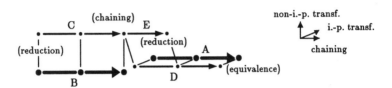

A: The board is dented.
B: The wrench is dropped.

Answering Questions of Type 1

At this point, PATHFINDER is ready to process questions concerning the described activity. Section 2.2 listed the four types of questions fielded by PATHFINDER. The following paragraphs describe how each of these four types may be answered. As a first example, consider the following question of type 1.

What happens to the speed of the wrench?

To answer this type of question, a composite event trace is constructed by merging all of the traces in the association structure. As each trace's contents are included in the composite trace, its time points and objects are mapped, if necessary, to make them consistent with other assertions already included in the composite trace. (Intuitively, one may think of projecting each trace through all mappings tied to associations linking that trace with other traces situated "closer to the viewer" in three-dimensional association structure diagrams such as depicted above.) A composite trace constructed for the current example is depicted in Figure 4.3. In this figure, the original description events are listed on top, with brackets indicating the portions of the overall activity corresponding to their occurrence.

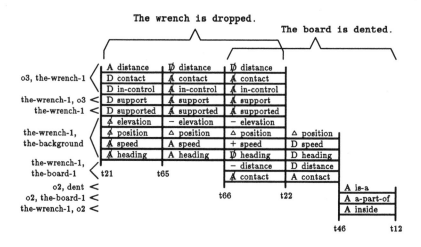

Figure 4.3
Composite trace for the denting/dropping example.

In answering the above question, PATHFINDER extracts the fragment of the composite trace having to do with the speed of the wrench, forming a new trace as follows:

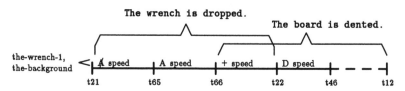

Finally, it translates this trace into simplified English and inserts context-specifying qualifications (e.g., "As the wrench is dropped, ...") each time the activity progresses past the start of a new event from the original description. For the above question, the response returned by PATHFINDER is as follows:

> First, as the wrench is dropped, the speed of the
> wrench does not appear. Next, the speed of the wrench
> appears. Next, as the board is dented, the speed of
> the wrench increases. Next, the speed of the wrench
> disappears.

As an extension of this capability, a program like PATHFINDER could also be made to "fill out" the composite trace to include change specifications for all concerned attribute-object combinations over all concerned intervals. This would constitute a form of STRIPS assumption [Fikes and Nilsson, 1971] applied to change information. For instance, an IN-CREASE specified in the composite trace could be extended into an IN-CREASE for following or preceding intervals as well, a CHANGE into a CHANGE, and so forth, with the non-continuable change specifications APPEAR and DISAPPEAR extended to NOT-DISAPPEAR and NOT-APPEAR, respectively, for future intervals and NOT-APPEAR and NOT-DISAPPEAR, respectively, for past intervals.

While this is a rather straightforward extension, PATHFINDER simply answers based on information explicitly included in the composite trace. Given the composite trace diagramed in Figure 4.3, other questions of type 1 are answered by PATHFINDER as follows:

```
What happens to the elevation of the wrench?

    First, as the wrench is dropped, the elevation of the
    wrench does not change. Next, the elevation of the
    wrench decreases. Next, as the board is dented, the
    elevation of the wrench decreases.

What happens to the distance between the wrench and the
board?

    First, as the board is dented, the distance between the
    wrench and the board decreases. Next, the distance
    between the wrench and the board disappears.
```

Additionally, PATHFINDER can answer questions of type 1 regarding hypothesized objects (e.g., the object that drops the wrench, the dent that appears in the board); however, a question of type 4 must be asked first in order to provide PATHFINDER with a candidate external name for such an object (e.g., "Does the hand drop the wrench?" followed by "What happens to the contact between the hand and the wrench?")

Answering Questions of Type 2

Questions of type 2 ask about relationships between particular events in the description. For the current example, there are only two possible questions of this type—the following question and a similar question with the two events interchanged.

> How does the denting of the board relate to the
> dropping of the wrench?

To answer a question of this type, we must first extract the portion of the association structure connecting the two events in question. This can be done by conducting a depth-first search starting at either of the two events and working through the set of associations connecting all events in the association structure. For the current example, the two named events are the only events of concern, and thus the entire association structure is relevant and specifies the path of association from the first event to the second event. The path is as follows:

> The board is dented. (original form—trace A)
>   → EQUIVALENCE
> The board is dented. (transformed—trace D)
>   → REDUCTION
> The board is dented. (transformed—trace E)
>   → CHAINING (inverse)
> The wrench is dropped. (transformed—trace C)
>   → REDUCTION (inverse)
> The wrench is dropped. (original form—trace B)

From this point, an answer to the above question may be formed in four steps:

1. The association path is partitioned into segments, with each segment containing traces all derived from the same description or precedent event. For the above association path, there are two such segments, the first containing traces A, D and E, and the second containing traces C and B.

2. For each segment, a single trace most representative of the concerned description or precedent event is selected. If the original trace for the description or precedent event is included, it is selected; otherwise, the trace having been transformed the fewest number of times from the original form is selected. For the above

association path, both segments contain the original forms of the traces; thus, these traces (A and B) are selected.[6]

3. Next, the relationship between each consecutive pair of selected events is summarized by noting the single association of highest priority. For the purposes of this chapter, the three types of associations employed are prioritized as indicated in Table 4.1.

4. Finally, the selected traces and correspondingly-selected associations are expressed in simplified English. Selected traces are specified by retrieving the English event references originally used for these events (e.g., "The wrench is dropped.") Selected associations are described using the English characterizations given in Table 4.1. If there is not a single association of highest priority between two selected traces, but rather two associations of highest priority oriented in different directions (e.g., a chaining association in the forward direction plus a chaining association in the reverse direction), then the above-described prioritization scheme cannot be used. In this case, PATHFINDER defaults to a specification of the *temporal* relationship between the two selected traces, this based on calculations from the time points included in the traces. Five possible temporal indications are then utilized:

> "... occurs at the beginning of ..." / "... begins with ..."
> "... occurs at the end of ..." / "... ends with ..."
> "... coincides with ..."

Here, "coincides with" is used as a catch-all specification, stating simply that the specified events overlap temporally to some degree.

For the above question and association path, we have two selected traces, trace A and trace B, with a chaining association in the inverse direction chosen to specify the relationship between these two events. The response returned is thus as follows:

> The denting of the board is caused by the dropping of the wrench.

---

[6] Other examples in the book illustrate circumstances where the original trace for an event does not occur along the association path between two other events, yet a transformed image of the first event does.

Priority	Association type	As expressed in English
1.	CHAINING	"...causes..." / "...is caused by..."
2.	REDUCTION	"...is a part of..." / "...involves..."
3.	EQUIVALENCE	"...is equivalent to..."

Table 4.1
Prioritization and English translations for chaining, reduction and equivalence associations as appear in the course of elaborating partial matches between event traces.

Answering Questions of Type 3

Questions of types 3 and 4 are answered using the same mechanism as for questions of type 2, except that further association must be performed first. Questions of type 3 ask about plausible causal connections. For the current example, such a question is as follows:

How could the dropping of the wrench cause the wrench to bounce off the board?

Because this question involves a new type of event, an event definition is also supplied prior to the question. The definition is as follows:

Object 21 bouncing off object 22 translates to the following event. First, the position of object 21 changes, the speed of object 21 does not disappear, the heading of object 21 does not disappear, the distance between object 21 and object 22 decreases, and the contact between object 21 and object 22 does not appear. Next, the position of object 21 changes, the speed of object 21 disappears, the heading of object 21 disappears, the distance between object 21 and object 22 disappears, and the contact between object 21 and object 22 appears. Next, the position of object 21 changes, the speed of object 21 appears, the heading of object 21 appears, the distance between object 21 and object 22 appears, and the contact between object 21 and object 22 disappears. Next, the position of object 21 changes, the speed of object 21 does not disappear, the heading of object 21 does not disappear, the distance between object 21 and object 22 increases, and the contact between object 21 and object 22 does not appear.

The event trace produced by applying the above event definition in the context of the submitted question is shown in Figure 4.4 (trace F). To incorporate this event into the current association structure, the matcher is run to identify partial matches between the new event and other events in the association structure. This matching cycle illustrates an additional aspect of the association process not involved in the preceding discussion. When a partial association structure already exists, we need only consider matches involving a subset of "active" traces in that structure. Referring back to the association structure existing at this point, we can see that traces C and E may be ignored, as all matches involving these traces will have corresponding matches involving traces B and D, these matches scored equivalently or higher than the matches for C and E. Likewise, trace A may also be ignored, because its matches will be reflected in matches to trace D. We may thus consider only traces B and D to be "active" for the purposes of generating new associations.

When PATHFINDER's matcher is invoked to find partial chaining and restatement matches between the new event, trace F, and the currently active traces, B and D, 18 partial matches are identified. Of these, the partial restatement match described in Figure 4.4 is ranked highest, involving an overlap between the beginning stages of the "bouncing" event and the beginning stages of the "denting" event.[7] The elaboration of this partial match into a sequence of associations is illustrated in the following diagram. Here, an equivalence association maps time points in trace D to equivalent time points (in trace H) consistent with the time points of trace F. Next, traces H and F are connected via reduction associations to a common subset of assertions, trace G.

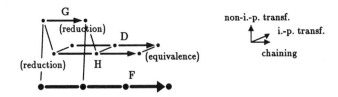

D: The board is dented. (transformed once)
F: The wrench bounces off the board.

---

[7] To steer the association process toward the construction of a suitable *causal* path of association for questions of type 3, heuristics having to do with connecting statements are incorporated, as described in chapter 7.

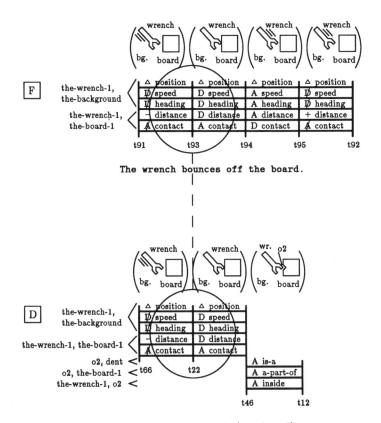

Figure 4.4
Partial match involved in answering "How could the dropping of the wrench cause the wrench to bounce off the board?"

Combined with the initial association structure fragment, the complete association structure at this point is as follows:

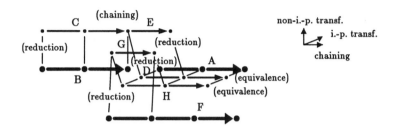

A: The board is dented.
B: The wrench is dropped.
F: The wrench bounces off the board.

We must now extract an association path connecting the dropping of the wrench with the bouncing of the wrench off the board. This path is outlined below.

> The wrench is dropped. (original form—trace B)
>   → REDUCTION
> The wrench is dropped. (transformed—trace C)
>   → CHAINING
> The board is dented. (transformed—trace E)
>   → REDUCTION (inverse)
> The board is dented. (transformed—trace D)
>   → EQUIVALENCE
> The board is dented. (transformed—trace H)
>   → REDUCTION
> The wrench bounces off the board (transformed—trace G)
>   → REDUCTION (inverse)
> The wrench bounces off the board. (original form—trace F)

From this path, three significant traces are selected, trace B, trace D (being transformed the fewest number of times from trace A, which falls outside this association path), and trace F. A single chaining association in the forward direction has highest priority for mention between trace B and trace D. Between trace D and trace F, however, two reduction associations in opposite directions have highest priority. As described above, PATHFINDER defaults to a temporal characterization in this case. Here, neither event begins or ends the other (trace D could conceivably extend *beyond* the end of trace F), so this relationship is described as simply "coincides with." The complete answer returned by PATH-FINDER is as follows. Because the question is posed hypothetically, the answer is phrased in a similar way.

```
The dropping of the wrench could cause the denting of
the board, which could coincide with the wrench
bouncing off the board.
```

Answering Questions of Type 4

Finally, we consider two questions of type 4. The first question is as follows (including an event definition for "falling"):

```
Object 21 falling translates to the following event.
Concurrently, object 21 remains not supported, the
position of object 21 changes, the speed of object 21
increases, the heading of object 21 does not disappear,
and the elevation of object 21 decreases.

Does the wrench fall?
```

The event trace produced for the wrench falling is as follows.

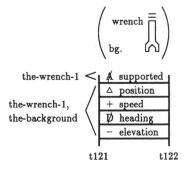

This trace matches best with a portion of the third transition in trace B ("The wrench is dropped.") In the elaboration of this partial match, additional assertions must be deleted from trace B, but not from the new trace, trace F, as all of its assertions are matched in trace B. The association path connecting trace F to the existing portion of the association structure is thus as follows.

> The wrench falls. (original form—trace F)
>   → REDUCTION (inverse)
> The wrench is dropped. (transformed—trace G)
>   → EQUIVALENCE
> The wrench is dropped. (original form—trace B)

This association path is then used to answer the question. As there is a single reduction association of highest priority, the characterization "is a part of" is used:

> Yes. The wrench falling is a part of the dropping of
> the wrench.

Questions of type 4 may also be used to ask whether a particular object has participated in a previously-mentioned event. The following question is an example:

> Does the wrench dent the board?

By constructing an event trace depicting the event referenced in the question and then associating this event trace with events previously depicted in the association structure, a strong match is generated with the original event "The board is dented."—this trace involving a hypothesized object later matched with the wrench. The new match does not violate constraints of the association process by equating different objects, and thus elaboration of the partial match proceeds, generating a single equivalence association and producing the following response:[8]

> Yes. The wrench denting the board is equivalent to the
> denting of the board.

---

[8] Actually, as described in chapters 6 and 8, PATHFINDER performs one additional check when answering questions of type 4. This check may result in a qualified response of "Perhaps." rather than "Yes."

4.3   Matches Involving Precedent Events

A Second Example

In this section, we continue with an abbreviated example involving a causal description including a precedent event. This example illustrates a situation where, in order to associate the events appearing in a causal description, the comprehender must postulate the occurrence of an additional event to fill a gap in the described activity. For our characterization of the causal reconstruction problem relative to a program serving as the comprehender, we have stipulated that all supplementary information relevant to comprehension be included in the input file; thus, we must provide a reference and event definition indicating the possibility of such a precedent event occurring. However, in order to ease the transition to a more complex version of the causal reconstruction task, where a program relies on an internal knowledge base of events and rules of restatement rather than requiring these to be externally supplied, we keep precedent events separate from the remainder of the causal description and describe their activity in terms of generic objects unrelated to the participants in the causal description. Further, precedent events are posed as *optional* for inclusion in the association structure, whereas the description events must necessarily be associated with one another.

The causal description for this example is as follows, describing activity involved in the firing of a pistol:

```
The trigger moves.  The hammer is released.
```

To this description, we add supplementary information in the form of event definitions for the two events "moving" and "releasing," plus a single precedent event of "unlatching," specified by both an event reference for the precedent event and an accompanying definition. The supplementary information specific to the precedent event is listed below.[9]

```
Object 21 unlatches object 22.

The unlatching of object 22 by object 21 translates to
the following event.  First, the position of object 21
```

---

[9]PATHFINDER employs a number of simple syntactic transformation rules in order to recognize matches between different forms of specification for events (e.g., matching the statement "Object 21 unlatches object 22." with the expression "The unlatching of object 22 by object 21 ... ").

changes, the speed of object 21 does not disappear, the
heading of object 21 does not disappear, the distance
between object 21 and object 22 does not appear, the
contact between object 21 and object 22 does not
disappear, and the restraint of object 22 by object 21
does not disappear. Next, the position of object 21
changes, the speed of object 21 does not disappear, the
heading of object 21 does not disappear, the distance
between object 21 and object 22 appears, the contact
between object 21 and object 22 disappears, and the
restraint of object 22 by object 21 disappears.

Figure 4.5 illustrates the three event traces generated for this example.
Nine partial matches are identified by PATHFINDER, the strongest of
which is a partial chaining match from the precedent event, trace C,
to the "releasing" event, trace B. This match involves three definite
changes: an appearance of distance, a disappearance of contact, and a
disappearance of restraint between two objects. Following an elaboration
of this partial match, the following association structure fragment is
generated. (By convention, precedent events are depicted using heavy,
dashed arrows.)

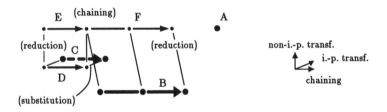

A: The trigger moves.
B: The hammer is released.

C: Object 21 unlatches object 22.

One difference between the above association structure fragment and
those described in previous examples concerns the information-preserving transformation used to bring objects and time points of one trace
into the context of another trace's activity. Here, a *substitution* transformation has been used—drawing a parallel between descriptions of
different events—rather than an *equivalence* association—relating alternate descriptions of the same event. As the precedent event involves

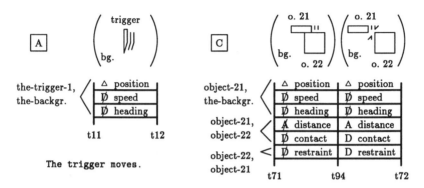

Object 21 unlatches object 22.

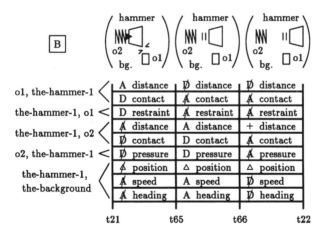

The hammer is released.

Figure 4.5
Event traces for "The trigger moves. The hammer is released."

physically different objects and has occurred at a different time than
the activity concerned by the "releasing" event, a substitution association is appropriate for this context.

Following the first cycle of association, there remain trace A, depicting
the trigger moving, and three active traces from the associated fragment:
trace B, depicting the releasing of the hammer; trace D, depicting the
trigger unlatching the hammer; and trace C, the original precedent event
depicting object 21 unlatching object 22. Unlike the example described
in the previous section, where one of the two traces linked by an equivalence association is "deactivated" for further matching, we retain both
the precedent and its substituted image as "active" traces, so that we
may both use the description-specific version of the precedent and possibly generate new uses of the original precedent event.

There are six partial matches between trace A and the three active
traces of the initial association structure fragment. Strongest among
these is a partial chaining match from trace A to trace D (the trig-
ger/hammer version of the unlatching event). Elaborating this partial
match produces the following completed association structure.[10]

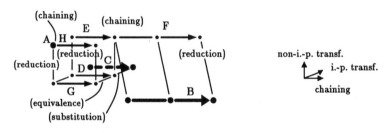

A: The trigger moves.
B: The hammer is released.

C: Object 21 unlatches object 22.

Answering Questions

For this example, we consider only questions of types 1 and 2—questions
concerning the association structure resulting from direct processing
of the causal description. In subsequent examples, the discussion of

----

[10]Regarding traces A and H in this diagram: trace A consists of a single transition
(the large dot), while H consists of two transitions, the first of which is identical to
the transition for trace A and thus coincides with it in the diagram.

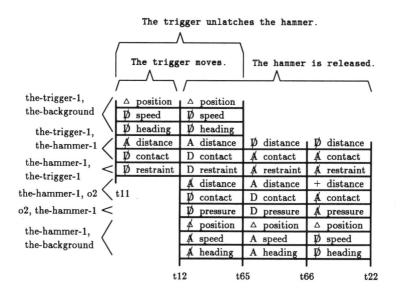

Figure 4.6
Composite trace for the trigger/hammer description.

question-answering is omitted altogether where inspection of the association structure and original event traces is sufficient to reveal the answers PATHFINDER would generate for questions of types 1 and 2.

First, a question of type 1:

> What happens to the restraint of the hammer by the
> trigger?

A composite trace for this example is shown in Figure 4.6. As before, the composite trace is formed by merging traces in the association structure, mapping objects and time points to a consistent set of such quantities. The precedent trace, trace C, is excluded from this process, as it describes a separate activity occurring at a different time from the rest of the activity involved in the description (the substitution association is taken as an indication that the precedent trace constitutes a separate activity.) Parts of the composite trace are generated from both description events and the mapped precedent involving the trigger unlatching the hammer. From this composite trace, the question concerning restraint may be answered as follows:

> First, as the trigger moves, the restraint of the
> hammer by the trigger does not disappear. Next, as the
> hammer is released, the restraint of the hammer by the
> trigger disappears. Next, the restraint of the hammer
> by the trigger does not appear.

As a second illustration of question-answering for this example, consider the following question of type 2:

> How does the trigger moving relate to the releasing of
> the hammer?

Answering of this question proceeds as described in the previous section, starting with an inspection of the association structure to determine a path of association between the specified events. This path of association is listed below.

> The trigger moves. (original form—trace A)
>   → CHAINING
> The trigger unlatches the hammer. (transformed—trace H)
>   → REDUCTION (inverse)
> The trigger unlatches the hammer. (transformed—trace G)
>   → EQUIVALENCE
> The trigger unlatches the hammer. (transformed—trace D)
>   → REDUCTION
> The trigger unlatches the hammer. (transformed—trace E)
>   → CHAINING
> The hammer is released. (transformed—trace F)
>   → REDUCTION (inverse)
> The hammer is released. (original form—trace B)

From this path, three traces are selected: trace A, trace D and trace B. The first and third of these are description events in their original form. The second is the minimally transformed version of the precedent event. Between each pair of these events, a single chaining association has highest priority and is thus used to summarize these sequences of associations. In English, the events are referenced using their original English form (here, as extracted from the question itself), with the exception of the transformed precedent event, which is described by taking the original English form for the precedent ("Object 21 unlatches object 22.") and replacing "object 21" with "the trigger" and "object 22" with "the hammer," in line with the substitution mapping producing trace D from the the original precedent trace, trace C. (The presence of a substitution association instead of an equivalence association signals a need for describing trace D using its own objects rather than those of trace C.) The answer returned by PATHFINDER is as follows:

```
The trigger moving causes the trigger to unlatch the
hammer, which causes the releasing of the hammer.
```

5 Inference, Background Statements and Assumptions

This chapter describes three simple extensions to the matching and elaboration process outlined in chapter 4. These extensions are: (1) the incorporation of deductive inference into the causal reconstruction process, (2) the utilization of background (static) information, and (3) the identification of assumptions made during matching, such that they may be listed in response to questions submitted to the program.

In connection with these extensions, two additional input quantities are included relative to the framework of the previous chapter: background statements and rules of inference. Background statements are included so that input descriptions may specify static properties and relationships that hold for the duration of a described activity. Additionally, background statements are permitted within the supplementary information as a means of providing additional static information relevant to a described activity. Rules of inference are included within the supplementary information and serve to inform the program of relevant patterns of deduction over transition space representations.

5.1   Overview

Employing Inference

There are two related applications of inference with respect to the transition space representation. First, inference can be used to extend the sets of assertions contained in particular event traces, thereby facilitating new partial matches between event traces or strengthening existing partial matches. Second, inference can be used to check partial matches for consistency once they are selected for elaboration, this in light of object and time point equivalences introduced by the partial matches.

Orthogonal to the issue of *when* inference is to be used, we may also consider what *types* of inference may be of use. Two types of inference present themselves: inference concerning predicates in the transition space representation, and inference concerning attributes in the representation.

As defined in chapter 3, each of the predicates used in our realization of transition space decomposes into a set of assertions involving only the primitives EQUAL, NOT-EQUAL, GREATER and NOT-GREATER. Taking advantage of this fact, we may conduct inference over predicates by focusing entirely on relationships between these four primitive predicates. Higher-level predicates may be converted into their corresponding EQUAL/GREATER-level expansions prior to inference, and following inference, the resulting set of assertions may be condensed where possible to redescribe the activity in terms of the higher-level defined predicates. It is a rather simple matter to enumerate logical relationships between EQUAL, NOT-EQUAL, GREATER and NOT-GREATER, and such rules are directly implemented within the PATHFINDER program. The following are a few examples of these rules:

> EQUAL(?attribute, ?object-1, ?t1, ?object-2, ?t2)
> $\Longrightarrow$ EQUAL(?attribute, ?object-2, ?t2, ?object-1, ?t1)

> EQUAL(?attribute, ?object-1, ?t1, ?object-2, ?t2)   AND
> GREATER(?attribute, ?object-2, ?t2, ?object-3, ?t3)
> $\Longrightarrow$ GREATER(?attribute, ?object-1, ?t1, ?object-3, ?t3)

> NOT-GREATER(?attribute, ?object-1, ?t1, ?object-2, ?t2)   AND
> NOT-GREATER(?attribute, ?object-2, ?t2, ?object-1, ?t1)
> $\Longrightarrow$ EQUAL(?attribute, ?object-1, ?t1, ?object-2, ?t2)

In addition, PATHFINDER uses a similar set of rules to detect logical inconsistencies. Two examples of such rules are as follows:

> NOT-EQUAL(?attribute, ?object-1, ?t1, ?object-1, ?t1)
> $\Longrightarrow$ ... inconsistency

> EQUAL(?attribute, ?object-1, ?t1, ?object-2, ?t2)   AND
> GREATER(?attribute, ?object-1, ?t1, ?object-2, ?t2)
> $\Longrightarrow$ ... inconsistency

In contrast to inference regarding predicates, inference regarding attributes relies on a potentially limitless set of rules. Such rules can express symmetric or transitive relationships for binary attributes:

> PRESENT(contact, <?o1, ?o2>, ?t1)
> $\Longrightarrow$ PRESENT(contact, <?o2, ?o1>, ?t1)

PRESENT(above, <?o1, ?o2>, ?t1)
$\implies$ NOT-PRESENT(above, <?o2, ?o1>, ?t1)

PRESENT(inside, <?o1, ?o2>, ?t1)   AND
PRESENT(inside, <?o2, ?o3>, ?t1)
$\implies$ PRESENT(inside, <?o1, ?o3>, ?t1)

Or, they may express arbitrary relationships between different attributes:

PRESENT(contact, <?o1, ?o2>, ?t1)
$\implies$ NOT-PRESENT(distance, <?o1, ?o2>, ?t1)

PRESENT(inside, <?o1, ?o2>, ?t1)   AND
PRESENT(above, <?o2, ?o3>, ?t1)
$\implies$ PRESENT(above, <?o1, ?o3>, ?t1)

In keeping with our requirement that all relevant background knowledge be supplied with a causal description, relevant rules of inference are included in the supplementary information, using a form that incorporates two specifications of activity (similar in form to the body of an event definition) and a single connecting statement linking the two specifications of activity and involving the verb "implies." As an example, the following segment specifies the last rule listed above:

> Concurrently, object 1 is inside object 2, and object 2 is above object 3. The preceding statement implies the following statement. Object 1 is above object 3.

To carry out inference on an event trace or set of event traces, PATH-FINDER converts the collective set of assertions to equivalent assertions involving (NOT-)EQUAL and (NOT-)GREATER and applies all available rules of inference, including both the built-in rules for (NOT-)EQUAL and (NOT-)GREATER and any explicitly entered rules for inference over attributes. Application of these rules follows the format of a forward-chaining production system, with inference activity continuing until no further consequences can be derived.

One additional strategy has been found to improve considerably the time efficiency of this process in PATHFINDER. Rather than focusing on individual EQUAL/GREATER-level relationships between attribute–object–time-point triples, a database of *equivalence classes* of these triples is set up. For example, from the assertion

EQUAL(speed, <object-1, the-background>, t11,
                    <object-2, the-background>, t11)

we may set up an equivalence class containing two attribute–object–time-point triples:

Equivalence class 1:
    { (speed, <object-1, the-background>, t11),
       (speed, <object-2, the-background>, t11) }

By maintaining all specifications of GREATER, NOT-EQUAL and NOT-GREATER relationships with respect to equivalence classes of attribute-object-time-point triples, rather than the individual members of these classes, much redundant inference can be avoided. To see this, consider what happens when one triple in such an equivalence class is determined to be NOT-EQUAL to another triple in another class. By simply recording a NOT-EQUAL relationship between the two classes, we avoid the necessity of having to independently discover and record each pairwise NOT-EQUAL relationship between a member of the first class and a member of the second class. Following termination of the inference process, individual relationships implied by the database of related equivalence classes can be quickly reconstructed.

In the framework of the transition space representation, inference amounts to a non-information-preserving transformation (i.e., information is added by this transformation). In diagraming association structures involving non-information-preserving transformations, we take the convention of "upwards" corresponding to "less information"—at least where it is possible to make such claims.[1] Following this convention, an

---

[1] By definition, a non-information-preserving transformation does not belong to an inverse pair of transformations. This does not require that each such transformation strictly decrease or increase the information content of a trace, however. Such a transformation might remove some types of information while adding assumptions regarding other types of information.

event trace produced by inference conducted on another event trace will be situated *below* that trace as follows:

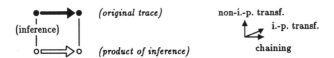

Here, we depict the product of inference using an arrow in outline, adhering to the following convention: description events and precedent events are depicted as thick arrows (precedents are dashed), all traces produced independently of the matching process are indicated in outline (this includes products of inference and products of exploratory transformations), and all traces produced in the course of elaborating partial matches are depicted using thin arrows.

As stated above, there are two ways in which inference may contribute to causal reconstruction in transition space. The first is in service of making partial matches possible or strengthening existing matches. To this end, PATHFINDER attempts inference on all of the initial traces in the association structure (this includes events referenced in the causal description and precedents supplied in the supplementary information). If inference succeeds in extending the set of assertions in a trace, a trace depicting the product of inference is inserted into the association structure, associated with the original trace via an "inference" association. Following subsequent application of exploratory transformations, as outlined in chapter 1 and detailed in chapter 6, inference is again attempted on the products of transformation. Because a trace produced by inference on another trace contains all assertions of the original trace plus new assertions, the original trace is marked "inactive" with regard to the determination of partial matches and performance of exploratory transformations.

Regarding the use of inference to detect inconsistencies, whenever a partial match is elaborated into a set of full associations, a check is made to see whether the object and time-point equivalences introduced by the match generate logical contradictions with regard to the assertions contained in the matched traces. For example, one trace may assert that an object increases in speed over an interval, and a second trace may assert that the object decreases in speed over a second interval. If the

Priority	Association type	As expressed in English
1.	CHAINING	"...causes..." / "...is caused by..."
2.	REDUCTION	"...is a part of..." / "...involves..."
3.	INFERENCE	"...implies..." / "...is implied by..."
4.	EQUIVALENCE	"...is equivalent to..."

Table 5.1
Prioritization and English translations for association types arising from the use of inference in conjunction with the elaboration of partial matches between event traces.

two traces are matched together in such a way that the first interval is equated with the second interval, an inconsistency arises, and the partial match must be abandoned. An example of inference used in this manner appears in the next section.

For question answering where inference is involved, we need to make only minor changes to the procedures outlined in the previous chapter. For questions of type 1, no changes are required, as all traces in the association structure are merged to form a composite trace from which the answer is generated, and a trace produced by inference on another trace will simply contribute a few new assertions to the composite trace. For questions of the remaining three types, we need to insert the "inference" association into the prioritization of associations, so that under the proper circumstances the program may respond that one event implies another. From the set of descriptions tested on PATHFINDER, it appears suitable to insert the "inference" association between the "reduction" and "equivalence" associations, producing the prioritization scheme depicted in Table 5.1. Thus, if two selected traces are joined by an association path consisting of an inference association followed by an equivalence association, the overall association will be summarized as one of inference, and so forth.

Making Use of Background Statements

The second extension discussed in this chapter has to do with the inclusion of background statements in the input supplied to the program. These statements may appear in both the causal description and supplementary information. By permitting such statements in either location, we may then test the program on causal descriptions extracted from sources such as encyclopedias—these descriptions possibly containing explicit background statements—while also facilitating the inclusion of additional information as required for comprehension—this along the lines of the added precedent events, rules of inference and so forth. In effect, a distinction can be made between background statements that might normally be supplied to *humans* set to the task of causal reconstruction, and additional background statements required when a program with an empty knowledge base is set to the task.

Background statements can often contribute to the process of inference. Because the assertions generated from background statements are time-independent, they are maintained separately from the time-dependent information of event traces and are thus not directly involved in the matching process between event traces. Indeed, in the interest of increasing the efficiency of the matching process, PATHFINDER routinely removes from event traces all time-specific assertions covered by assertions maintained in its base of background assertions.

The following are examples of simple background statements expressible using the grammar introduced in chapter 2.

> The block is a physical object.
> The beam is not flexible.
> The support of object 1 by object 2 is present.
> The elevation of the ceiling exceeds the elevation of the floor.

These statements are translated into simple assertions involving the defined predicates PRESENT, NOT-PRESENT, MATCH, NOT-MATCH, EXCEED and NOT-EXCEED, as described in chapter 3. Due to the time-invariant nature of these assertions, by convention we use the value "null" where a time point is required by these predicates:[2] The following assertions represent each of the background statements listed above.

> PRESENT(is-a, <the-block, physical-object>, null)
> NOT-PRESENT(flexible, the-beam, null)
> PRESENT(support, <object-1, object-2>, null)
> EXCEED(elevation, <the-ceiling, the-floor>, null)

Once a base of background assertions has been set up, rules of inference are applied to extend the set of background assertions, producing

---

[2] The use of "null" in place of an explicit time point also occurs in specifying temporal relationships between time points—e.g., "PRESENT(after, <t2, t1>, null)"—in the definitions for the ten change characterizations provided in chapter 3.

new assertions of the same time-independent nature. Later, whenever inference is to be applied to a specific event trace or set of event traces, the background assertions are instantiated to each specific time point of the involved event traces, augmenting the set of assertions from which inference may draw new consequences. In this manner, background statements may contribute both to the extension of event traces in preparation for matching and the checking of partial matches for consistency.

Identifying Supporting Assumptions

The third extension described in this chapter involves the program noting particular assumptions made in the course of chaining matches. This has to do with precedent events, as the events referenced in the causal description itself are accepted unquestioningly as having occurred. When a precedent event is incorporated into the overall model of the activity, then if that precedent is the consequent of a chaining association, it is informative to consider whether all assertions in the initial transition of that precedent are covered by assertions in the corresponding interval of the antecedent trace. If not, then the remaining, uncovered assertions must be counted as assumptions. Section 5.4 provides an example of the recording of assumptions, for use in question-answering by the program.

5.2   Employing Inference

This section presents four simple examples illustrating the use of inference in PATHFINDER. For the first three of these examples, inference is used to facilitate matching. The fourth example involves inference used to detect a logical inconsistency resulting from a particular partial match.

Inference Regarding Predicates

For the first example, the following causal description and accompanying event definitions are provided:

```
Vehicle 1 decreases in speed to match vehicle 2.
Vehicle 2 increases in speed to match vehicle 1.
```

Object 11 decreasing in speed to match object 12
translates to the following event. Concurrently, the
position of object 11 changes, the speed of object 11
decreases, the heading of object 11 does not disappear,
the position of object 12 changes, the speed of object
12 does not disappear, and the heading of object 12
does not disappear. At that point, the speed of object
11 matches the speed of object 12.

Object 21 increasing in speed to match object 22
translates to the following event. Concurrently, the
position of object 21 changes, the speed of object 21
increases, the heading of object 21 does not disappear,
the position of object 22 changes, the speed of object
22 does not disappear, and the heading of object 22
does not disappear. At that point, the speed of object
21 matches the speed of object 22.

This example illustrates a situation where inference strengthens a partial match already present between two traces. In this case, the inference involves the symmetric property of the predicate EQUAL.

Applying the above event definition to the two events referenced in the causal description, the following two event traces are produced:

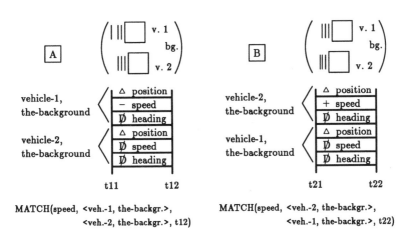

MATCH(speed, <veh.-1, the-backgr.>,
      <veh.-2, the-backgr.>, t12)

MATCH(speed, <veh.-2, the-backgr.>,
      <veh.-1, the-backgr.>, t22)

While there does exist a partial match between these two event traces, the match concerns only the fact that both objects are moving and does not include the fact that at the end of the interval they are moving at the same speed, this due to the reversed ordering of arguments to the relevant "MATCH" assertions. However, when PATHFINDER applies its built-in rules for inference at the level of assertions involving EQUAL, GREATER, NOT-EQUAL and NOT-GREATER, augmented versions of the two event traces are produced, as follows:

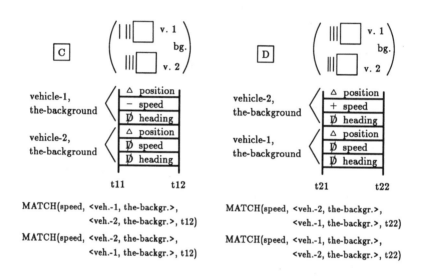

MATCH(speed, <veh.-1, the-backgr.>,
                    <veh.-2, the-backgr.>, t12)
MATCH(speed, <veh.-2, the-backgr.>,
                    <veh.-1, the-backgr.>, t12)

MATCH(speed, <veh.-2, the-backgr.>,
                    <veh.-1, the-backgr.>, t22)
MATCH(speed, <veh.-1, the-backgr.>,
                    <veh.-2, the-backgr.>, t22)

At this point, the association structure fragment may be diagramed as follows:

A: Vehicle 1 decreases in speed to match vehicle 2.
B: Vehicle 2 increases in speed to match vehicle 1.

Here, the traces produced by inference are marked as active for purposes of matching, and the original traces are marked as inactive.

Elaborating the partial restatement match between the two traces produced by inference, the final association structure for this example is as diagramed below:

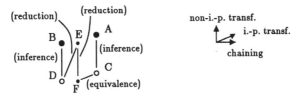

A: Vehicle 1 decreases in speed to match vehicle 2.
B: Vehicle 2 increases in speed to match vehicle 1.

Here, both trace D and trace F contain information not contained in the other (concerning speeding up and slowing down of the objects), and thus reduction transformations must be applied in both directions to produce a complete match at trace E, diagramed below. (By convention, complete restatement matches with no time point/object equivalences are depicted by a single trace rather than two identical traces joined by an equivalence association.)

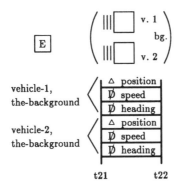

MATCH(speed, <veh.-1, the-backgr.>, <veh.-2, the-backgr.>, t22)

MATCH(speed, <veh.-2, the-backgr.>, <veh.-1, the-backgr.>, t22)

Inference Regarding Attributes

The second example involves inference based on properties of individual attributes. The causal description for this example is as follows:

> The rocket propels the jet of exhaust. The jet of
> exhaust moves away from the rocket.

Given event definitions for "propelling" and "moving away," the following event traces are produced:

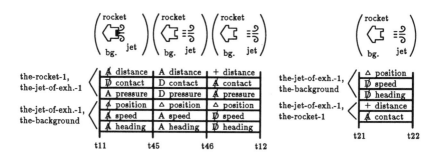

As in the previous example, a partial match does exist but this match is strengthened following the application of inference. Here, however, the inference to be conducted concerns not predicates but attributes: "distance" and "contact." As such rules are not built into PATHFINDER, the following four specifications are included in the supplementary information to PATHFINDER:

> The distance between object 21 and object 22 is
> present. The preceding statement implies the following
> statement. The distance between object 22 and object
> 21 matches the distance between object 21 and object
> 22.

> The distance between object 31 and object 32 is not
> present. The preceding statement implies the following
> statement. The distance between object 32 and object
> 31 is not present.

> The contact between object 41 and object 42 is present.
> The preceding statement implies the following
> statement. The contact between object 42 and object 41
> is present.

```
The contact between object 51 and object 52 is not
present. The preceding statement implies the following
statement. The contact between object 52 and object 51
is not present.
```

By specifying not only that the presence of distance between a first
and second object implies the presence of distance between the second
and first object, but also that the two distances *match* in value, inference
conducted at the level of the primitive predicates EQUAL, GREATER,
NOT-EQUAL and NOT-GREATER will cause in all increases and decreases in one direction of distance to generate corresponding increases
and decreases in the other direction of distance. The event traces produced by inference conducted on the original traces are depicted below.

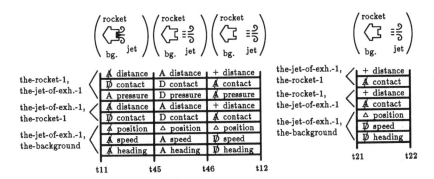

A partial restatement match between the two products of inference is
elaborated in a similar manner to the previous example, producing the
following association structure.

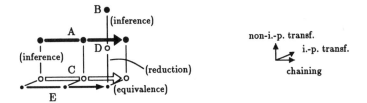

```
A: The rocket propels the jet of exhaust.
B: The jet of exhaust moves away from the rocket.
```

Inference between Attributes

The third example is rather simple, but illustrates two additional facets of inference: inference *between* attributes and inference which *creates* a partial match where none existed prior to inference. The input description for this example is as follows:

```
The elevation of the ball increases.  The ball moves.
```

Given this description, plus a definition for "moving," the following event traces result:

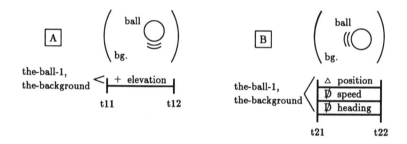

Of course, a change in elevation constitutes a change in three-dimensional position as well. Given the following rules of inference, PATH-FINDER is able to recognize this correspondence.

```
The elevation of object 11 increases.  The preceding
event implies the following event.  The position of
object 11 changes.

The elevation of object 21 decreases.  The preceding
event implies the following event.  The position of
object 21 changes.

The position of object 31 does not change.  The
preceding event implies the following event.  The
elevation of object 31 does not change.
```

Applying these rules to the original traces, an extension for trace A is generated (but not for trace B), as follows:

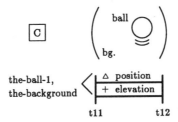

The resulting partial restatement match between this trace and the original trace for the ball moving leads to the following association structure:

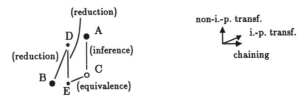

A: The elevation of the ball increases.
B: The ball moves.

Testing Partial Matches for Consistency

The final example of this section illustrates the use of inference in checking partial matches for consistency. In this case, inference results in the avoidance of an undesirable match. The input description for this example is as follows:

The arrow is released. The arrow strikes the target.

Given event definitions for "releasing" and "striking," the following two event traces are generated. For the "releasing" event:

	A distance	$\emptyset$ distance	$\emptyset$ distance
o1, the-arrow-1			
	D contact	$\cancel{A}$ contact	$\cancel{A}$ contact
the-arrow-1, o1	D restraint	$\cancel{A}$ restraint	$\cancel{A}$ restraint
the-arrow-1, o2	$\cancel{A}$ distance	A distance	+ distance
	$\emptyset$ contact	D contact	$\cancel{A}$ contact
o2, the-arrow-1	$\emptyset$ pressure	D pressure	$\cancel{A}$ pressure
the-arrow-1,	$\cancel{A}$ position	$\triangle$ position	$\triangle$ position
the-background	$\cancel{A}$ speed	A speed	$\emptyset$ speed
	$\cancel{A}$ heading	A heading	$\emptyset$ heading
	t11	t45	t46	t12

Here, two hypothetical objects are introduced via the event definition: a latch-like object ("o1") that relinquishes contact and restraint on the arrow, and a spring-like object ("o2") that propels the arrow once unlatched. For the "striking" event, the following trace results:

	$\triangle$ position	$\triangle$ position
the-arrow-1,	$\emptyset$ speed	D speed
the-background	$\emptyset$ heading	D heading
the-arrow-1,	$-$ distance	D distance
the-target-1	$\cancel{A}$ contact	A contact
	t21	t64	t22

For these two traces, the strongest partial match is a partial chaining match from the "releasing" event (third transition) to the "striking" event. This match involves the following four assertions from the "releasing" event:

CHANGE(position, <the-arrow-1, the-background>, t46, t12)
NOT-DISAPPEAR(speed, <the-arrow-1, the-background>,
                          t46, t12)
NOT-DISAPPEAR(heading, <the-arrow-1, the-background>,
                          t46, t12)
NOT-APPEAR(contact, <the-arrow-1, o2>, t46, t12)

and the following four assertions from the "hitting" event:

CHANGE(position, <the-arrow-1, the-background>, t21, t64)
NOT-DISAPPEAR(speed, <the-arrow-1, the-background>,
                          t21, t64)
NOT-DISAPPEAR(heading, <the-arrow-1, the-background>,
                          t21, t64)
NOT-APPEAR(contact, <the-arrow-1, the-target-1>, t21, t64)

The first three assertions of each set produce a reasonable match between the two traces, linking movement of "the-arrow-1" from "t46" to "t12" with similar movement from "t21" to "t64." However, the matching of statements concerning "contact" additionally equates "o2" (the spring that propelled the arrow) with "the-target-1." Because the arrow is specified as remaining not in contact with both objects and because these objects are not known to be distinct from one another, the match extends to equate these two objects.

The problem with this match is that the arrow is moving *away* from the spring that propelled it, while it is moving *toward* the target. This is explicitly represented in the disparity between the assertion

INCREASE(distance, <the-arrow-1, o2>, t46, t12)

in the "releasing" trace and

DECREASE(distance, <the-arrow-1, the-target-1>, t21, t64)

in the "striking" trace. Unfortunately, from the standpoint of matching, this only means that the partial match identified between the two traces

will not include the assertions concerning "distance," as neither statement covers the other. By performing inference on the collective set of
assertions contained in the two traces, however, the inconsistency can
be detected. In particular, the INCREASE assertion specifies that its
indicated distance is GREATER at the second time point, while the DE-
CREASE assertion specifies that its indicated distance is GREATER at
the first time point. Given a record of object and time point equivalences
for the match, then depending on the order in which rules of inference
are applied, transitivity of the GREATER predicate will generate one
of the following two assertions:

> GREATER(distance, <the-arrow-1, the-target-1>, t46,
> <the-arrow-1, the-target-1>, t46)

or

> GREATER(distance, <the-arrow-1, the-target-1>, t12,
> <the-arrow-1, the-target-1>, t12).

At this point, one of PATHFINDER's built-in rules for detecting inconsistency fires, causing PATHFINDER to terminate its processing of
the partial match in question and remove the corresponding entry from
the agenda. Before discarding the partial match completely, however, it
checks to see if there are any reduced partial matches meriting further
consideration as new entries in the agenda. For a partial match involving mappings between N pairs of objects or time points, PATHFINDER
generates a set of N reduced partial matches, in each case excluding one
of the mapped pairs along with all assertions involving objects or time
points of the excluded pair. For the above example, one such reduced
match omits the mapping from "o2" to "the-target-1," retaining only
the mapping between "t46" and "t21" and between "t12" and "t64."
This reduced match thus excludes the assertions concerning "contact,"
yet retains the assertions concerning "position," "speed" and "heading."
On the next iterative cycle of the association process, this reduced match
ranks highest among the available partial matches for consideration, and
thus PATHFINDER proceeds by elaborating this partial match. In this

case, no inconsistencies are detected during the required inference check. The following association structure results:

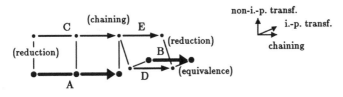

A: The arrow is released.
B: The arrow strikes the target.

with the complete chaining match between traces C and E as follows:

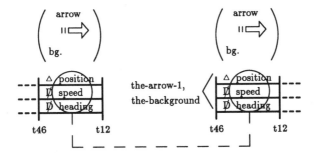

5.3 Making Use of Background Statements

A First Example

This section presents two brief examples concerning the incorporation of background statements into the causal reconstruction process. In the first example, the combination of a background statement and assertions specific to an event trace produces, via inference, a new partial match relevant to the association process. For this example, the causal description is as follows:

The ball is inside the basket. The basket descends to the floor. The ball remains above the floor.

Given a definition for "descending to," PATHFINDER produces the following event traces for the referenced events in this description:

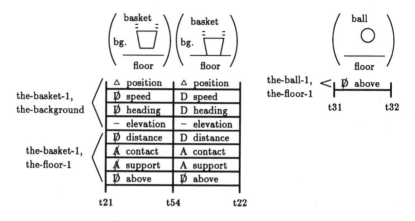

The background statement in the causal description ("The ball is inside the basket.") translates to the following time-independent assertion, which is maintained by PATHFINDER in a separate base of background assertions:

PRESENT(inside, <the-ball-1, the-basket-1>, null)

Also for this example, the following rule of inference has been provided to the program:

```
Concurrently, object 11 is inside object 12, and object
12 is above object 13. The preceding statement implies
the following statement. Object 11 is above object 13.
```

Whenever PATHFINDER conducts inference on an event trace or set of event traces, it instantiates all background assertions to the specific time points of the traces in question and includes the new instantiated assertions in the inference process. For the above trace describing the basket descending to the floor, three instantiated background assertions are included, as follows:

PRESENT(inside, <the-ball-1, the-basket-1>, t21)
PRESENT(inside, <the-ball-1, the-basket-1>, t54)
PRESENT(inside, <the-ball-1, the-basket-1>, t22)

These three statements, coupled with statements from the event trace indicating that the basket is above the floor at each of the indicated time points, lead through inference to the following new assertions:

PRESENT(above, <the-ball-1, the-floor-1>, t21)
PRESENT(above, <the-ball-1, the-floor-1>, t54)
PRESENT(above, <the-ball-1, the-floor-1>, t22)

In general, PATHFINDER always strives to maintain event traces in a maximally "condensed" form, utilizing assertions involving higher-level defined predicates wherever possible as a substitute for combinations of assertions involving lower-level defined predicates or primitive-level predicates. In this case, from the original dynamic assertions in the "descending" trace, it is known that "t54" is after "t21" and that "t22" is after "t54." These temporal ordering assertions in combination with the above PRESENT assertions condense to form the following two dynamic assertions:

NOT-DISAPPEAR(above, <the-ball-1, the-floor-1>, t21, t54)
NOT-DISAPPEAR(above, <the-ball-1, the-floor-1>, t54, t22)

Finally, when these two dynamic assertions appear in the inference-generated image of the original "descending" trace, two partial matches appear with respect to the second original event. By the heuristics employed in PATHFINDER, neither match is preferred to the other, thus PATHFINDER chooses one at random. The following association structure results:

A: The basket descends to the floor.
B: The ball remains above the floor.

A Second Example

In the second example, background information contributes to the selection of one match over a competing match. Here, the supplied causal description is as follows:

> The support of the screw by the table is present. The
> hand ungrasps the screw. The screw collides with the
> wrench.

Provided with definitions for "ungrasping" and "colliding with," the following event traces result:

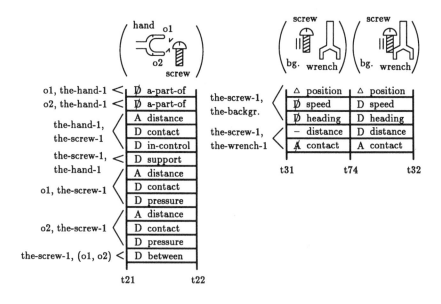

For the sake of illustration, suppose the program is given two precedents: "dropping" an object, and "letting" an object "roll."[3] Given

---

[3] Due to limitations of the simplified English syntax employed here, the second of these must be described as one object "letting roll" a second object.

suitable definitions for these events, the following event trace is produced for the "dropping" precedent:

object-21, object-22 ⟨	A distance	Ɗ distance	Ɗ distance
	D contact	Ⱥ contact	Ⱥ contact
	D in-control	Ⱥ in-control	Ⱥ in-control
object-22, object-21 <	D support	Ⱥ support	Ⱥ support
object-22 <	D supported	Ⱥ supported	Ⱥ supported
object-22, the-background ⟨	Ⱥ position	△ position	△ position
	Ⱥ speed	A speed	+ speed
	Ⱥ heading	A heading	Ɗ heading
	Ⱥ elevation	− elevation	− elevation
	t81	t105	t106 · · · t82

For the "letting roll" precedent, the following trace is generated:

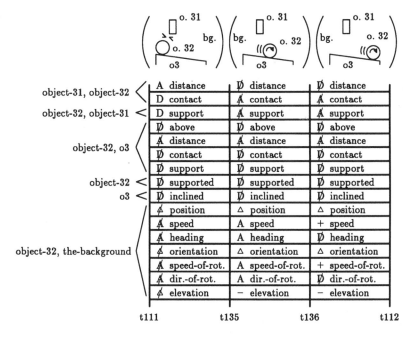

object-31, object-32 <	A distance	Ɗ distance	Ɗ distance
	D contact	Ⱥ contact	Ⱥ contact
object-32, object-31 <	D support	Ⱥ support	Ⱥ support
object-32, o3 ⟨	Ɗ above	Ɗ above	Ɗ above
	Ⱥ distance	Ⱥ distance	Ⱥ distance
	Ɗ contact	Ɗ contact	Ɗ contact
	Ɗ support	Ɗ support	Ɗ support
object-32 <	Ɗ supported	Ɗ supported	Ɗ supported
o3 <	Ɗ inclined	Ɗ inclined	Ɗ inclined
object-32, the-background ⟨	Ⱥ position	△ position	△ position
	Ⱥ speed	A speed	+ speed
	Ⱥ heading	A heading	Ɗ heading
	Ⱥ orientation	△ orientation	△ orientation
	Ⱥ speed-of-rot.	A speed-of-rot.	+ speed-of-rot.
	Ⱥ dir.-of-rot.	A dir.-of-rot.	Ɗ dir.-of-rot.
	Ⱥ elevation	− elevation	− elevation
	t111	t135	t136 · · · t112

Ignoring the background information provided, there are two possible reconstructions of the described scenario: (1) ungrasping the screw results in a dropping of the screw, leading to the screw hitting the wrench, and (2) ungrasping the screw starts the screw rolling, leading to it hitting the wrench.[4]

The following rule of inference helps resolve the ambiguity presented by the initial description and supplied precedent events:

> The support of object 41 by object 42 is present. The
> preceding statement implies the following statement.
> Object 41 is supported.

Given this rule, plus the background statement that the screw is supported by the table, an inference contradiction arises when partial matches involving the dropping precedent are considered (the screw is determined to be both supported and not supported). As a result, PATHFINDER reconstructs the scenario drawing on other partial matches, chaining from the "ungrasping" event to the "letting roll" precedent and from this precedent to the "colliding" event, yielding the following association structure:

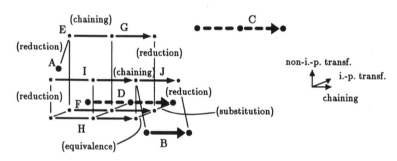

A: The hand ungrasps the screw.
B: The screw collides with the wrench.

C: Object 21 drops object 22.
D: Object 31 lets roll object 32.

---

[4] Actually, by supplying two precedents in this manner, we have violated Grice's maxim of relation—one of the supplied precedents must be irrelevant. However, because this situation relates to the broader issue of how a program with a pre-existing knowledge base of events, rules of restatement and so forth might reconstruct described scenarios provided *without* supplementary information, we temporarily suspend the requirements.

5.4   Identifying Supporting Assumptions

The final example for this chapter concerns the recording and recalling of assumptions made in the course of matching. For this example, the following description is supplied:

> The steam rises. The steam contacts the metal plate.

Given event definitions for "rising" and "contacting," PATHFINDER generates two event traces:

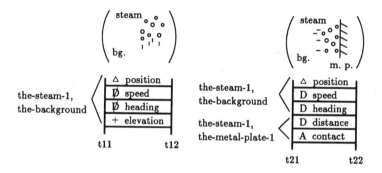

Also, PATHFINDER is provided with a precedent event "rise into contact with," as follows:

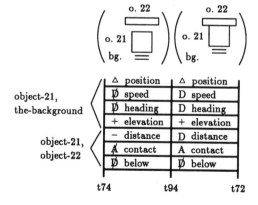

Reconstructing the scenario by elaborating top-ranked partial matches, the following association structure results:

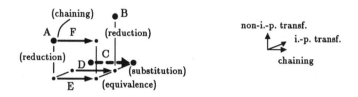

A: The steam rises.
B: The steam contacts the metal plate.

C: Object 21 rises into contact with object 22.

In this association structure, traces D and E are derived from the precedent trace and depict the steam rising into contact with the metal plate. From the reduction transformation applied to trace E in order to produce a complete chaining match with trace A, it is apparent that the following three assertions in the opening interval of trace E are not matched in the antecedent, trace A:

DECREASE(distance, <the-steam-1, the-metal-plate-1>,
              t11, t12)
NOT-APPEAR(contact, <the-steam-1, the-metal-plate-1>,
              t11, t12)
NOT-DISAPPEAR(below, <the-steam-1, the-metal-plate-1>,
              t11, t12)

Because precedents are taken to be events occurring previously in different contexts and only tentatively relevant to the current scenario, it is informative to record the fact that such assertions are unmatched and recall this information when answering questions. Thus, PATHFINDER provides an optional mode of operation for which questions of types 2, 3 and 4 produce compound responses, as illustrated below.

How does the steam rising relate to the steam contacting the metal plate?

The steam rising causes the steam to rise into contact with the metal plate, which involves the steam contacting the metal plate.

> For the steam rising into contact with the metal plate,
> it is assumed that at the beginning, the distance
> between the steam and the metal plate decreases, the
> contact between the steam and the metal plate does not
> appear, and the steam remains below the metal plate.

Stated another way, the scenario as reconstructed would be deemed inconsistent if it were discovered that any of the assumed conditions were false; i.e., if the steam were to be rising yet moving away from the metal plate, or rising while already in contact with the metal plate, or rising yet not from below the metal plate.

6 Exploratory Transformations

This chapter describes the application of transformations in an exploratory manner, generating alternate descriptions of events for use in the matching process. This provides a mechanism by which a program may bridge a range of discontinuities arising from the writer's use of analogy or abstraction in the input description. To facilitate this additional processing, a new variety of supplementary information is considered, the *rule of restatement*. Minor alterations in the matching heuristics and question answering procedures are also required.

6.1 Overview

How Exploratory Transformations Work

When applied to particular event traces, exploratory transformations produce alternate representations of the indicated events, these new representations possibly at higher or lower levels of abstraction relative to the original traces, or employing synonym terms, or involving a metaphorical reinterpretation of activity in terms of different types of objects and different attributes. Conceptually, we may think of each original event trace—representing the literal interpretation of an event referenced in the causal description—as being expanded into a small *cluster* of related events and event descriptions, each of which may participate in the association process. Partial matches involving such transformed images of event traces may then associate these events with other events specified at different levels of abstraction or in terms of different underlying metaphors.

It should be noted, however, that in all cases, exploratory transformations produce *plausible* redescriptions of events—redescriptions that leave room for error. For example, a particular transformation might summarize the event of one object coming into contact with a part of a second object as the first object coming into contact with the whole—the second object itself. However, it is conceivable that the first object might already be in contact with some other part of the second object and thus, overall, the first object would then simply remain in contact with the second object. For this reason, transformed images of events are granted a probationary status, to be accepted only when elaborated partial matches link these images to other known occurrences.

Two broader questions are not addressed in this book. These are:
(1) how a program might *learn* new transformations to apply to event
traces (e.g., learn new analogies between events or new ways of stating
activity at different levels of abstraction), and (2) how a program might
heuristically determine which transformations—as retrieved from a large
knowledge base—are most relevant to a particular comprehension situation. In keeping with our definition of the causal reconstruction problem
relative to a program with an empty knowledge base, all transformations
to be used by the program must find motivation in supplementary information provided to the program. Thus, in a manner paralleling the
input of rules of inference, we now permit the inclusion of *rules of restatement*, as, for example, the following entry:

> The restraint of object 1 by object 2 is present. The preceding
> statement is equivalent to the following statement. Object 1 is
> restrained by object 2.

Three verb groups are permitted within the connecting statement linking the two parts of a rule of restatement: "is equivalent," "parallels"
and "summarizes." The use of these variants is described later in this
section. In the above example, two specifications of restraint—both
acceptable by the simplified English grammar used in PATHFINDER—
are declared to be equivalent. This produces a simple transformation as
follows (again, variables begin with "?"):

> **transformation type:** equivalence
> **first scenario:**
>   PRESENT(restraint, <?object-1, ?object-2>, ?t1)
> **second scenario:**
>   PRESENT(restrained, <?object-1, ?object-2>, ?t1)
> **bindings:** { [restraint → restrained] }

An individual transformation is applied to an event trace by matching either the first or second scenario in its specification with a subset
of the assertions in the event trace. For every such match, those assertions in the event trace that are involved in the match are removed
from the event trace and replaced with suitably mapped assertions from
the other scenario in the transformation's specification. Often, rules of
restatement are supplied in *clusters,* with each rule specifying what to

do in a particular circumstance: presence of a phenomenon, absence of a phenomenon, change, non-change, and so forth. In such cases, the individual transformations produced by these rules are grouped together to form larger, more comprehensive transformations to be applied as a unit and subsequently indicated by a single association in the association structure.[1]

As a simplification, if the transformation generated from a rule of restatement involves a complete match between its two scenarios (the above transformation is of this variety, as are transformations of type "substitution" and "generalization," described later), it is augmented to include a binding list specifying associated pairs of time points, objects, reference standards and attributes between the two sides of the transformation. Whenever such a transformation is found to be applicable to an event trace, the event trace is additionally transformed by a substitution of terms according to this binding list. In many cases, this simplification permits a single rule of restatement covering, say, presence of a particular phenomenon, to take the place of a large cluster of rules detailing alternate circumstances.

For sake of illustration, suppose the above transformation is applied to the following event trace ("unlatching" from section 4.3):

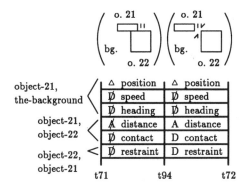

Two matches for the first scenario of the transformation are found (involving time points "t71" and "t94"). Replacing the matched statements

---

[1] By convention, PATHFINDER collects rules of restatement into clusters when the rules involve common sets of participating objects (e.g., "object 201" and "object 202").

from the event trace with new statements derived from the second scenario and then mapping the rest of the statements in the event trace according to the binding list of the transformation, the following event trace is produced:

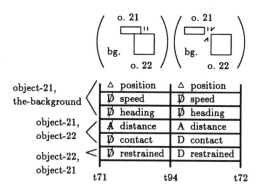

Types of Exploratory Transformations

As described in previous chapters, we draw a distinction between information-preserving transformations, which belong to inverse pairs of transformations on event traces in transition space, and non-information-preserving transformations, which do not belong to such inverse pairs. Following is a list of exploratory information-preserving and non-information-preserving transformations handled by PATHFINDER; this list parallels the list given in chapter 1, but provides a bit more detail regarding several of the varieties. Specific examples involving each of these types of transformations appear in sections 6.2 and 6.3.

Information-preserving exploratory transformations:

Equivalence. Replacement of time points, objects, reference standards or attributes with *synonym* quantities, producing an alternate specification of the same event.

Substitution. Replacement of time points, objects, reference standards or attributes with *different, but parallel* quantities in a new context, producing a specification of an event distinct from the original event, yet parallel in the types of changes involved.

Non-information-preserving exploratory transformations:

Generalization. Replacement of a reference standard (e.g., an object type such as "container") with a new, more general reference standard (e.g., "physical-object").

Interval composition. Merging of two adjacent time intervals into a single composite interval, with changes specified according to the composition of the changes in the original two intervals.

Attribute composition. Reexpression of activity originally involving a set of related attributes (e.g., "height," "width" and "depth") with activity involving a single, encompassing attribute (e.g., "size").

Object composition. Reexpression of activity originally involving the parts of an object with activity involving the whole object.

Attribute-object reification. A transformation replacing activity involving a particular attribute (e.g., "speed") with activity involving a new object representing that attribute applied to its argument (e.g., "the-speed-of-vehicle-51").

Event-attribute reification. A transformation replacing part of an event trace (e.g., changes involved in an object's motion) with an assertion involving a new attribute applied to one of the participating objects (e.g., "moving" applied to an object).

Event-object reification. A transformation replacing part of an event trace with assertions involving a new object representing the replaced activity (e.g., an object representing a collision, with other objects "engaged-in" the collision object).

Intuitively, information-preserving transformations correspond to analogical associations, and non-information-preserving transformations correspond to abstraction associations, but this is not entirely accurate. For example, in drawing an analogy between two events, the "core" of the association might be a substitution of object types and attributes between the two behaviors (an information-preserving transformation), but additionally, it may be necessary to delete irrelevant information from one or the other trace before the substitution may be made (a non-information-preserving transformation). Likewise, information-preserving transformations, especially equivalence transformations, may be required in the course of relating two events described at different levels of abstraction.

English expression used	Association type
"...is equivalent to..."	EQUIVALENCE
"...parallels..."	SUBSTITUTION
"...summarizes..."	GENERALIZATION,
/ "...is summarized by..."	COMPOSITION, and
	REIFICATION

Table 6.1
English expressions for use in rules of restatement, and corresponding association
types for generated exploratory transformations.

As described previously, in the diagraming of association structure
fragments, information-preserving transformations are depicted by alignment in the depth dimension, and non-information-preserving transformations are depicted by alignment in the vertical dimension. In addition,
the arrows depicting transformed images of event traces are diagramed
in outline, similar to the products of inference as described in chapter 5:

(information-preserving transformation)   *(non-information-preserving transformation)*

Extensions to the Operation of PATHFINDER

All of the exploratory transformations applied by PATHFINDER origi-
nate in rules of restatement provided in the supplementary information
to the program. For purposes of question-answering, it is necessary
for PATHFINDER to distinguish between "equivalence" and "substitution" information-preserving transformations, and between information-
preserving and non-information-preserving transformations. Thus, three
different verb groups are employed, as listed in Table 6.1. Note that this
input convention does not require that the human who composes the supplementary information have specific knowledge of the internal workings
of PATHFINDER: he or she may rely on intuitive judgment regarding
the suitability of using "is equivalent to," "parallels" or "summarizes"
to characterize the relationship between two accounts of activity.

Exploratory transformation of event traces is conducted in the second phase of operation for PATHFINDER—that is, following the initial parsing and formation of event traces, and preceding the association phase (see section 1.4). The second phase begins with inference carried out on each of the original event traces depicting referenced events and precedents. The images of these traces under inference are next transformed where possible via exploratory transformation clusters applied in either the "forward" or "reverse" direction.[2] Transformed images of traces are immediately subjected to an additional round of inference, leading to one of three results: (1) abandonment of the transformed image if a contradiction arises, (2) generation of a further, inference-transformed image trace if inference adds new assertions, or (3) no additional effect if inference does not add new assertions and no contradiction is found. As new traces are generated via transformation and inference, they are inserted into the association structure, with appropriate associations indicating their origins. The process then continues recursively, with the products of transformation and inference subjected to further transformation and inference where possible.

There are several possible ways to bound the exploratory transformation process, so that it does not extend into an infinite expansion of transformed images into new transformed images. One simple way is to limit the number of times any event trace may be transformed. This has a disadvantage in that the choice of such a limit will necessarily be somewhat arbitrary. An alternative technique is to explicitly check that each newly-generated event trace is not covered by an existing event trace known to the system. This will curtail a variety of endless chains of transformations, yet it will also fail to curtail others such as infinite sequences of object composition transformations postulating new parts of parts of an object. A simple alternative to these approaches has been employed in PATHFINDER: each sequence of transformation-induced associations leading from an original description event or precedent may contain only a single application of any particular transformation cluster, either in the forward or reverse direction. Note, however, that this technique takes advantage of the fact that only a limited number of

---

[2] The bidirectional applicability of transformation clusters applies also to non-information-preserving transformations. However, the two directions of application need not constitute *inverses* of one another, as a careful examination of the transformations illustrated in section 6.3 indicates.

rules of restatement are included in the supplementary information to
PATHFINDER. For a comprehension program required to selectively
apply transformations drawn from a large pre-existing knowledge base,
this technique would have to be modified—presumably to incorporate
heuristics or to limit the exploration to a fixed set of abstraction levels
and analogically-related domains (see section 10.2 for further discussion
of this issue).

Changes to the association phase (phase 3) are minimal. Because
PATHFINDER's application of exploratory transformations produces
explicit associations recorded in the association structure, each original
trace is already associated with all of its transformed images. In the
association phase, then, it is only necessary to look for partial matches
between the clusters of traces formed by the exploratory transformation process. PATHFINDER runs its matcher on all pairs of events
in different clusters, identifying both partial chaining and partial restatement matches as before. Assembling the partial matches into an
agenda, PATHFINDER employs the scoring heuristics outlined in chapter 4, with the inclusion of one additional heuristic, italicized in the list
below. (Note that this is still not a complete list of PATHFINDER's
heuristics as presented in chapter 1 and detailed in appendix A. The
remaining heuristics are discussed in chapter 7.)

Matching between transitions.   Definite changes (APPEAR, DIS-
APPEAR, CHANGE, INCREASE and DECREASE) are weighted
most, other dynamic assertions next and static assertions least.

Proximity to description events.   Penalties are introduced for
matches involving precedent events *or exploratory transformations
of events.*

Narrative ordering. Preference is given to chaining matches between
events referenced consecutively in the description.

Current status of the association structure.   Penalties are introduced for matches providing a second antecedent or consequent for
an event, matches between events already connected via associations, and matches involving hypothesized objects (e.g., a conjectured part of a physical object).

Types of associations.   Partial restatement matches are penalized
slightly relative to partial chaining matches.

Priority	Association type	As expressed in English
1.	SUBSTITUTION	"...parallels..."
2.	CHAINING	"...causes..." / "...is caused by..."
3.	REDUCTION	"...is a part of..." / "...involves..."
4.	GENERALIZATION, COMPOSITION, and REIFICATION	"...summarizes..." / "...is summarized by..."
5.	INFERENCE	"...implies..." / "...is implied by..."
6.	EQUIVALENCE	"...is equivalent to..."

Table 6.2
Prioritization and English translations for association types, as used by
PATHFINDER to describe sequences of associations.

The rationale for this new heuristic is as follows: suppose an exploratory
transformation affects only part of an event trace, leaving the remaining
portion unchanged. If a second trace matches the unchanged portion, it
will match with both the original trace and its transformed image. To
avoid inclusion of an irrelevant association in the sequence of associations
connecting the first trace to the second trace, then, we should discourage
use of the partial match involving the transformed image of the first
trace.

In the fourth phase of operation, question-answering, additional
changes are required in order to handle reconstruction involving exploratory transformations. In particular, the new association types
"substitution," "generalization," "composition" and "reification" must
be inserted into the prioritization of association types used in answering
questions of types 2, 3 and 4. On the basis of the examples tested on
PATHFINDER, a suitable prioritization was determined to be as shown
in Table 6.2.

A further modification is required concerning the answering of questions of type 4 (asking whether a particular event has occurred). Because
exploratory transformations raise *plausible* redescriptions of events, not
necessary ones, a path of association connecting the event in question
with events in the association structure may not guarantee occurrence
of that event. To compensate for this, PATHFINDER performs an additional check to see whether or not the assertions of the questioned event
are covered in a composite trace of the activity as used to answer ques-

tions of type 1. If so, it answers "Yes." followed by a summarization of the path of association. If not, it begins with "Perhaps." and qualifies all verbs in the summarized path through the inclusion of "could." An example involving this extra check in answering questions of type 4 appears at the end of chapter 8.

6.2   Information-Preserving Transformations

We now proceed with a number of examples illustrating the use of exploratory transformations in causal reconstruction. This section concerns information-preserving transformations; the next section concerns non-information-preserving transformations.

Equivalence

The first example involves the use of an equivalence transformation similar to the one illustrated in section 6.1. The input description for this example is as follows:

```
The block collides with the stone.  The block becomes
in contact with the stone.
```

Given a definition for "collide" consistent with previous examples, the following two event traces result for this description:

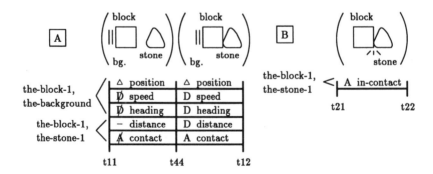

As such, no partial match exists between the two traces, and causal reconstruction will fail. Including the following rule of restatement makes causal reconstruction possible:

```
The contact between object 11 and object 12 is present.
The following statement is equivalent to the preceding
statement. Object 11 is in contact with object 12.
```

This rule produces a transformation that may be applied in the forward direction to trace A and in the reverse direction to trace B. The original traces and their transformed images are then as follows:

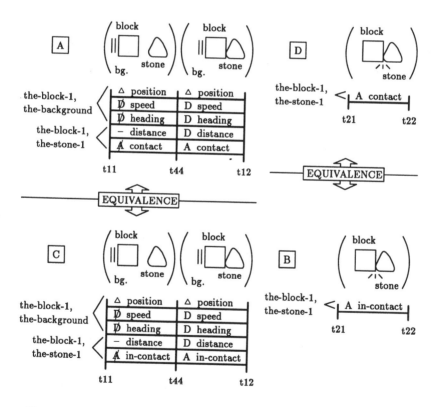

Two partial matches result: from trace A to trace D and from trace B to trace C. Both are scored equivalently and would produce the same question-answering behavior for PATHFINDER. Suppose the match between trace A and trace D is chosen. Elaborating this partial match into an additional equivalence association (involving a replacement of time points) and a reduction association (removing extra assertions from trace A), the following association structure results:

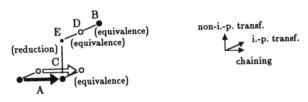

A: The block collides with the stone.
B: The block becomes in contact with the stone.

Substitution of Object Types

This example and the next two involve transformations of the substitution variety. As noted above, substitution transformations/associations relate event traces depicting *different* events that parallel one another in some way. This contrasts with equivalence transformations/associations, which relate different specifications of the *same* event.

The first substitution example involves a replacement of object types and concerns the following causal description and included precedent event:

The block starts to push from above on the water. The
water starts to push from below on the block.

Object 21 compresses spring 22.

Using event definitions supplied for "pushing from above" and "pushing from below," PATHFINDER constructs two event traces depicting the events specified in the causal description. These two traces are diagramed below.

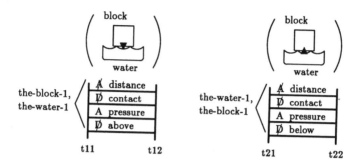

Given a definition for "compressing," the following event trace is generated for the precedent event:

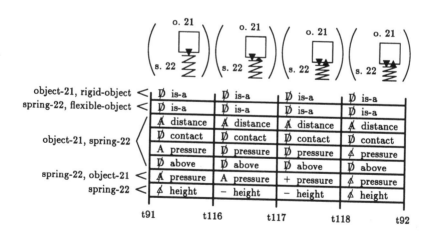

Intuitively, it would seem that the supplied precedent serves well to fill a causal gap between the two events in the causal description; however, several pieces of supplementary information must be supplied before PATHFINDER can reconstruct the described scenario. First, background information must be supplied describing the types of the participants ("The block is a rigid object. The water is a liquid.") Next, rules of inference must be supplied relating "above" to "below" and specifying symmetric properties for "distance" and "contact."

Given the above supplementary information, there remains a sizable block to reconstruction. For one thing, the program must be told that, strictly speaking, liquids are not flexible objects:

```
Liquid 61 is a liquid. The preceding statement implies
the following statement. Liquid 61 is not a flexible
object.
```

However, in some circumstances it is useful to reason about the behavior of quantities of liquid as if they were flexible objects (e.g., when pressure appears). This may be expressed by the following rule of restatement:[3]

```
Concurrently, liquid 71 is a liquid, and the pressure
between object 72 and liquid 71 is present. The
following statement parallels the preceding statement.
Concurrently, object 81 is a flexible object, and the
pressure between object 82 and object 81 is present.
```

This rule generates a substitution transformation, which in turn may be applied to the precedent event, producing a new, related precedent event involving compression of a liquid by a rigid object. Given this new precedent, PATHFINDER is able to elaborate partial matches with the original description events without generating a logical inconsistency concerning the object type associated with "the water." The gener-

---

[3] Note that this rule not only indicates a general relationship between two scenarios, but is also constructed in a manner implying a particular *mapping* of quantities between the scenarios. As discussed in section 4.1, the program is provided with such rather explicit specifications of analogies where substitution of reference standards or attributes is involved.

ated association structure (including inference associations concerning
"above," "below," "distance" and so forth) is as follows:

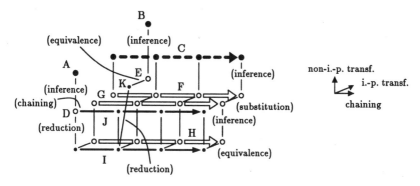

A: The block starts to push from above on the water.
B: The water starts to push from below on the block.

C: Object 21 compresses spring 22.

When asked how the first description event relates to the second,
PATHFINDER may now respond:

> The block starting to push from above on the water
> causes the block to compress the water, which involves
> the water starting to push from below on the block.

Substitution Regarding Spatial Orientation

The second substitution example concerns reorientation of an event di-
rectionally in space. While the transition space representation does not
capture complex spatial knowledge concerning shapes, directions, textures, and so forth, it does capture the range of propositional spatial
relationships, and in certain instances it is necessary to "rotate" an
event in space by transforming these relationships. For this example,
PATHFINDER is given the following causal description and precedent
event:

> Object 1 starts to push on object 2. Object 1 starts
> to move to the left.

> Object 31 pushes forward off object 32.

Here, the description events depict one spatial orientation (object 1 to the left of and adjacent to object 2, then moving to the left), while the precedent event depicts another spatial orientation of objects (object 31 in front of object 32, then moving forward). Specifically, the following event traces are generated for the description events:

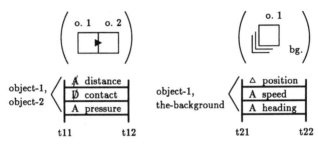

MATCH(heading,
    < object-1, the-background >,
    < the-leftward-direction, the-bg. >, t22)

For the precedent event, the following trace is generated:

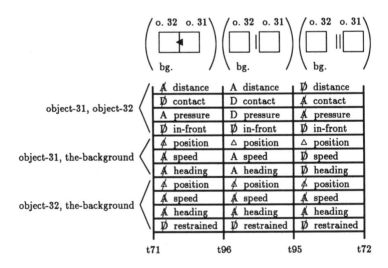

MATCH(heading, < object-31, the-background >,
    < the-forward-direction, the-background >, t95)

In its original form, the supplied precedent does not assist in causal reconstruction. However, the precedent can be of assistance if the program is provided with a rotational transformation connecting the two involved orientations of activity:

the-leftward-direction ⟷ the-forward-direction

in-front-of ⟷ to-the-right-of
to-the-right-of ⟷ behind
behind ⟷ to-the-left-of
to-the-left-of ⟷ in-front-of

This transformation may be expressed as four rules of restatement, one of which is given below.

```
Concurrently, object 41 is to the left of object 42,
and the heading of object 41 matches the heading of the
leftward direction. The following statement parallels
the preceding statement. Concurrently, object 51 is in
front of object 52, and the heading of object 51
matches the heading of the forward direction.
```

The exploratory transformation and association phases for this example proceed as for the previous example, with the generation of a new, transformed version of the precedent (involving one object pushing *leftward* off another), followed by an association of the description events via partial matches with the new version of the precedent.

An additional remark is warranted regarding the question answering phase for this example. When a question of type 2 is posed to the program, the use of a simple rule of thumb permits a response that explicitly characterizes the utilized precedent as metaphorical:

```
Object 1 starting to push on object 2 causes object 1
metaphorically to push forward off object 2, which
involves object 1 starting to move to the left.
```

The rule of thumb is as follows: if a utilized precedent has been formed by a substitution involving a mapping of *attributes* and not just reference standards, then the word "metaphorically" is used to qualify any reference to the precedent in a question response. Motivating this rule of thumb is the observation that such transformations recast an activity not just in terms of different types of objects (as in the preceding example), but more radically in terms of different *behavior*—parallel changes in different attributes of participating objects.

Substitution of Attributes: A Second Example

The final example for this section concerns a more complex substitution of attributes between events in different physical domains. Here, the following causal description and precedent are provided to PATHFINDER:

```
The radio wave is transmitted into space.  The strength
of the radio wave decreases.

Liquid 11 spreads thin over surface 12.
```

A simple definition for "transmitting" is used, producing the following two traces for the description events:

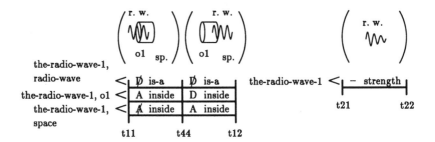

For the precedent event, the following trace is produced:

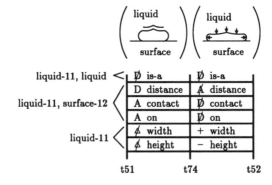

From a human perspective, it is plausible to reconstruct the described situation by "thinking about a liquid spreading thin over a surface." For PATHFINDER, the precedent in its original form does not aid in causal reconstruction, as the two scenarios involve different attributes and reference standards. However, given two rules of restatement describing an analogy between radio signals and liquids, a transformation of the precedent event may be effected, yielding a second precedent in the radio signal domain. One of the rules supplied to PATHFINDER is listed below and specifies a correlation between the strength of a radio wave in space and the height of a liquid on a surface.

> Concurrently, wave 21 remains a radio wave, wave 21 remains inside space 22, and the strength of wave 21 does not disappear. The following event parallels the preceding event. Concurrently, liquid 31 remains a liquid, liquid 31 remains on surface 32, and the height of liquid 31 does not disappear.

The second rule is similar, specifying a correlation between the coverage of a radio wave in space and the width of a liquid on a surface. Applying these rules, the following transformed image of the original precedent is generated:

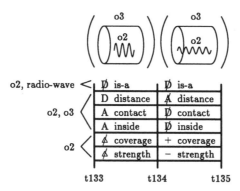

Given the new precedent, suitable partial matches are found and elaborated, producing a complete association structure in which the new precedent fills a causal gap between the two description events.

As in the preceding example, a question of type 2 will be answered in a manner that explicitly notes the metaphorical use of the precedent:

```
How does the transmitting of the radio wave into space
relate to the strength of the radio wave decreasing?
```

```
The transmitting of the radio wave into space causes
the radio wave metaphorically to spread thin over
space, which involves the strength of the radio wave
decreasing.
```

Other Information-Preserving Transformations

The above transformations map time points, objects, reference standards, attributes and tuples of these quantities in a global manner—that is, independent of particular contexts in which the quantities appear. A further information-preserving transformation called an *interchange* transformation involves an exchange or permutation of quantities within an event trace, but limited to certain contexts within the trace. An especially interesting variety of interchange transformation is one that forms a *retrograde* of an activity, this by renaming time points within the context of assertions regarding temporal ordering, such that if a particular time point was previously designated as occurring after a second time point, the second time point is then designated as occurring after the first. Note that for such transformations, however, the time points must *not* be renamed globally, as this would simply produce an alternate, forward version of the original event trace, with different labels for time points.

Other varieties of interchange transformations may exchange the roles of *objects* within an event trace (while retaining the distinct static properties of these objects), or they may rearrange temporal intervals in arbitrary ways with or without forming retrogrades of these intervals (e.g., "catching" involves a falling followed by appearance of control, while "dropping" involves a disappearance of control followed by falling). The associations generated by such transformations could possibly be of use in organizing a large knowledge base of events or in performing causal reconstruction from a limited knowledge base. However, as for the other information-preserving exploratory transformations described above, specific rules of restatement would be required to motivate particular interchange transformations, because arbitrary rearrangements will by no means generally produce physically realizable events from other physically realizable events.

6.3 Non-Information-Preserving Transformations

This section presents a number of examples involving the seven varieties of non-information-preserving exploratory transformations listed in section 6.1.

Generalization

We begin with an example involving a generalization transformation. As described in section 6.1, generalization transformations replace a reference standard (e.g., "steel") with a more general reference standard (e.g., "metal"). The input description for this example is as follows:

    The block starts to push on the sponge. The sponge is
    compressed.

Given generic event definitions for the events "start to push on" and "compress"—these definitions consistent with previous examples concerning these events—the following event traces are generated. For the block starting to push on the sponge:

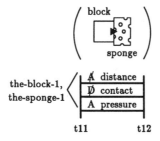

For the sponge being compressed:

	t21–t86	t86–t87	t87–t88	t88–t22
o1, rigid-object <	Ð is-a	Ð is-a	Ð is-a	Ð is-a
the-sponge-1, <	Ð is-a	Ð is-a	Ð is-a	Ð is-a
flexible-object	Ⱥ distance	Ⱥ distance	Ⱥ distance	Ⱥ distance
	Ð contact	Ð contact	Ð contact	Ð contact
o1, the-sponge-1	A pressure	Ð pressure	Ð pressure	Ⱥ pressure
	Ð above	Ð above	Ð above	Ð above
the-sponge-1, o1 <	Ⱥ pressure	A pressure	+ pressure	Ⱥ pressure
the-sponge-1 <	Ⱥ height	− height	− height	Ⱥ height

t21   t86   t87   t88   t22

While a partial match does indeed exist between these two representations, this match is strengthened by including the following rule of restatement in the supplementary information:

```
Object 21 is a sponge. The following statement
summarizes the preceding statement. Object 21 is a
flexible object.
```

This rule produces a non-information-preserving transformation of type generalization. The transformation is used in combination with background information regarding the participating objects ("The block is a rigid object. The sponge is a sponge.") to produce transformed images of the original traces, recasting activity regarding "the sponge" as a sponge in terms of activity regarding it as a flexible object, and vice-versa. Following the application of exploratory transformations, PATHFINDER elaborates a partial chaining match from a generalized image of the pushing event to the original trace for the compressing event. Included in this match is an assertion that "the sponge" is a flexible object. The generated association structure is diagramed below:

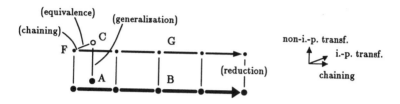

A: The block starts to push on the sponge.
B: The sponge is compressed.

It should be noted that a rule of inference would also work here (replacing "summarizes" in the above rule with "implies"), the only difference being that for inference, the assertion that "the sponge" is a flexible object would be used to *augment* the event trace, rather than substituting for the original assertion that "the sponge" is a sponge. In general, inference can be used in this way in place of generalization; however, we might expect that retention of information at multiple levels of abstraction would reduce the overall efficiency of the matching process on larger examples and in the more general context of systems possessing enough innate background knowledge to facilitate selective targeting of particular levels of abstraction for exploration.

Interval Composition

The next example concerns interval composition—the merging of two temporal intervals into a single, composite interval. The description for this example is as follows:

The wheel slows. The wheel stops.

Supplied with event definitions for "slowing" and "stopping," PATH-
FINDER generates the following two event traces:

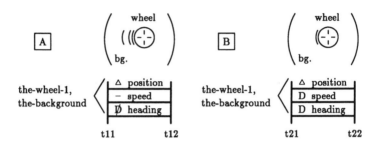

For a human reader, there are actually two plausible reconstructions of
this scenario: one in which the slowing causes the stopping, and another
in which the slowing is actually contained within the stopping, as the
initial portion of that event. In this example, PATHFINDER is supplied
with supplementary information relevant to the latter interpretation. In
the larger context of a program capable of backtracking or exploring
multiple paths of association in parallel, we might expect that both
alternatives would be explored, with one interpretation chosen on the
basis of compatibility with other events and their associations in the
overall reconstruction.

For this example, PATHFINDER is supplied with the following rule
of restatement:

```
First, the position of object 21 changes, the speed of
object 21 decreases, and the heading of object 21 does
not disappear. Next, the position of object 21
changes, the speed of object 21 disappears, and the
heading of object 21 disappears. The following event
summarizes the preceding event. Concurrently, the
position of object 21 changes, the speed of object 21
disappears, and the heading of object 21 disappears.
```

Graphically, the transformation specified by this rule is as follows:

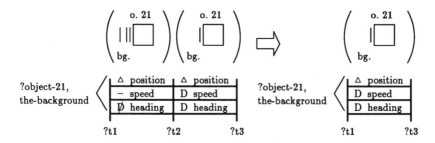

?object-21,
the-background

?t1   ?t2   ?t3

?object-21,
the-background

?t1   ?t3

Applied in the reverse direction to the stopping event, above, the transformation produces the following event trace:

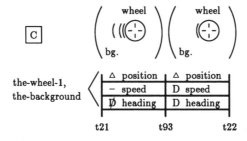

the-wheel-1,
the-background

t21   t93   t22

In turn, this trace yields a partial match with the slowing event and produces the following overall association structure:

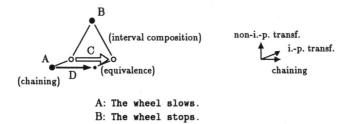

A: The wheel slows.
B: The wheel stops.

Attribute Composition

The next example involves attribute composition, in which activity concerning several attributes is replaced by activity concerning a single, encompassing attribute. The initial description for this example is as follows:

```
The block combines with the pile of blocks.  The pile
of blocks gets taller.
```

Given definitions for "combine with" and "get taller," the following event traces are produced:

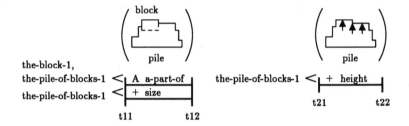

As such, no match exists between the two event representations. However, with the additional specification of the following rule of restatement, a match is facilitated:

```
Concurrently, the height of object 21 increases, the
width of object 21 does not change, and the depth of
object 21 does not change.  The following event
summarizes the preceding event.  The size of object 21
increases.
```

The transformation generated by this rule can be applied in the reverse direction to the first trace, producing the following trace:

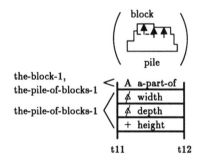

A partial restatement match between this event and the second description event may then be elaborated.

Object Composition

The final example of composition-type transformations involves object composition, in which assertions regarding part of an object are replaced by assertions regarding the whole object. The input description for this example is given below:

```
The hub is a part of the wheel, and the hub is
restrained by the wheel. The wheel turns. The hub
turns.
```

The first sentence of the description provides two background statements. Given a definition for "turns," the two event references in the description translate to the following event traces:

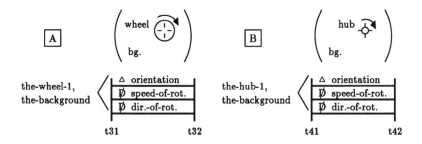

Although a partial match exists between these two traces, it relies on a mapping equating "the wheel" with "the hub." As described previously, PATHFINDER rejects partial matches that equate distinct objects in the description. Thus, this match cannot be used for causal reconstruction. In order to facilitate reconstruction, a rule of restatement such as the following is required:

```
Concurrently, object 11 remains a part of object 12,
object 11 remains restrained by object 12, and object
11 turns. The following event summarizes the preceding
event. Object 12 turns.
```

This rule produces an object composition transformation similar to the one described in chapter 1. Applying this transformation in both directions where applicable to the above traces, three transformed images are produced, as diagramed in Figure 6.1.

Trace C hypothesizes a part of "the wheel" that is restrained by it and that is turning. Trace E reexpresses turning of "the hub"—known from background assertions to be a part of "the wheel" and restrained by "the wheel"—in terms of turning of "the wheel." Trace D goes in the other direction, hypothesizing a further part of "the hub" that is restrained by it and that is turning. Six partial matches arise, corresponding to each of traces A and C matched with each of traces B, D and E. The partial match between traces A and B is ruled out because it equates "the wheel" with "the hub." The partial matches between traces A and D, C and E, C and B and C and D are penalized because they involve hypothesized objects. Similarly, the matches between C and E and between C and D are penalized relative to the others because each involves two exploratory traces, not just one. This leaves the partial match between trace A and trace E as the strongest match. An elaboration of this partial match produces the following association structure (here, including unused exploratory traces and associations):

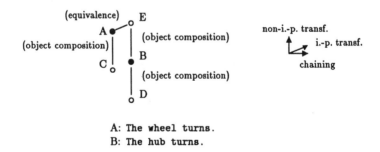

A: The wheel turns.
B: The hub turns.

Attribute-Object Reification

The remaining three examples in this section concern the use of *reification* transformations. This term is used here in a manner consistent with

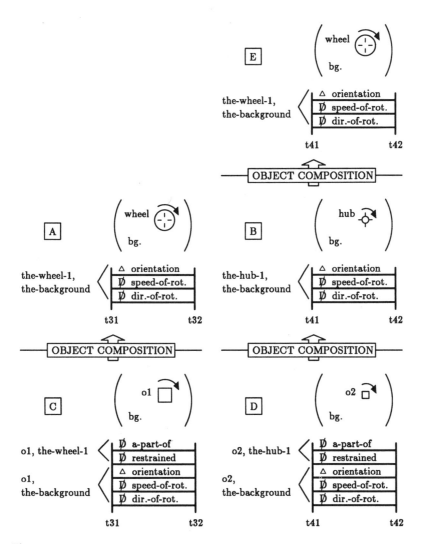

Figure 6.1
Exploratory transformation of traces for "The wheel turns." and "The hub turns."

usage elsewhere in artificial intelligence (e.g., [Genesereth and Nilsson, 1987]) to mean an extension of the set of symbols available to a representation, such that the representation may explicitly refer to quantities not previously representable or represented only in an indirect, unnamed manner.

Attribute-object reification involves the creation of a new object to represent a particular attribute applied to one or more of the participants in a causal scenario. The causal description below illustrates the utility of this type of transformation:

```
The block enters the water.  The water reduces the
speed of the block.
```

The interesting feature of this example has to do with the event "reduces." Suppose we provide a definition evoking a literal interpretation of this event: one object applies pressure to a second object and thereby removes a piece of the second object. Given this definition, along with a definition for "enters," the following event traces are generated for the two description events:[4]

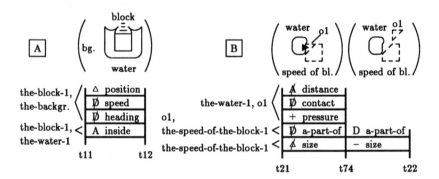

---

[4] The event definition for "reduces" complies with conventions regarding usage of transition space (section 3.2) in that it jointly covers occurrences such as a sponge reducing grease buildup on a surface—in which the removed portion remains in contact with the object doing the reducing—and occurrences such as a whittling knife reducing a bump on a piece of wood—in which the removed portion does not remain in contact with the object doing the reducing.

PATHFINDER instantiates the supplied, literal definition for "reduces" in terms of the specified objects "the water" and "the speed of the block." The resulting trace B thus depicts a generated decrease in "size" for the quantity "the-speed-of-the-block-1."

Given traces A and B, there is a considerable disparity between the two specifications of activity, yet one that may still be bridged through the incorporation of appropriate, generic supplementary information. First, the program has no knowledge that an object entering a liquid can slow down. The following two precedent events provide this background knowledge:

```
Object 21 comes into contact with liquid 22 by entering
liquid 22.

Object 31 is slowed by contact with object 32.
```

Given definitions for these two precedents, the following traces are added to the association structure:

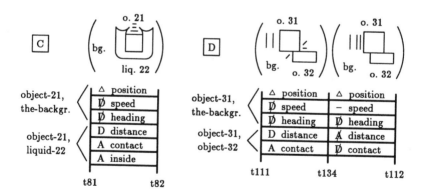

As a result of the inclusion of these two precedent events, PATH-FINDER elaborates a sequence of two partial matches, the first associating trace A with trace C, and the second chaining a transformed image of trace C to trace D. One product of this sequence of elaborations is the following intermediate trace, formed by a substitution operation on trace D and specifying the speed of the block decreasing as a result of the block contacting the water:

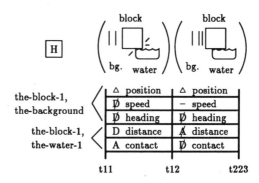

	Δ position	Δ position	
the-block-1, the-background	Ø̸ speed	− speed	
	Ø̸ heading	Ø̸ heading	
the-block-1, the-water-1	D distance	Å distance	
	A contact	Ø̸ contact	

t11   t12   t223

However, this account still does not match the "reducing" event, above, because that event specifies its decrease in speed indirectly as a decrease in "size" for a quantity representing the speed of an object. Restatement rules of the attribute-object reification variety bridge this kind of gap. A appropriate rule for this case is given below and described in the following text.

```
Concurrently, the speed of object 41 remains a
measurement of speed for object 41, and the speed of
object 41 decreases. The following event summarizes
the preceding event. The size of the speed of object
41 decreases.
```

There are two noteworthy aspects to this rule. First, as a means of anchoring the otherwise arbitrary quantity "the speed of object 41," the first scenario in the rule includes a specification that this quantity is a measurement of "speed" for "object 41." Second, it should be noted that the phrase "the speed of object 41" appears twice in an unusual context within the rule. Specifically, in the clauses "*the speed of object 41* remains a measurement of speed for object 41" and "the size of *the speed of object 41* decreases," the phrase—parsed as an attribute expression— must be treated as an object in order to apply PATHFINDER's built-in translation rules for forming transition space assertions. (In a similar manner, an object is formed for such a phrase in the sentence "The water reduces *the speed of the block.*" in the initial description, in order to apply the supplied event definition for "reduces.") Thus, given the rule as stated, the following simple transformation is produced:

transformation type: attribute-object-reification
first scenario:
    NOT-DISAPPEAR(
        a-measurement-of,
        <?the-speed-of-object-41, <speed, ?object-41>>,
        ?t1, ?t2)
    DECREASE(speed, <?object-41, the-background>, ?t1, ?t2)
second scenario:
    DECREASE(size, ?the-speed-of-object-41, ?t1, ?t2)
bindings: {}

In combination with two other rules of restatement regarding speed not changing and increasing, respectively, this rule expresses a relationship between alternate specifications in terms of "speed" and "size" that is broadly applicable to the interpretation of such events as "reducing," "trimming," "adding to" and "building up" the speed of an object. Given these rules, the following transformed image of the "reducing" event is generated during the exploratory transformation stage of PATHFINDER's processing:

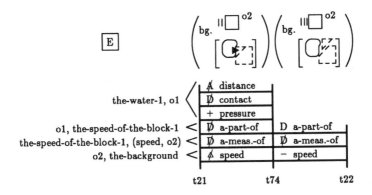

As a result, a partial match is generated between this transformed image of the "reducing" trace and trace H, shown previously, completing a path of association between the original two events. The final association structure for this example is as follows:

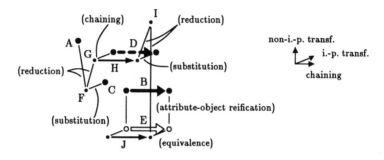

A: The block enters the water.
B: The water reduces the speed of the block.

C: Object 21 comes into contact with liquid 22 by entering liquid 22.
D: Object 31 is slowed by contact with object 32.

Asked how the two original events relate to one another, PATH-FINDER responds:

> The block entering the water is a part of the block coming into contact with the water by entering the water, which causes the block to be slowed by contact with the water, which coincides with the water reducing the speed of the block.

Event-Attribute Reification

The event-attribute reification transformation replaces part of an event (i.e., several dynamic assertions) with assertions involving a new attribute applied to one or more of the participants. For example, changes involved in motion might be replaced by an attribute "moving" applied to the object in motion. The following description illustrates the use of this type of transformation:

```
The light strikes the floor.   The floor remains
illuminated.
```

Given a simple definition for "strikes," the following event traces are generated:

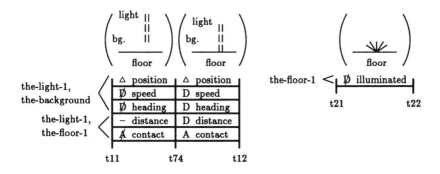

As such, no partial match exists between the two traces. A partial match appears, however, given a relevant rule of restatement:

```
Concurrently, illuminated remains an assertion of
illumination, object 11 remains a physical object,
light 12 remains a beam of light, object 11 remains
opaque, the distance between light 12 and object 11
disappears, and the contact between light 12 and object
11 appears.  The following event summarizes the
preceding event.  Concurrently, object 11 remains a
physical object, and object 11 remains illuminated.
```

This rule generates an event-attribute reification transformation. Its distinguishing feature is a statement to the effect that a particular attribute is "an assertion of" a type of event. The remainder of the rule replaces activity involved in that type of event with a single assertion utilizing the specified attribute. Applied in the reverse direction to the second trace above, the following transformed image is produced:[5]

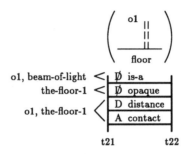

Elaborating a partial match between this trace and the trace depicting the light striking the floor, the following association structure is generated:

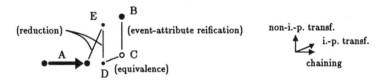

A: The light strikes the floor.
B: The floor remains illuminated.

This produces the following answer to a question of type 2:

The light striking the floor ends with the floor
remaining illuminated.

Event-Object Reification

The final example in this chapter concerns event-object reification. This transformation is similar to event-attribute reification, except that a

---

[5] In this case, PATHFINDER has also been supplied with a background statement asserting that "illuminated" is an assertion of "illumination," and thus no assertion to this effect appears in the transformed image trace.

part of an event is replaced by a new *object* representing that activity. For this example, the input description is as follows:

```
The cue ball transfers the motion to the eight ball.
The eight ball rolls into the pocket.
```

Given a literal event definition for "transferring"—one in which a first participant relinquishes to a second participant the property of being "in possession of" a specified object—the following trace is generated for the first event:

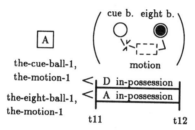

Given an event definition for "rolling into," the following event trace is generated for the second event:

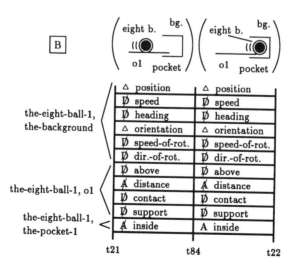

In the supplementary information supplied to PATHFINDER, background statements assert that "the motion" is an event, and, in particular, that it is an occurrence of the event type "motion." In addition, PATHFINDER is given a precedent event "Object 21 starts and continues to move." as illustrated below:

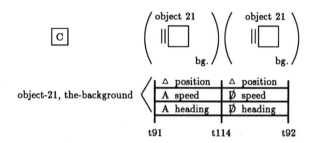

Supplied only with the above-listed information, PATHFINDER has no basis for determining a suitable relationship between the first event and the other two events. Again, appropriate, generic supplementary information can facilitate a bridging of the gap. First, two rules of restatement are supplied, describing an equivalence between the metaphorical specification of an object being "in possession of" an event and a more conventional and event-specific specification of the object being "engaged in" the event.

```
Concurrently, event 31 is an event, and object 32 is in
possession of event 31.  The preceding statement is
equivalent to the following statement.  Concurrently,
event 31 is an event, and object 32 is engaged in event
31.

Concurrently, event 31 is an event, and object 32 is
not in possession of event 31.  The preceding statement
is equivalent to the following statement.
Concurrently, event 31 is an event, and object 32 is
not engaged in event 31.
```

Applied to trace A, this cluster of rules produces the following transformed image:

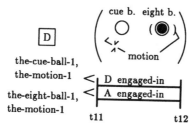

At this point, trace D may be transformed by a second cluster of rules of restatement—these rules of the event-object reification variety. Each member of this cluster of rules describes a set of changes in "position," "speed" and "heading" of an object as applies to one of four situations: appearance, non-appearance, disappearance or non-disappearance of the object being "engaged in" an event depicting motion. The rule for "appearance" is given below:

```
Concurrently, event 41 remains an occurrence of motion,
the position of object 42 changes, the speed of object
42 appears, and the heading of object 42 appears. The
following event summarizes the preceding event. Object
42 becomes engaged in event 41.
```

This cluster of rules applies in the reverse direction to trace D, and in two distinct ways. First, disappearance of "the-cue-ball-1" being engaged in "the-motion-1" is transformed into a set of changes reflecting a stopping motion for that object. Second, appearance of "the-eight-ball-1" being engaged in "the-motion-1" is transformed into a set of changes reflecting a starting motion for that object. As a result, the transformation of trace D by this cluster of rules produces the following image trace:

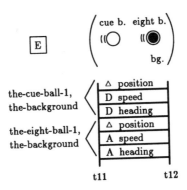

Given all of the above pieces of supplementary knowledge, a partial match is found for the "transferring" event. This match chains trace E, above, to the precedent event, trace C. Following the elaboration of this match, a second partial chaining match is elaborated between a transformed image of the precedent event and the second description event ("rolling into") as depicted by trace B. The resultant association structure is as follows:

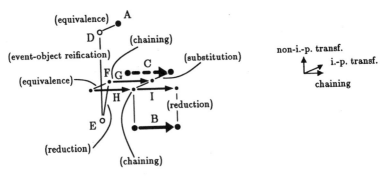

A: The cue ball transfers the motion to the eight ball.

B: The eight ball rolls into the pocket.

C: Object 21 starts and continues to move.

Given this structure, a question of type 2 evokes the following response from PATHFINDER:

```
The cue ball transferring the motion to the eight ball
causes the eight ball to start and continue to move,
which causes the eight ball to roll into the pocket.
```

7 Making Use of Connecting Statements

Causal descriptions often contain statements and other grammatical devices that explicitly indicate various associations between events. This chapter explores the incorporation of stylized "connecting statements" serving in this capacity; for example, "The striking of the cartridge causes the gunpowder to explode." Such statements may indicate direct or *indirect* associations between events, and thus it is up to the program to work out the details of precisely how the specified events might fit together as parts of a larger activity. In many cases, it would seem that connecting statements serve to disambiguate descriptions that could otherwise yield several plausible interpretations. This use of connecting statements is explored in the examples presented in this chapter.

The overview section describes the input of connecting statements and their incorporation into the causal reconstruction process. The remaining two sections present examples involving connecting statements used to specify temporal ordering associations between events, and connecting statements used to specify other relationships between events.

7.1 Overview

Input Conventions for Connecting Statements

Consider the following simple description:

> The ball moves. The block is hit.

If we disregard the narrative ordering of the events as presented, there are two plausible reconstructions of this scenario. In the first, it is the moving ball that hits the block. In the second, the block is first hit by something else, then moves against the ball, resulting in the ball moving. Natural language provides a number of devices by which such ambiguities may be eliminated. For example, the narrative ordering of events may be reversed or further roles of objects specified, as in the following examples:

> The block is hit. The ball moves.
> The ball moves and hits the block.
> The block is hit against the ball. The ball moves.

Connecting statements and the grammatical devices they represent provide a more general mechanism of explicitly indicating relationships between events. For example, information about the relative temporal ordering of events may be provided, as in the following variants of the above description:

> The block is hit after the ball moves.
> After the ball moves, the block is hit.
> The block is hit, and then the ball moves.

Or, associations of other varieties may be specified, as in the following examples involving specification of causal relationships:

> The ball moves, causing the block to be hit.
> The ball moves as a result of the block being hit.
> When the block is hit, this leads to the ball moving.

Many of the above examples employ grammatical constructions beyond the capabilities of PATHFINDER; however, the *content* of these constructions can be captured in PATHFINDER's input syntax. For statements regarding temporal ordering of events, PATHFINDER processes explicit references to the beginning or end of an event (the "time-point-expression" construct listed in the syntax for PATHFINDER in chapter 2). This construct is illustrated in the following statement:

> The beginning of the ball moving is after the end of the hitting
> of the block.

In addition, this construct may appear within event definitions, making it possible to define more complex temporal relationships between events (e.g., "occurs during," "occurs at the beginning of," and so forth). An example of such a definition appears in the next section.

For other specifications of association between events, a syntax paralleling the syntax of statements appearing in rules of restatement can be used:

> The structure expanding causes the component to move.
> The pile growing summarizes the pile increasing in height.

The electric current traveling from the first junction to the second junction is equivalent to the electric current passing through the filament.

For such statements, PATHFINDER accepts the same range in specifications as used by the program itself in answering questions about relationships between events. Thus, the following instances of "connecting material" are permitted: "parallels," "causes," "is caused by," "is a part of," "involves," "summarizes," "is summarized by," "implies," "is implied by," and "is equivalent to." By convention, no *new* events may be introduced in connecting statements supplied to PATHFINDER: all indicated events must have previously been specified using event references.[1]

Extensions to the Operation of PATHFINDER

Both temporal ordering statements and the more general statements of interassociations between events share a similar input specification syntax. However, PATHFINDER uses two different mechanisms to process these two varieties of statements. For statements of temporal ordering, PATHFINDER makes use of the inference process employed in checking elaborated partial matches for consistency. For example, if one event is specified as occurring after a second event, yet a chaining association is elaborated leading from that first event to the second event, a logical inconsistency will arise in the form of a loop of temporal ordering statements, with the first event specified as occurring both before and after the second event. Section 7.2 illustrates the use of inference in this manner to process temporal ordering statements.

For other specifications of association between events, PATHFINDER makes use of a separate mechanism that monitors the system of inter-event associations indicated by the association structure and the set of candidate partial associations appearing in the agenda. This mechanism employs a slightly weakened version of the facilities PATHFINDER has for answering questions of types 2, 3 and 4 (describing inter-event relationships). When PATHFINDER is presented with a connecting statement specifying that one event is related to another by a particular type

---

[1] This convention was adopted for simplicity; however, it would not be difficult to extend PATHFINDER to permit new specifications of events within connecting statements.

of association (e.g., "causes" or "is a part of"), the program tests partial matches in the agenda for compliance with this statement, using the following rule:

A connecting statement is fulfilled by a partial match when that partial match completes a path of association between the two events specified in the connecting statement, and the type of association indicated by the connecting statement appears in the correct orientation along the path, does not appear in the reverse orientation along the path, and, if the specified association type is other than a chaining association, no chaining associations occur along the path.

Thus, if a first event has been specified as causing a second event, the elaborated partial match must complete a path of association which when traversed from the first event to the second event contains a chaining association in the forward direction and no chaining associations in the reverse direction. If a first event has been specified as being "a part of" a second event, then the path of association completed by elaboration of the partial match must contain a reduction association in the reverse direction (from a reduced to a non-reduced description), no reduction association in the forward direction, and no chaining associations.

As noted above,[this scheme for assessing compliance with connecting statements relies on a weaker characterization of paths of association than used by PATHFINDER to answer questions. Here, we do not require that the indicated association type be the association *of highest priority* along the path in question, just that it be present in the correct orientation (plus the other considerations listed above). For the examples run on PATHFINDER, this weaker characterization was found to be more suitable.

In checking to see whether candidate partial matches fulfill previously-supplied connecting statements, PATHFINDER has two concerns: (1) partial matches explicitly fulfilling particular connecting statements should be given preference over partial matches not fulfilling any connecting statement, and (2) partial matches creating a path of association between two events that violates a particular connecting statement should be abandoned. These two components are thus added to the set of heuristics PATHFINDER uses to evaluate partial matches, producing the following (complete) set of heuristics for PATHFINDER (heuristics related to the extensions described in this chapter are italicized):

Matching between transitions. Definite changes (APPEAR, DIS-APPEAR, CHANGE, INCREASE and DECREASE) are weighted most, other dynamic assertions next and static assertions least.

Proximity to description events. Penalties are introduced for matches involving precedent events or exploratory transformations of events.

Narrative ordering. Preference is given to chaining matches between events referenced consecutively in the description.

Current status of the association structure. Penalties are introduced for matches providing a second antecedent or consequent for an event, matches between events already connected via associations, and matches involving hypothesized objects (e.g., a conjectured part of a physical object).

Types of associations. Partial restatement matches are penalized slightly relative to partial chaining matches. Also, *matches not fulfilling any connecting statements are penalized slightly, and matches violating a connecting statement are penalized heavily.*

In addition to the consideration of connecting statements when ranking partial matches for elaboration, PATHFINDER also checks for compliance with connecting statements once a selected partial match has been elaborated. This is because there are some instances in which it is computationally expensive to determine fully whether the elaboration of a partial match will produce an association of a particular variety (e.g., a reduction association in one direction or the other), without actually going through the operations involved in elaborating the partial match in question.

The final extension of PATHFINDER related to connecting statements involves questions of type 3. As described in chapter 4, these questions ask the program about plausible causal connections (e.g., "How could the water boiling cause the steam to condense on the metal plate?") As such, these questions implicitly insist that any path of association PATHFINDER establishes between the indicated events must be a *causal* path. This is precisely the effect produced by a connecting statement, and thus in processing questions of type 3, PATHFINDER constructs a new connecting statement explicitly indicating the desired causal relationship, enters this statement into its list of supplied connecting statements, and thus steers its association process toward identification of a suitable causal path of association between the two indicated events.

7.2   Temporal Ordering Statements

An Initial Version of the Example

To illustrate the use of connecting statements of the temporal ordering variety, consider the following description:

```
The ball rises.  The ball falls.  The rising by the
ball occurs after the falling by the ball.
```

Given definitions for "rise" and "fall," the following event traces are produced for the two description events:

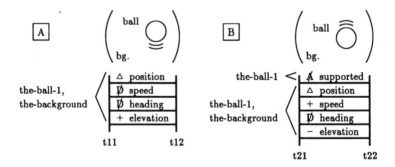

To these events, we add the following two precedent events:

```
Object 31 is overcome by gravity.
```

```
Object 41 bounces vertically off object 42.
```

Given suitable definitions, the following trace is produced for the first precedent event:

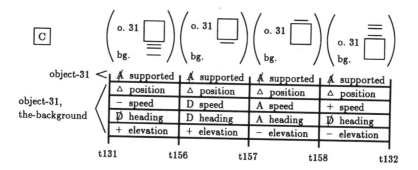

object-31	$\mathcal{A}$ supported	$\mathcal{A}$ supported	$\mathcal{A}$ supported	$\mathcal{A}$ supported
	△ position	△ position	△ position	△ position
object-31,	− speed	D speed	A speed	+ speed
the-background	$\cancel{D}$ heading	D heading	A heading	$\cancel{D}$ heading
	+ elevation	+ elevation	− elevation	− elevation

t131   t156   t157   t158   t132

For the second precedent:

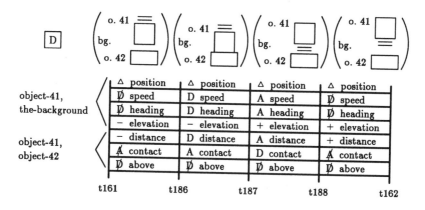

	△ position	△ position	△ position	△ position
object-41,	$\cancel{D}$ speed	D speed	A speed	$\cancel{D}$ speed
the-background	$\cancel{D}$ heading	D heading	A heading	$\cancel{D}$ heading
	− elevation	− elevation	+ elevation	+ elevation
object-41,	− distance	D distance	A distance	+ distance
object-42	$\mathcal{A}$ contact	A contact	D contact	$\mathcal{A}$ contact
	$\cancel{D}$ above	$\cancel{D}$ above	$\cancel{D}$ above	$\cancel{D}$ above

t161   t186   t187   t188   t162

If we ignore the connecting statement appearing in the input description, there are two ways to reconstruct the described scenario: (1) the rising ball could be overcome by gravity, leading to it falling, or (2) the falling ball could bounce vertically off something, leading to it rising.[2]

---

[2] As in section 5.3, we have temporarily suspended the requirements regarding Grice's maxim of relation, supplying more precedent events than necessary for causal reconstruction. This approximates some aspects of the situation faced by a program relying on internal background knowledge, parts of which may be irrelevant to a described situation. As will be seen for this example, however, one possible response by PATHFINDER is to freely incorporate both precedents when its heuristics lead it to do so.

Given the connecting statement "The rising by the ball occurs after the falling by the ball." the ambiguity of the input description and supplied precedents is resolved. First, PATHFINDER is supplied with a simple definition for the event "occurs after," as follows:

```
Object 21 rises.  Object 22 rises.  The rising by
object 21 occurs after the rising by object 22.  The
occurring translates to the following statement.  The
beginning of object 21 rising is after the end of
object 22 rising.
```

This event definition is somewhat unusual in structure because the statement being provided with a definition (sentence 3) refers to two other events. These events appear as sentences 1 and 2. Instantiating this definition for the original connecting statement appearing in the input description, the following assertion is created:

PRESENT(after, <t11, t22>, null)

In order to perform the inference needed to detect compliance with this connecting statement, PATHFINDER must be supplied with two rules of inference, as follows:

```
Concurrently, time 51 is after time 52, and time 52 is
after time 53.  The preceding statement implies the
following statement.  Time 51 is after time 53.

Time 61 is after time 62.  The preceding statement
implies the following statement.  Time 62 is not after
time 61.
```

Given the above supplementary information, the first partial match chosen for elaboration is a partial restatement match from the end of trace C to trace B (the ball is overcome by gravity and starts falling). Elaboration of this partial match produces no logical inconsistencies. Next, a partial chaining match is selected, linking trace A to the transformed image of trace C produced during elaboration of the first partial match (i.e., the ball rising causes the ball to be overcome by gravity).

However, when this partial match is elaborated, a logical inconsistency arises regarding the ordering of time points. With the inclusion of the connecting statement above, the rising activity is thus specified as occurring both before and after the falling activity. Elaboration of this second partial match is then abandoned. From this point two additional partial matches are elaborated: a partial chaining match from the transformed image of trace C to trace D (the ball being overcome by gravity leads to the ball bouncing vertically off something), and a partial restatement match from the end of the ball bouncing vertically off something to the ball rising—trace A. For these partial matches, no inconsistency arises, and in the end, the rising event is indeed specified as occurring after the falling event.

Following the association process, the association structure is as illustrated below:

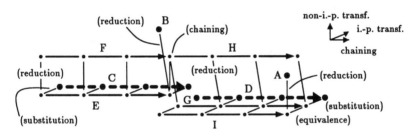

A: The ball rises.
B: The ball falls.

C: Object 31 is overcome by gravity.
D: Object 41 bounces vertically off object 42.

Alternate Versions of the Example

Now consider what happens when the same causal description is entered, except that the accompanying connecting statement is reversed, so that the falling activity is specified as occurring after the rising activity:

The ball rises. The ball falls. The falling by the
ball occurs after the rising by the ball.

The new connecting statement produces the following assertion:

PRESENT(after, <t21, t12>, null)

Given the same precedent events and rules of inference as in the above example, the new association sequence is as follows. As before, the first partial match elaborated is a partial restatement match from trace C to trace B (the ball is overcome by gravity and starts falling). Next, however, the partial chaining match from A to the transformed image of C succeeds (the ball rising causes the ball to be overcome by gravity), as no logical inconsistency arises with respect to the assertion generated for the new connecting statement. For this example then, the association process completes after two iterations, producing the following association structure:

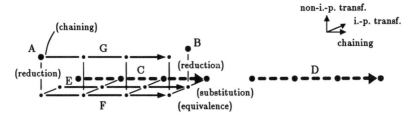

A: The ball rises.
B: The ball falls.

C: Object 31 is overcome by gravity.
D: Object 41 bounces vertically off object 42.

If the connecting statement is omitted altogether from the input description, the association process proceeds in a manner identical to the above sequence for the input description with reversed connecting statement. The association structure generated for this case is then identical to the one illustrated above.

7.3   Other Specifications of Association

An Initial Version of the Example

This section illustrates the use of connecting statements concerning other types of associations between events. As described in section 7.1, PATH-

FINDER checks for compliance with such connecting statements by conducting an analysis of paths of association proposed for completion in the association structure. An initial variant of the input description to be discussed in this section appears below.

```
The electric current travels from the first circuit
junction to the second circuit junction. The electric
current passes through the filament. The electric
current traveling from the first circuit junction to
the second circuit junction causes the electric current
to pass through the filament.
```

Ignoring the accompanying connecting statement, there are three ways to associate the events referenced in the description: (1) the electric current could travel from the first to the second circuit junction and then *continue* by passing through the filament, (2) the filament could be situated between the first and second circuit junctions, so that the electric current passing through the filament *coincides with* its traveling between the circuit junctions, and (3) the electric current could first pass through the filament, then continue by traveling between the circuit junctions (this third possibility is, of course, discouraged by PATHFINDER's narrative ordering heuristics).

For this example, event definitions produce the following traces for the referenced events. For the "traveling" event:

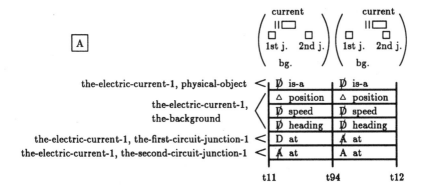

For the "passing through" event:

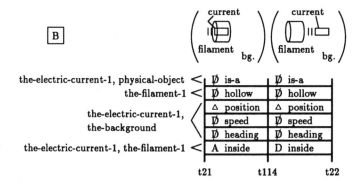

Because the event definitions supplied for this example concern physical objects rather than electric currents, an initial amount of transformation is needed before matching may proceed. Similar to the "substitution" examples appearing in chapter 6, we provide background statements concerning the types of the participating quantities, and a rule of inference asserting that electric currents are not physical objects:

> The electric current is an electric current. The first
> circuit junction is a physical object. The second
> circuit junction is a physical object. The filament is
> a physical object.

> Quantity 21 is an electric current. The preceding
> statement implies the following statement. Quantity 21
> is not a physical object.

Next, we supply PATHFINDER with two rules of restatement stating that electric currents may be viewed as physical objects where the attributes "at" and "inside" are concerned. In the second rule, we further state that for an electric current to be inside a physical object, the object must be "conductive," whereas for a physical object to be inside another physical object, the latter must be "hollow."

> Concurrently, quantity 31 is an electric current,
> object 32 is a physical object, and quantity 31 is at
> object 32. The following statement parallels the
> preceding statement. Concurrently, object 41 is a

physical object, object 42 is a physical object, and
object 41 is at object 42.

Concurrently, quantity 51 is an electric current,
object 52 is a physical object, object 52 is
conductive, and quantity 51 is inside object 52. The
following statement parallels the preceding statement.
Concurrently, object 61 is a physical object, object 62
is a physical object, object 62 is hollow, and object
61 is inside object 62.

Applying transformations generated by these rules of restatement to
the event traces for the description events, the following traces are produced. For the "traveling" event:[3]

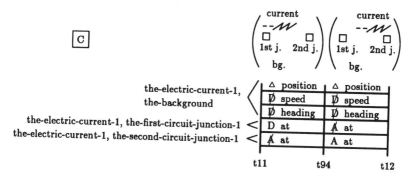

For the "passing through" event:

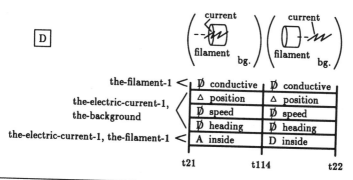

---

[3] In these traces, no assertions appear regarding the fact that the electric current
is an electric current, because PATHFINDER routinely removes from all event traces
those assertions matched by background statements.

At this point, three candidate partial matches appear: two directions of partial chaining matches between traces C and D, and a single, two-transition partial restatement match between traces C and D. These partial matches correspond to the three possible reconstructions of the input description mentioned previously.

Given the connecting statement appearing in the above description ("The electric current traveling from the first circuit junction to the second circuit junction causes the electric current to pass through the filament.") the heuristics used by PATHFINDER eliminate from consideration both the partial restatement match from trace C to trace D and the partial chaining match from trace D to trace C. PATHFINDER thus selects the partial chaining match from trace C to trace D and elaborates it, producing the following association structure:

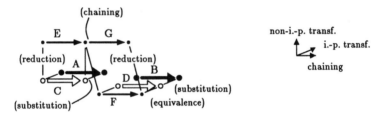

A: The electric current travels from the first circuit junction
   to the second circuit junction.
B: The electric current passes through the filament.

A Second Version of the Example

Alternatively, suppose the input description is supplied with a different connecting statement as follows:

> The electric current travels from the first circuit
> junction to the second circuit junction. The electric
> current passes through the filament. The electric
> current traveling from the first circuit junction to
> the second circuit junction is equivalent to the
> electric current passing through the filament.

Given the same supplementary information as described above, PATH-FINDER's heuristics now eliminate from consideration both candidate partial chaining matches, from trace C to trace D and from trace D to trace C, leaving the partial restatement match to be elaborated. For this variant of the example, then, the following association structure results:

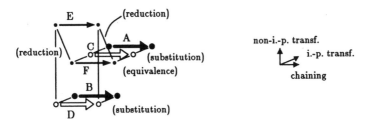

A: The electric current travels from the first circuit junction to the second circuit junction.
B: The electric current passes through the filament.

8 An Extended Example

This chapter brings together much of the discussion in the preceding chapters by detailing the operation of PATHFINDER in processing the causal description introduced in chapter 1, regarding the exposure of film in a camera. The discussion proceeds sequentially through the four phases of operation for PATHFINDER, from parsing and encoding of input specifications, to the application of exploratory transformations and inference, to the association process, and finally to the answering of a range of questions for the example.

8.1 Phase 1: Parsing and Encoding the Input

Appearing below is the original description listed in chapter 1, as drawn from the *Encyclopedia Americana* ([Grolier Inc., 1989], v. 5, p. 265). As noted in chapter 1, these sentences appear at the beginning of the entry for "camera" in that source. (The entry continues by describing what happens when the film is developed.)

> **CAMERA.** The basic function of a camera is to record a permanent image on a piece of film. When light enters a camera, it passes through a lens and converges on the film. It forms a latent image on the film by chemically altering the silver halides contained in the film emulsion.

Converting the description so that it conforms to the input syntax of PATHFINDER, the following simplified version is produced. While a number of simplifications have been made regarding grammatical devices used, the *vocabulary* of the description remains largely unchanged, especially regarding verbs.[1]

```
The camera records the image on the film.  The
recording of the image is a function of the camera.
The light enters the camera.  The light passes through
the lens.  The light converges on the film.  The light
forms the image on the film.  The light chemically
```

---

[1] Note, however, that all reference problems have been removed from the description by replacing "it" with an appropriate antecedent. This simplification and others are listed in chapter 2.

```
alters the silver halides.  The silver halides are
contained in the emulsion.  The emulsion is a part of
the film.
```

The simplified causal description above contains six event references and three background statements. The event references are as follows:

```
The camera records the image on the film.
The light enters the camera.
The light passes through the lens.
The light converges on the film.
The light forms the image on the film.
The light chemically alters the silver halides.
```

The background statements are as follows:

```
The recording of the image is a function of the camera.
The silver halides are contained in the emulsion.
The emulsion is a part of the film.
```

The first of these background statements is motivated by the sentence beginning "The basic function of a camera is..." in the original description. The second is motivated by the phrase "...contained in the film emulsion." The third is motivated by the noun phrase "film emulsion." Of these three statements, the first is parsed and encoded by PATHFINDER, but finds no further use in the association process. The second and third statements are used by PATHFINDER in conducting inference.

In addition to these statements, it could be argued that the use of the word "by" in the final sentence of the original description constitutes a connecting statement roughly equivalent to the following statement conforming to the input syntax for PATHFINDER:

```
The light forming the image on the film summarizes the
light chemically altering the silver halides.
```

Statement type	Quantity
background statement	8, regarding object types
event definition	6, one for each referenced event
precedent event	1, change of appearance from chemical transformation
rule of inference	5
rule of restatement	8

Table 8.1
Supplementary information provided for the camera example.

While PATHFINDER can process the description with this connecting statement included, it can also process the description without such a statement, and as the latter situation is more difficult, it is this situation that is presented here.

As described in chapter 2, PATHFINDER accepts five varieties of supplementary information. Table 8.1 summarizes these quantities for the camera description input file.

The supplementary background statements supplied to PATHFINDER are as follows:

```
The camera is a physical object.  The image is a visual
pattern.  The film is a physical object.  The light is
a beam of light.  The lens is a physical object.  The
silver halides are a physical object.  The emulsion is
a physical object.  The emulsion is a mixture.
```

Next, the six event definitions are given. In keeping with the general philosophy of the approach, these definitions are not particularized to the precise circumstances of the camera scenario; rather, they depict commonly-occurring situations involving generic objects (mostly *physical* objects). For the first two events, concerning "recording on" and "entering," the event definitions are as follows:

```
Object 1 recording information 2 on medium 3 translates
to the following event.  First, object 1 remains a
physical object, information 2 remains a piece of
```

information, medium 3 remains a physical object, event
4 remains an event, object 1 becomes engaged in event
4, and information 2 remains not accessible from medium
3. Next, object 1 remains a physical object,
information 2 remains a piece of information, medium 3
remains a physical object, event 4 remains an event,
object 1 becomes not engaged in event 4, and
information 2 becomes accessible from medium 3.

Object 11 entering object 12 translates to the
following event. Concurrently, object 11 remains a
physical object, object 12 remains a physical object,
object 12 remains hollow, the position of object 11
changes, the speed of object 11 does not disappear, the
heading of object 11 does not disappear, and object 11
becomes inside object 12.

Instantiated to the context of the events referenced in the description,
these definitions yield the following event traces:

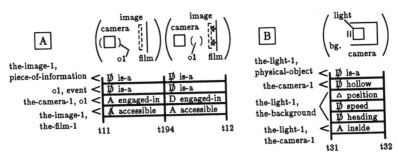

The camera records the image on the film.   The light enters the camera.

Here, the recording event has been represented at a level of abstraction
depicting the camera as "engaged in" a reified event-object "o1." An
abstract description as such would seem to be motivated in this case, as
there are many ways to record a piece of information (writing or typing,
using a tape recorder, recording on film, storing on a computer memory

chip, and so forth), such that the only common elements held between these events are as depicted in the above event trace.[2]

The next two event definitions are for "passing through" and "converging on," as follows. Here, "converging on" is depicted in terms of an object moving into contact and ending "on" a second object, with a corresponding decrease in the size of the first object, as when a set of moving objects (e.g., a team of emergency vehicles, or a set of coordinated streams of water) "converges on" a location.

Object 21 passing through object 22 translates to the following event. First, object 21 remains a physical object, object 22 remains a physical object, object 22 remains hollow, the position of object 21 changes, the speed of object 21 does not disappear, the heading of object 21 does not disappear, and object 21 becomes inside object 22. Next, object 21 remains a physical object, object 22 remains a physical object, object 22 remains hollow, the position of object 21 changes, the speed of object 21 does not disappear, the heading of object 21 does not disappear, and object 21 becomes not inside object 22.

Object 31 converging on object 32 translates to the following event. First, object 31 remains a physical object, object 32 remains a physical object, the position of object 31 changes, the speed of object 31 does not disappear, the heading of object 31 does not disappear, the distance between object 31 and object 32 decreases, the contact between object 31 and object 32 does not appear, object 31 remains not on object 32, and the size of object 31 decreases. Next, object 31 remains a physical object, object 32 remains a physical object, the position of object 31 changes, the speed of object 31 disappears, the heading of object 31 disappears, the distance between object 31 and object 32 disappears, the contact between object 31 and object 32 appears, object 31 becomes on object 32, and the size of object 31 decreases.

---

[2] Alternatively, a program like PATHFINDER could be configured to perform word sense disambiguation as it reconstructs a scenario, selecting from a family of alternative particularizations of an event based on compatibility with other events in the scenario. This task has been left for future exploration.

The event traces generated for the corresponding description events are then:

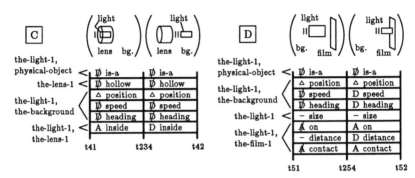

The light passes through the lens.   The light converges on the film.

The remaining two event definitions concern "forming on" and "chemically altering." These definitions are given below. The definition for "forming on" is specialized to formation of a visual pattern on an object; however, as for "recording on," above, the definition characterizes activity at an abstract level involving a reified event, as there are many ways in which even this specialized type of event may occur (marking as with a pencil or paintbrush, etching or carving using a sharp object, stamping an impression into a surface, projecting an image, and so forth).

Object 41 forming image 42 on object 43 translates to the following event. First, object 41 remains a physical object, image 42 remains a visual pattern, object 43 remains a physical object, event 44 remains an event, object 41 becomes engaged in event 44, the appearance of object 43 does not change, and image 42 remains not on object 43. Next, object 41 remains a physical object, image 42 remains a visual pattern, object 43 remains a physical object, event 44 remains an event, object 41 becomes not engaged in event 44, the appearance of object 43 changes, and image 42 becomes on object 43.

Object 51 chemically altering object 52 translates to
the following event. First, object 51 remains a
physical object, object 52 remains a physical object,
object 52 remains made of substance 53, object 52
remains not made of substance 54, the distance between
object 51 and object 52 disappears, and the contact
between object 51 and object 52 appears. Next, object
51 remains a physical object, object 52 remains a
physical object, object 52 becomes not made of
substance 53, object 52 becomes made of substance 54,
the distance between object 51 and object 52 does not
appear, and the contact between object 51 and object 52
does not disappear.

Given these definitions, the following event traces are produced for
the corresponding description events:

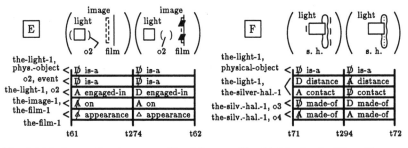

The light forms the image on the film.   The light chemically alters
                                          the silver halides.

In line with the creation of hypothetical objects to represent participants
appearing in an event definition but not named in the corresponding
event reference, "o3" and "o4" have been created to represent particular
substances making up the silver halides before and after the chemical
alteration event.

Next, a single precedent event and definition are supplied to PATH-
FINDER. This event involves an object undergoing a chemical transfor-

mation and concurrently changing appearance. This event is crucial to understanding the described scenario: without knowledge that an object may change appearance as it changes its chemical composition, there is no basis for drawing a connection between chemical alteration of the silver halides and formation of an image on the film.[3] The event reference and definition for the precedent event are as follows:

```
Object 61 changes appearance from chemical
transformation.

Object 61 changing appearance from chemical
transformation translates to the following event.
Concurrently, object 61 remains a physical object,
object 61 becomes not made of substance 62, object 61
becomes made of substance 63, and the appearance of
object 61 changes.
```

This event reference and definition produce the following event trace:

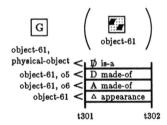

Object 61 changes appearance from chemical transformation.

Next, PATHFINDER is supplied with five rules of inference, listed below. These rules assert that a beam of light is not a physical object,

---

[3] On a related issue, it may be noted that the original description speaks of "latent" versus "permanent" images, indicating that the film may not actually change appearance until developed. In spite of this, it would nevertheless appear necessary that a comprehender, whether human or program, *think* in terms of a change of appearance, such that a connection to formation of an image may be made.

that an object contained in a mixture is a part of that mixture, that a part of a part of an object is itself a part of the object, and that a visual pattern is accessible from an object or medium precisely when it may be characterized as being "on" that object or medium.[4]

> Object 71 is a beam of light. The preceding statement implies the following statement. Object 71 is not a physical object.

> Concurrently, object 81 is a mixture, object 82 is a physical object, and object 82 is contained in object 81. The preceding statement implies the following statement. Object 82 is a part of object 81.

> Concurrently, Object 91 is a part of object 92, and object 92 is a part of object 93. The preceding statement implies the following statement. Object 91 is a part of object 93.

> Concurrently, image 101 is a visual pattern, and image 101 is on object 102. The preceding statement implies the following statement. Image 101 is accessible from object 102.

> Concurrently, image 111 is a visual pattern, and image 111 is not on object 112. The preceding statement implies the following statement. Image 111 is not accessible from object 112.

Finally, eight rules of restatement are provided to PATHFINDER. The first three of these, listed below, concern an analogical mapping

---

[4] The last two rules have been entered as inference rules rather than equivalence rules because the condition of a visual pattern being "on" an object would seem to imply more than simply being "accessible from" the object (i.e., the object is presumably modified in some property such as appearance, too).

between beams of light and physical objects. In particular, the first
two rules state that when a beam of light is characterized as "inside"
or having "contact" with a physical object, the beam of light may be
viewed as if it were itself a physical object inside or in contact with that
physical object. For the analogy involving the attribute "inside," there
is an additional mapping between the enclosing object being "hollow"
in the physical object case, versus "transparent" for the case involving
a beam of light.

The third rule below illustrates the specification of rules of restatement
incorporating assertions at higher levels of abstraction—here, the rule
involves events treated as abstract objects. The rule states that if a
beam of light engages in an event, leading to a change of appearance in a
quantity, that beam of light may be viewed as a physical object engaging
in an event, leading to a change of appearance in the quantity. This
rule applies in a range of circumstances involving events characterized
at an abstract level, including the case of a beam of light "forming"
a visual pattern on an object—as occurs in the causal description—
and also events such as the "splattering" of color on an object or the
"bleaching" of a surface.

```
Concurrently, quantity 121 is a beam of light, object
122 is a physical object, object 122 is transparent,
and quantity 121 is inside object 122. The following
statement parallels the preceding statement.
Concurrently, object 131 is a physical object, object
132 is a physical object, object 132 is hollow, and
object 131 is inside object 132.
```

```
Concurrently, quantity 141 is a beam of light, object
142 is a physical object, and the contact between
quantity 141 and object 142 is present. The following
statement parallels the preceding statement.
Concurrently, object 151 is a physical object, object
152 is a physical object, and the contact between
object 151 and object 152 is present.
```

```
First, quantity 161 remains a beam of light, event 162
remains an event, and quantity 161 becomes engaged in
```

event 162. Next, object 163 remains a physical object,
and the appearance of object 163 changes. The
following event parallels the preceding event. First,
object 171 remains a physical object, event 172 remains
an event, and object 171 becomes engaged in event 172.
Next, object 173 remains a physical object, and the
appearance of object 173 changes.

The remaining five rules of restatement concern summarization of
specifications of activity in terms of other specifications of activity: a
visual pattern generalized as a piece of information, part of an object
changing appearance summarized as the whole object changing appearance, and contact between an object and a part of a second object summarized as contact between the object and the second object itself. Note
that in keeping with the general nature of rules of restatement, these
rules suggest *plausible* alternate characterizations, which may not always
be applicable. (For instance, if a part of an object changes appearance,
it may be hidden within the whole and thus the whole may not change
appearance.) As such, we depend on the association process to choose
between alternate characterizations of activity proposed through the use
of these rules of restatement.[5]

Image 181 is a visual pattern. The following statement
summarizes the preceding statement. Image 181 is a
piece of information.

Concurrently, object 191 remains a part of object 192,
and the appearance of object 191 changes. The
preceding event is summarized by the following event.
The appearance of object 192 changes.

---

[5] Indeed, two additional rules of restatement have been excluded from the set provided to PATHFINDER, because they describe circumstances deemed insufficiently plausible to merit inclusion. The first excluded rule complements the second rule listed here and describes a situation in which no change in appearance for part of an object is summarized as no change in appearance for the whole. In this case, some other part of the whole could still change appearance, leading to the whole changing appearance. The second excluded rule complements the last three listed here and describes a situation in which no appearance of contact with a specified part of an object is summarized as no appearance of contact with the whole. In this case, contact with some other part of the whole could still take place, leading to an overall appearance of contact with the whole.

Concurrently, object 201 remains a part of object 202,
the distance between object 203 and object 201
disappears, and the contact between object 203 and
object 201 appears. The preceding event is summarized
by the following event. Concurrently, the distance
between object 203 and object 202 disappears, and the
contact between object 203 and object 202 appears.

Concurrently, object 201 remains a part of object 202,
the distance between object 203 and object 201 does not
appear, and the contact between object 203 and object
201 does not disappear. The preceding event is
summarized by the following event. Concurrently, the
distance between object 203 and object 202 does not
appear, and the contact between object 203 and object
202 does not disappear.

Concurrently, object 201 remains a part of object 202,
the distance between object 203 and object 201 appears,
and the contact between object 203 and object 201
disappears. The preceding event is summarized by the
following event. Concurrently, the distance between
object 203 and object 202 appears, and the contact
between object 203 and object 202 disappears.

8.2   Phase 2: Applying Exploratory Transformations

Having completed the first phase of operation—parsing of the input text
and translation to a set of event traces—PATHFINDER proceeds with
phase 2, application of exploratory transformations and inference to the
set of event traces. The results of this step are presented in overview only
here, with a more detailed description of particular transformed images
of traces appearing below in the discussion of the association process for
this example. Figure 8.1 diagrams the clusters of transformed images
produced for each of the original event traces for this example. Note
that each of the traces B, C, D, E and F has been transformed by a
substitution operation, mapping it from an initial specification in terms

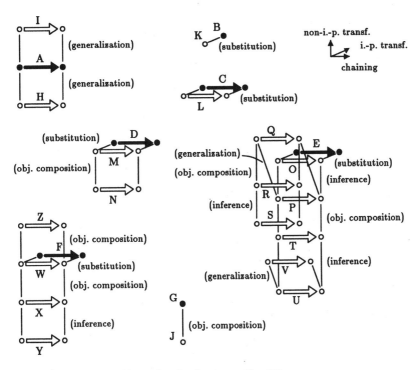

A: The camera records the image on the film.
B: The light enters the camera.
C: The light passes through the lens.
D: The light converges on the film.
E: The light forms the image on the film.
F: The light chemically alters the silver halides.

G: Object 61 changes appearance from chemical transformation.

Figure 8.1
Status of the association structure following the application of exploratory
transformations and inference.

of physical objects to one involving a beam of light. As these original traces are logically inconsistent when combined with background knowledge that "the light" is a beam of light, they are excluded from the matching process, and only the logically consistent transformed images of these traces are considered. Additionally, many of the traces have been transformed via inference and non-information-preserving transformations, as motivated by rules of inference and rules of restatement in the input file.

8.3 Phase 3: Associating the Events

Keeping Figure 8.1 handy as a reference, we now proceed with a discussion of the association process for this example. PATHFINDER executes six iterations of its association cycle in order to associate the seven clusters of event traces.

In selecting partial matches for elaboration, PATHFINDER detects a number of instances of equated description objects. In each case, it removes the offending partial match from the agenda and inserts a reduced match excluding the particular binding responsible for the equated description objects, as described previously. These operations will not be mentioned in the following summary of the association process.

On the first cycle, the program selects from a field of 120 candidate partial matches. The match chosen for elaboration is a partial chaining match from trace M (a transformed image of trace D—"The light converges on the film.") to trace Z (an image of trace F—"The light chemically alters the silver halides.") This particular match and elaboration were discussed in detail in chapter 1. Of interest is the fact that in elaborating this partial chaining match, PATHFINDER has formed a bridge between descriptions at two levels of abstraction. Trace D depicts the light interating with *the film*, whereas trace F depicts the light interacting with *the silver halides*—these being contained within, hence part of, the emulsion, which is a part of the film. An exploratory transformation of the object composition variety has been applied to trace F, producing trace Z, which depicts the light as coming into contact with the film rather than the silver halides.

Diagramed below are traces M and Z and the assertions involved in the selected partial chaining match.

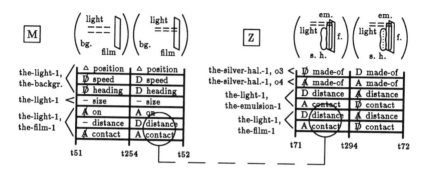

	Δ position	Δ position
the-light-1,	D̸ speed	D speed
the-backgr.	D̸ heading	D heading
the-light-1 <	− size	− size
	A̸ on	A on
the-light-1,	− distance	D distance
the-film-1 <	A̸ contact	A contact
	t51	t254	t52

	D̸ made-of	D made-of
the-silver-hal.-1, o3 <	A̸ made-of	A made-of
the-silver-hal.-1, o4 <	D distance	A̸ distance
the-light-1,	A contact	D̸ contact
the-emulsion-1 <	D distance	A̸ distance
the-light-1,	A contact	D̸ contact
the-film-1 <	t71	t294	t72

Elaboration of this partial chaining match yields the following association structure fragment. (For simplicity, this diagram and succeeding diagrams depicting association structure fragments for the camera example omit labels for chaining, reduction and equivalence associations generated in the elaboration of partial matches.)

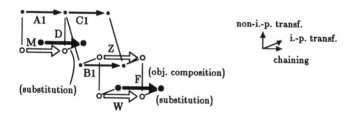

D: The light converges on the film.
F: The light chemically alters the silver halides.

The next two partial matches chosen for elaboration involve motion on the part of the beam of light and are facilitated in part by the narrative ordering heuristic in PATHFINDER. The first of these matches involves trace L (an image of trace C—"The light passes through the lens.") and trace M (the above-mentioned image of trace D—"The light converges on the film.") This partial match is diagramed below.

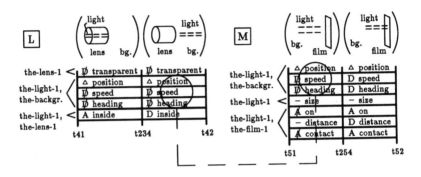

After the elaboration of this partial match, the relevant association structure fragment appears as follows:

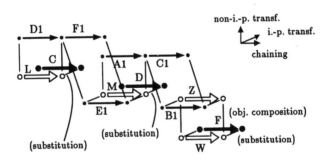

C: The light passes through the lens.
D: The light converges on the film.
F: The light chemically alters the silver halides.

Following this, the next partial match elaborated is a partial chaining match between trace K (an image of trace B—"The light enters the camera.") and trace L (the above-mentioned image of trace C—"The light passes through the lens.") This partial match is as follows:

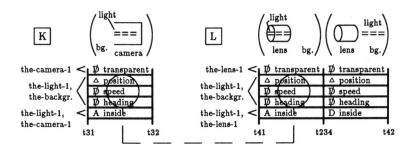

Elaboration of this partial match results in the following association structure fragment:

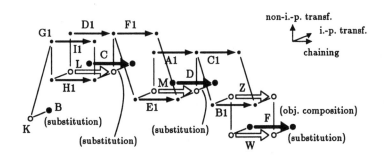

B: The light enters the camera.
C: The light passes through the lens.
D: The light converges on the film.
F: The light chemically alters the silver halides.

The fourth match elaborated is a partial restatement match between trace B1 (an equivalence image of trace Z, the abstracted image of trace F—"The light chemically alters the silver halides.") and the precedent

trace, G—"Object 61 changes appearance from chemical transformation.") This partial match is as follows:

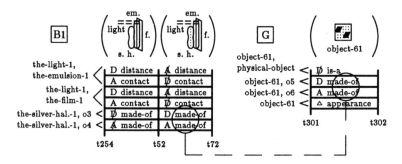

This match extends the association structure fragment as follows:

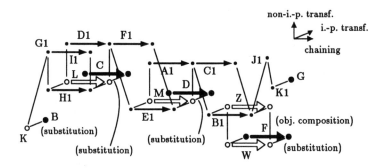

B: The light enters the camera.
C: The light passes through the lens.
D: The light converges on the film.
F: The light chemically alters the silver halides.

G: Object 61 changes appearance from chemical transformation.

Next, a partial restatement match is elaborated between trace K1
(the substituted version of the precedent trace, G—here, "The silver
halides change appearance from chemical transformation.") and trace
V (a transformed image of trace E—"The light forms the image on
the film.") Here, an object composition transformation applied in the
reverse direction has produced a transformed image of trace E in which a
hypothesized *part* of the film changes appearance. Change of appearance
in this part, "o65," is then matched with change of appearance in the

known part "the-silver-halides-1" in trace K1. The traces and partial match are as diagramed below:

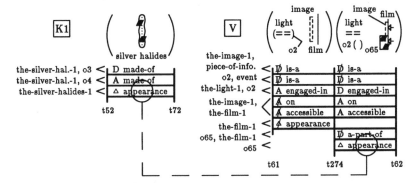

Elaboration of this partial match produces the following association structure fragment:

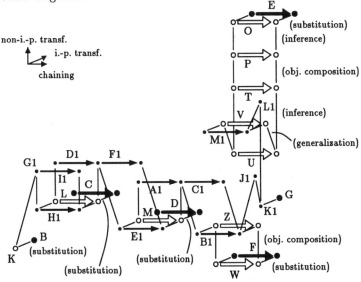

B: The light enters the camera.
C: The light passes through the lens.
D: The light converges on the film.
E: The light forms the image on the film.
F: The light chemically alters the silver halides.

G: Object 61 changes appearance from chemical transformation.

The sixth and final partial match elaborated is a partial restatement match between trace M1 (an equivalence image of trace V, the transformed image of trace E—"The light forms the image on the film.") and trace A—"The camera records the image on the film.") In this case, equally-ranked partial matches also exist between trace A and two other transformed images of trace E: trace P and trace U. These three matches all involve the same matched assertions, and question-answering is unaffected by the choice of which match to elaborate.

Traces M1 and A are diagramed below, along with the partial match to be elaborated. In this match, object "o2"—created to represent the event engaged in by the light as it forms the image on the film—has been matched with object "o1"—created to represent the event engaged in by the camera as it records the image on the film. This matching of hypothesized event-objects advances a hypothesis that a single event is responsible for both activities.

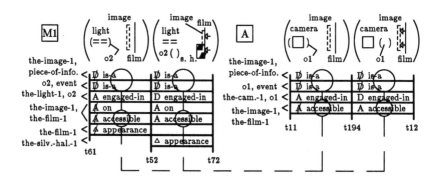

At this point, the association process is complete: all six of the original description events have been associated together. At this point, the association structure appears as diagramed in Figure 8.2.

8.4   Phase 4: Answering Questions

Having completed the association structure, PATHFINDER proceeds to answer questions. Chapter 1 described the answering of a single

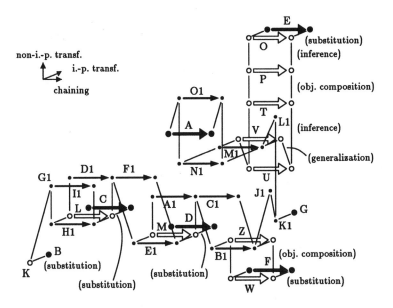

A: The camera records the image on the film.
B: The light enters the camera.
C: The light passes through the lens.
D: The light converges on the film.
E: The light forms the image on the film.
F: The light chemically alters the silver halides.

G: Object 61 changes appearance from chemical transformation.

Figure 8.2
Status of the association structure at the end of the association phase for the
camera description.

question of each variety for this example. These questions and additional
questions of the four varieties are discussed in the following paragraphs.

As described in previous chapters, questions of the first type concern
the time-varying status of particular attributes. Below are a number of
examples of questions of this type pertaining to the camera description.
These questions are accompanied by the answers returned by PATH-
FINDER.

```
When is the light inside the camera?

    As the light enters the camera, the light becomes
    inside the camera.

When is the light inside the lens?

    First, as the light enters the camera, the light
    becomes inside the lens. Next, as the light passes
    through the lens, the light becomes not inside the
    lens.

What happens to the distance between the light and the
film?

    First, as the light passes through the lens, the
    distance between the light and the film decreases.
    Next, as the light converges on the film, the distance
    between the light and the film disappears. Next, as
    the camera records the image on the film, the distance
    between the light and the film does not appear.

When is the light on the film?

    First, as the light passes through the lens, the light
    remains not on the film. Next, as the light converges
    on the film, the light becomes on the film.

When is the image on the film?

    As the camera records the image on the film, the image
    becomes on the film.

When is the image accessible from the film?

    As the camera records the image on the film, the image
    becomes accessible from the film.
```

What happens to the appearance of the film?

As the camera records the image on the film, the appearance of the film changes.

PATHFINDER's responses to several questions of type 2 are listed below. Paths of association underlying these responses may be discerned from Figure 8.2.

How does the light entering the camera relate to the light converging on the film?

The light entering the camera causes the light to pass through the lens, which causes the light to converge on the film.

How does the camera recording the image on the film relate to the light forming the image on the film?

The camera recording the image on the film coincides with the light forming the image on the film.

How does the light converging on the film relate to the light forming the image on the film?

The light converging on the film causes the light to chemically alter the silver halides, which ends with the silver halides changing appearance from chemical transformation, which occurs at the end of the light forming the image on the film.

Questions of types 3 and 4 are processed in the same manner as questions of type 2, except that further association is required before a path of association may be described. Following is an example of a question of type 3, concerning a plausible causal connection:

How could the building reflecting the light into the camera cause the light to converge on the film?

For this question, an event definition is provided for "reflecting into," producing the following trace for the event referenced in the question:

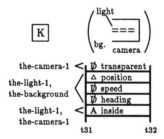

	t741	t766	t767	t768	t742
the-light-1, the-background	△ position	△ position	△ position	△ position	
	∅ speed	∅ speed	∅ speed	∅ speed	
	∅ heading	∅ heading	△ heading	∅ heading	
the-light-1, the-building-1	− distance	D distance	A distance	+ distance	
	A contact	A contact	D contact	A contact	
the-light-1, the-camera-1	∅ distance	∅ distance	− distance	− distance	
	A contact	A contact	A contact	A contact	
	A inside	A inside	A inside	A inside	

The above trace is associated with the existing set of event traces through elaboration of a partial restatement match involving the final transition of this trace and trace K (the substituted image of trace B— "The light enters the camera.") Trace K is as follows:

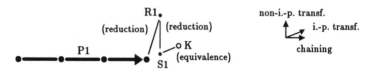

Elaborating this partial match produces the following sequence of associations extending the association structure diagramed in Figure 8.2:

R1•
(reduction) / (reduction)

P1

S1 ○ K (equivalence)

non-i.-p. transf.
i.-p. transf.
chaining

P1: The building reflects the light into the camera.
K: The light enters the camera. (transformed)

Having associated the new event with existing events in the association structure, PATHFINDER now describes the path of association between the two events named in the question. This path progresses from "The building reflects the light into the camera." through the new sequence of associations connecting this event with "The light enters the camera." and continues through previously-existing associations to reach "The light converges on the film." The answer returned by PATHFINDER is as follows:

```
The building reflecting the light into the camera could
end with the light entering the camera, which could
cause the light to pass through the lens, which could
cause the light to converge on the film.
```

Questions of type 4 ask if a new event may be used to paraphrase part of the activity. Following is a first example of this type of question for the camera description:

```
Does the light enter the lens?
```

In processing the original description, PATHFINDER has been given an event definition for "entering," and thus this definition is reused here. Because "the light" is a beam of light and not a physical object, the original trace produced is logically inconsistent; however, an exploratory transformation of the substitution variety maps this trace into the domain of beams of light, parallel to the treatment of "The light enters the camera." in the original description. The transformed image of this question event appears below as trace Q1. This trace has been matched via a partial chaining match with trace H1 (a transformed image of trace C—"The light passes through the lens.")

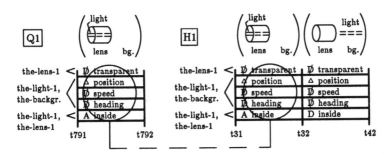

Given this path of association, PATHFINDER answers the question as follows:

```
Yes.  The light entering the lens causes the light to
pass through the lens.
```

The following question of type 4 illustrates a way of asking PATH-FINDER about the utilization of precedent events in its association structure:

```
Do the silver halides change appearance from chemical
transformation?
```

This question makes use of the event definition accompanying the precedent event "Object 61 changes appearance from chemical transformation." producing trace P1, below. In searching for a match, PATH-FINDER finds that the activity in question does indeed occur in trace K1, below, a substituted version of the precedent event.

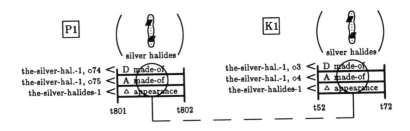

This enables PATHFINDER to answer in the affirmative. Because the two events linked by the relevant path of association are both expressed in the same way in English, PATHFINDER suppresses the second sentence of its response ("The silver halides changing appearance from chemical transformation is equivalent to the silver halides changing appearance from chemical transformation.") PATHFINDER's answer is thus simply:

```
Yes.
```

The following question of type 4 illustrates PATHFINDER's handling of paths of association involving exploratory transformations in this context.

```
Does the light come into contact with the emulsion?
```

Given a definition for "coming into contact," PATHFINDER produces the event trace P1, below. By utilizing its repertory of exploratory transformations, PATHFINDER also generates an abstracted image of trace P1 (trace S1), involving the light coming into contact with the film rather than with the emulsion. Given PATHFINDER's heuristics, the highest-ranked partial match is one associating this transformed image with trace E1 (the transformed image of trace D—"The light converges on the film.")

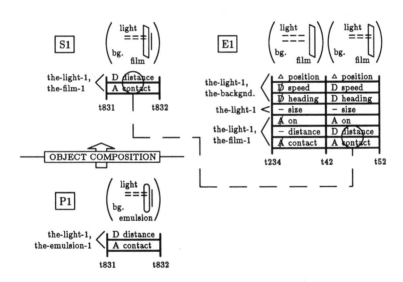

Note that the selected match, while it does associate the new event with an event known to the system, nevertheless matches on the basis of the light coming into contact with the film rather than with the emulsion. As such, contact between the light and the emulsion is only conjectured by the match, not firmly established.[6] This results from the fact that

---

[6] In this case, a competing partial match from P1 to a transformed image of trace F—"The light chemically alters the silver halides."—is penalized relative to the above match, as it introduces a redundant antecedent for the matched trace.

exploratory transformations introduce *plausible* redescriptions of events, not necessary ones. As mentioned in chapter 6, PATHFINDER compensates for this aspect of exploratory transformations by checking to see whether all assertions of the target event for a question of type 4 are covered in a composite trace for the originally-described activity. If so, PATHFINDER answers "Yes." followed by a summarization of the generated path of association. For the above question, PATHFINDER does indeed find that all assertions of the new event are covered in the composite trace, and thus it answers as follows:

> Yes. The light coming into contact with the emulsion
> is a part of the light converging on the film.

To contrast with the above question, suppose the following question of type 4 is posed to PATHFINDER:

> The film leader is a physical object. The film leader
> is a part of the film.
>
> Does the light come into contact with the film leader?

Here, an identical path of association is found, connecting the new event with "The light converges on the film." In this case, however, the subsequent check to see if all assertions of the new event are covered in the composite trace results in failure. When this happens, PATHFINDER qualifies its answer as "Possibly." followed by a description of the plausible path of association:

> Possibly. The light coming into contact with the film
> leader could be a part of the light converging on the
> film.

9 Related Literature

The research described in this book draws inspiration from and shares a number of goals with a broad base of research in artificial intelligence, psychology, linguistics and philosophy. This chapter explores some of the work forming this foundation.

9.1 Research in Artificial Intelligence

Six tasks are used to organize the discussion of related research in artificial intelligence. These are: reasoning about physical systems, reasoning about time, causal modeling, analogical reasoning, reasoning in support of communication, and natural language understanding.

Reasoning about Physical Systems

In the area of reasoning about physical systems, work in qualitative physics is perhaps most closely related to the research described here. Seminal work in qualitative physics is reported in [Forbus, 1984], [de Kleer and Brown, 1984] and [Kuipers, 1986]. This work deals primarily with the task of reasoning about the global behavior of a physical system from knowledge of the behavior of individual components in that system. Of particular relevance to the causal reconstruction problem are two aspects of this work. First, by representing physical activity at a detailed level in terms of time-varying parameters of participating objects, a good deal of leverage is gained toward the determination of whether particular behaviors may be exhibited by particular physical systems. Second, by representing values and changes in these parameters in a qualitative way, a computational savings is realized, coupled with a tolerance for low-resolution input information.

The transition space representation exhibits many similarities with the representations appearing in qualitative physics; however, due to the particular nature of the causal reconstruction task, there are some differences as well. The most central difference is a grounding of the representation in *language*, rather than in a scientific model of a target physical behavior. This has an effect of bringing into the representation a range of phenomena recognized and articulated by humans, yet normally not included in scientific accounts of activity: objects such as beams of light, radio signals, sounds, dents, paths and so forth, and attributes like "support," "inside," "appearance," and "shape," which are often fundamentally qualitative in nature and rougher in granularity than the quantitative phenomena supporting many scientific models of behavior. As a consequence, the transition space representation tends to be somewhat more macroscopic, with events often spanning several qualitative states or operating regions of a device. Other differences with some the work in qualitative physics include a greater emphasis on representation at different levels of abstraction and in terms of different underlying analogies, and the use of heuristically-guided matching rather than constraint propagation as a mechanism for reasoning.

Related in some ways to the work in qualitative physics is the work in model-based reasoning [Davis, 1984], [Davis and Hamscher, 1988]. This work is rather broad in scope, incorporating quantitative calculations and often including an explicit representation of activity at different levels of abstraction. Model-based reasoning also emphasizes a scientific characterization of physical activity, as contrasted with the language orientation adopted in transition space. Some recent work is attempting to bridge these two general disciplines, including the linking of model-based reasoning with language-based explanations [Gruber, 1990], and the combination of model-based reasoning with specifications of the general context surrounding particular behaviors [Nayak *et al.*, 1992].

A number of other research efforts concerned with reasoning about physical systems have drawn wholly or in part on cognitive motivation. One example drawing partially on cognitive motivation is the work in naive physics [Hayes, 1985a] [Hayes, 1985b]. This work involves a blend of (1) detailed attention to the capture of a human-oriented ontology for representing physical situations, and (2) consideration of the ramifications of simple axiomatizations of physical phenomena, given an ability to perform deductive inference. In the first respect, this work has captured many conceptual notions utilized by humans in reasoning about physical activity: edges, surfaces, quantities of liquid, spaces and so forth. In relying on deductive inference for reasoning, however, some human-oriented styles of reasoning are excluded: reasoning by analogy, reasoning at different levels of abstraction, reasoning under uncertainty and so forth.

Work on the CYC project [Lenat *et al.*, 1986] is related in some respects to the work in naive physics. This work pays special attention to the capture of a human-oriented ontology of the world and furthermore extends to consideration of human-like reasoning capabilities regarding the use of analogy and abstraction. The orientation of the work on CYC is in many ways similar to that of the research described here. In an article by Lenat and Feigenbaum [1987], the authors outline three general principles summarizing this orientation: (1) the Knowledge Principle—that intelligent programs must have a great deal of knowledge to perform usefully, (2) the Breadth Hypothesis—that intelligent behavior depends on an ability to fall back on increasingly general knowledge and an ability to reason by analogy, and (3) a view of Artificial Intelligence as Empirical Inquiry—requiring an actual testing of theories on large problems. The Breadth Hypothesis is especially aligned with the orientation pursued here: in understanding causal descriptions, we have given particular attention to the use of information at different levels of abstraction and information accessible through the use of analogy.

On the other hand, there are also some differences between CYC and the work described here. For CYC, the objective is to acquire vast amounts of all types of knowledge, including knowledge about people, animals, institutions and so forth. To this end, knowledge is typically coded directly in the representational language used by the program, rather than being extracted from verbal descriptions provided to the program. Additionally, much effort has been exerted in CYC on human-directed organization of this massive amount of knowledge into classes of entities, microtheories and so forth. In the work described in this book, a complementary emphasis has been placed on automated detection of new associations among unorganized or unconnected fragments of knowledge—this in the specific context of postulating plausible connections among events referenced in causal descriptions.

Two additional cognitively-motivated approaches focusing on reasoning about physical behavior are the work in Functional Representation, as described in [Sembugamoorthy and Chandrasekaran, 1986], and the work on consolidation, as described in [Bylander and Chandrasekaran, 1985]. Functional Representation stresses a tightly interconnected, compiled representation of knowledge concerning structure, function and behavior of physical systems and components, such that a program may easily perform simple explanation and diagnosis tasks. This work represents activity in terms of the sorts of objects and events appearing in verbal descriptions of activity, but has not thus far emphasized language comprehension as a research task. The work on consolidation focuses on reasoning about physical behavior using local computations between pairs of interacting physical components, rather than the global sorts of computations required in qualitative physics. In the process of pursuing this objective, the work also targets a representational ontology related to human intuitive accounts of physical behavior. As with the Functional Representation work, this work has not emphasized language comprehension as a research task.

Other cognitively-oriented work in reasoning about physical behavior may be found in the literature on artificial intelligence in medicine (e.g., see [Patil, 1988]). The conceptual nature of quantities such as diseases and symptoms, as well as a need for such programs to communicate with humans has in many ways forced the incorporation of representational ontologies and styles of reasoning in line with human capabilities, as in the work on medical reasoning at multiple levels of abstraction [Patil *et al.*, 1981] and incorporating multiple reasoning techniques [Szolovits and Pauker, 1978].

Reasoning about Time

Also very relevant to the work described here is the literature on reasoning about time. A concise survey of this research appears in [Shoham and Goyal, 1988]. Some of this work has addressed the task of reasoning about temporal ordering information ([Allen, 1983], [Vilain, 1982], [Vilain and Kautz, 1986]), while other work has focused on reasoning about events and causality, including general purpose representations for temporal knowledge proposed by McDermott [1982] and Allen [1984]. McDermott's representation includes facilities for reasoning explicitly about continuous change, persistence of facts and the branching of alternate paths of temporal unfolding of events. Allen's representation captures simultaneous actions, and actions involving non-activity. Such approaches may mesh well with the transition space representation for checking postulated combinations of events for logical consistency.

Recently, there has been an exploration of the use of non-monotonic logic in reasoning about time, especially concerning the determination of plausible consequences of events or actions. Hanks and McDermott [1986] observed that for several varieties of non-monotonic logic, the rules for selection of default assumptions were insufficiently constraining to support the formation of rather simple predictions concerning the future. This has resulted in a search for stronger preference criteria by which a choice may be made between alternative default assumptions (e.g., [Shoham, 1986] [Morgenstern and Stein, 1988]). Separately, Doyle and Wellman have argued that "every universal theory of default reasoning will violate at least one reasonable principle of rational reasoning" [1989]. This sequence of results would seem to suggest that domain-specific heuristics may play a significant role in tasks such as prediction and explanation. It is possible that one useful heuristic for these tasks might be that of matching between transition-centered representations of events, as explored in this book.

Causal Modeling

Two research efforts in the area of causal modeling are those of Doyle [1988] [1989] and Pearl and Verma [1991]. While both efforts fit the characterization of causal modeling outlined in chapter 1, there are some differences between the two approaches. Doyle's approach is largely symbolic, consisting of a set of device models for individual physical mechanisms, plus a set of heuristics for assembling the devices into candidate models of a system, to be checked against input/output data using constraint propagation. Pearl and Verma's approach is largely probabilistic in nature, and in this case, the causal modeling program is allowed to interact with the system being modeled. Both approaches lend themselves to possible interaction with the approach described here in targeting the combined causal reconstruction/causal modeling problem occurring when a program is simultaneously presented with a causal description and a demonstration of a target physical behavior.

Also related to the causal modeling problem is the work of Iwasaki and Simon [1986] and de Kleer and Brown [1986]. In this work, a causal model is constructed not from empirical data concerning the behavior of an observed physical system, but from a system of equations already modeling that system in a non-causal way. As equations are intrinsically bidirectional in nature, causal information is not immediately apparent in such a formulation. Iwasaki and Simon look for smaller sets of variables that can be solved independently of other variables, while de Kleer and Brown consider the propagation of disturbances through the equations as a basis for inferring causal relations.

Analogical Reasoning

Taken in a broad sense, analogical reasoning encompasses a range of research in artificial intelligence, including not only work explicitly characterized as concerning analogical reasoning, but as well work in case-based reasoning, memory-based reasoning and explanation-based learning. Representative work explicitly characterized as concerning analogical reasoning includes that of Winston [1982], Gentner [1983] and Carbonell [1983]. Winston's approach stresses the use of causal relations in finding and elaborating analogies between source and target scenarios. Gentner's approach, proposed as a psychological theory and subsequently applied in artificial intelligence by Falkenhainer et al. [1986], stresses the use of both causal relations and other "higher-order" relations in working out analogies. Carbonell's approach applies analogy in the domain of planning, such that previous plans are retrieved and incrementally modified until they satisfy the requirements of a new situation.

For Winston's and Gentner's approaches—these dealing expressly with reasoning about external causal situations—events are represented by the equivalent of atomic formulae (e.g., "COLLIDE(o1, o2)"). This presents an opportunity regarding the transition space representation. Because transition space characterizes not only the occurrence of events, but also the types and sequencing of individual changes in their temporal unfolding, matching in transition space may be of use in adding further discriminatory power to these approaches in deciding which pairs of events ought to be brought into analogical association with one another.

Related work in case-based reasoning [Kolodner et al., 1985] [Hammond, 1986], memory-based reasoning [Stanfill and Waltz, 1986], and explanation-based learning [Mitchell et al, 1986] [DeJong and Mooney, 1986] also addresses the issue of using previous knowledge in new, possibly altered circumstances. Research in case-based reasoning and explanation-based learning has focused largely on situations involving planning and action, with less emphasis on situations involving physical causation. The memory-based reasoning paradigm is rather general in nature, constituting a shift of emphasis from inference, as normally applied in artificial intelligence applications, to massively parallel matching over a large base of stored knowledge. It is possible that this paradigm could be usefully applied to the causal reconstruction task, because much of

what PATHFINDER does in performing causal reconstruction amounts
to matching of the sort that could be executed efficiently in parallel.

Reasoning in Support of Communication

For reasoning in support of communication, the work of Rieger [1976]
constitutes an important precedent regarding the task of understanding descriptions of physical behavior. In this effort, Rieger outlines two
components: a representation for physical devices supporting simple reasoning about their behavior, and a discrimination network for locating
representations during language comprehension. To represent physical
devices, Rieger uses networks containing five types of quantities (actions, states, state changes, tendencies and "wants"), these connected
by 26 varieties of links incorporating several varieties of causation (including one-shot causation, continuous causation, and gated versions
of these two). To this Rieger adds a discrimination network, which is
used to locate relevant device models during the process of language
comprehension. In general, the approach carries a considerable intuitive
appeal; however, there are also some limitations to the approach. Wilks
[1977] argues that the set of causal link types is too large. Also, there
is no explicit specification of time in the representation, and no way to
combine previously unassociated physical mechanisms—that is, pairs of
mechanisms for which no explicit relationships have previously been inserted into the knowledge base. Finally, because the entire scheme was
never fully implemented and tested, it is somewhat difficult to assess its
ultimate potential.

Providing an original motivation for the research described in this
book was the Event Shape Diagram representation of Waltz [1982]. In
this representation, events are described in terms of the values of various
functions and assertions plotted against time (these roughly equivalent
to the attribute applications represented by individual rows in the diagrams for event traces), with additional assertions added to specify relationships between such plottings. Event Shape Diagrams can be used to
draw distinctions between closely related events (e.g., "eat," "swallow,"
"nibble" and "gulp"), or to process metaphorical references to events
(e.g., for a person to "eat up" compliments). The work described here
takes this idea one step further in additionally using detailed knowledge
of the temporal unfolding of events to distinguish descriptions at dif-

ferent levels of abstraction and to detect plausible causal associations between events.

A direct predecessor of the transition space representation is the Event Calculus representation [Borchardt, 1984] [Borchardt, 1985]. This representation also draws motivation from the work on Event Shape Diagrams and is directed at the task of automated recognition and summarization of events occurring in an observed scene, given a time-log of object positions, orientations and other simple properties as might be output from a computer vision system. The implemented program for this work accepts a simulated data stream as input, and produces as output a simplified English summarization of the activity. Individual occurrences of events are recognized in a hybrid top-down and bottom-up process involving the evaluation of particular event recognition rules stated in the Event Calculus language. This language bottoms out in simple operations on graphs plotting the values of various attributes against time.

One interesting difference between the Event Calculus representation and the transition space representation is that Event Calculus centers around *rules* for recognizing occurrences of events—these similar in appearance to nested subroutine calls in a programming language. Rules as such would seem to be less useful in detecting *similarities* between events as required for the causal reconstruction task. Thus, the transition space representation centers, rather, around the use of stereotypical *instances* of events. (Conversely, it should be noted, the use of stereotypical instances may be of less utility in recognizing occurrences of events, motivating a combined use of both representations for systems required to do both tasks. Whether or not this is so remains to be tested, however.)

Research by Siskind [1992] has addressed the combined task of recognizing occurrences of physical events in an animated movie and learning correspondences between these events and spatial motion verbs appearing in accompanying language commentary. The implemented system for this work starts by identifying rigid and flexible joints between primitive figures in the movie (line segments and circles). It then uses these joints to assemble the primitive figures into composite figures. Next, contact, support and other simple relations are used to partition the composite figures into different "planes" in the depth dimension. Finally, a filtering process identifies plausible mappings of composite figures and sequences of activity for these figures to objects and events appearing in the verbal commentary. The representation for events used by Siskind is roughly similar to that used here, grounding out in a specification of values and changes for simple perceptually-motivated attributes like position, orientation, contact and support.

Additional work relevant to the task of reasoning in support of communication includes: research on the START system ([Katz, 1988], [Katz and Levin, 1988]), regarding the encoding and transformation of natural language segments for effective retrieval in response to subsequent natural language queries; research by Batali [1991], regarding automated comprehension of text for describing and posing questions related to the use of physics formulae; and the Episodic Logic of Schubert and Hwang [1989], combining the use of episodic variables (reified events in the terminology used here) and probabilistic inference rules in a logic-based approach to narrative comprehension. A separate logic-based approach is described in [Hobbs et al., 1988], involving the use of abduction to handle reference ambiguities, compound nominals, syntactic ambiguity and instances of metonymy in input text.

Several implemented systems have focused on the integration of techniques for communication and reasoning about physical events and actions. The UC system [Wilensky et al., 1984] consults users on use of the UNIX operating system. This system combines language comprehension capabilities (including a treatment of ellipsis and reference problems), language generation, knowledge acquisition, and planning facilities in handling user queries. The EDISON program [Dyer *et al.*, 1987] permits incremental construction of a knowledge base of mechanical device models via entry of verbal descriptions and directly-coded diagrammatic representations relating component models known to the program. The program can then answer questions regarding device structure, function and operation and produce new device models in response to submitted goal statements. Work by Vere and Bickmore [1990] has produced a program situated in a simulated physical environment and integrating capabilities of simulated perception, language comprehension and generation, temporal reasoning, planning and episodic memory. Finally, work in the area of Intelligent Tutoring Systems strives to integrate communication and application-domain reasoning capabilities with such capabilities as user modeling and dialog management (e.g., see [Woolf, 1988]).

Natural Language Understanding

Research in natural language understanding targets a range of interconnected issues, from linguistic analysis (including syntactic analysis,
lexical disambiguation, semantic analysis, reference disambiguation, discourse analysis, and so forth) to the generation and indexing of knowledge structures supporting reasoning and question answering. This latter category of research is most relevant to the work described in this
book. A survey of this literature may be found in [Lehnert, 1988].

An influential body of work focusing on the generation and use of
knowledge structures in association with language comprehension is that
of Schank and his colleagues at Yale University [Schank and Riesbeck,
1981] [Dyer, 1983] [Kolodner, 1983] [Lehnert and Loiselle, 1989]. The
Conceptual Dependency representation forming the foundation for much
of that work reduces natural language statements to a largely canoni-
cal form employing a small set of primitive relationships between events,
animate agents and objects. This representation has been applied extensively in the domain of narrative comprehension and has been augmented
to include larger knowledge structures such as scripts, plans, goals, memory organization packets, and thematic abstraction units (see, for example, Dyer [1983]). Conceptual Dependency and transition space share a
notion of representing actions and events as stereotypical instances to
be matched with one another. The transition space approach may be
thought of as augmenting this matching process to include fine-grained
information concerning the sequencing and simultaneity of individual
changes expressible in language.

One especially interesting representational construct to emerge from
the Yale research effort is the Plot Unit, as described in [Lehnert and
Loiselle, 1989] and elsewhere. This construct captures the connectivity
of positive and negative events with respect to fulfillment of the goals
of participating agents, and related mental states of those agents. By
condensing stories along these lines, patterns of events may be recognized and parallels drawn between different stories. With respect to the
analysis of affect in narrative comprehension, plot units serve a similar
purpose as the event traces presented here.

Of separate interest is the work of Grosz [1977] concerning the use
of focus in task-oriented dialogues. This research provides a basis for
handling reference problems associated with physical objects that are

described but not named in a dialog. As noted in chapter 2, reference disambiguation has not been addressed in the work described here. Additionally, focus could be of use in the processing of larger causal descriptions—here, by limiting the extent to which the program must look for associations between a newly-referenced event and events previously referenced in the input text.

Also relevant is the work in spreading activation, including research by Quillian [1969], Collins and Loftus [1975], Alterman [1985], Norvig [1989] and others. Spreading activation involves a simultaneous propagation of several fronts of "activation" leading out from individual nodes in a semantic network, such that paths of association may be found whenever the expanding fronts of two concepts intersect. Quillian's program, the Teachable Language Comprehender, introduced the basic notion of spreading activation as used in automated language comprehension. To this, Collins and Loftus added a decreasing strength for activation as the front moves further away from a starting node, plus a thresholding operation to determine if an intersection between two fronts merits consideration as a path of association. More recently, Alterman has employed a similar approach in searching for "coherence" relations among events referenced in a piece of narrative text—these, according to Alterman, somewhat weaker in nature than causal associations, yet relevant to the question of whether two referenced events may be related. Finally, a separate variant of this process has been employed by Norvig, again for narrative understanding. Norvig's approach attaches labels to the "markers" passed in the spreading activation process. These labels are then used to restrict the types of links that may be traversed by the markers.

Much of the work in spreading activation has dealt with narrative understanding—that is, stories about human actions and their consequences. A possible difficulty for this approach concerning physical causality is that physical events are very context-dependent. For example, if a hand lets go of an object, the object will fall only if it is not otherwise supported. To represent this context in a semantic network, we must split event nodes into subnodes depicting special cases, and this subdivision becomes rather unwieldy if we consider the variety of possible contextual variations of each event and the fact that only some of variants of one event may be linked to variants of another event. Transition space captures this context directly as added assertions in an event trace. These added assertions are then incorporated into the matching and inference processes used to determine if two events may be related in a particular way.

A separate possible difficulty concerning the use of spreading activation is that this approach places a heavy burden on the knowledge engineer in charge of the network to explicitly enter all possible inter-event relationships—a task which becomes progressively more difficult as the size of the network increases. For the transition space representation, the inter-event associations are *implicit*. To enter a new event, we need only specify what happens during the event, resulting in an automatic association of that event with other events known to the system.

9.2   Research in Psychology

Perception of Events and Causality

The discussion of related research in psychology is subdivided into research concerning the perception of events and causality, and research in mental models. For this first category, a central relevant work is that of [Miller and Johnson-Laird, 1976]. This compilation of knowledge concerning human perception and verbal description of the world has been an important source of motivation for the research described in this book. In this work, Miller and Johnson-Laird characterize attributes as qualitative or quantitative in nature (pp. 12, 17, 30), as typically unary or binary (p. 323), and as describable primarily in terms of relative comparisons between values (p. 17). Additionally, time is viewed as a sequence of discrete moments (p. 77), necessitating a consideration of *two* time points when characterizing changes (p. 86). Events are taken as complex patterns of changes—specifically, changes of the type people talk about (pp. 79, 85, 87). Finally, and most important to the design of the transition space representation, causality is viewed as an association between changes or events (pp. 98, 491). In addition, there are a few differences between the transition space representation and the theory advanced by Miller and Johnson-Laird. In particular, the authors describe a sub-theory of "routines"—almost-conscious strategies employed by humans in comprehending language and answering questions. By this account, when presented with a verbal stimulus, people may either immediately execute the relevant routines to independently verify the stated account, or they may simply assume that the routines would succeed were they to be executed, and use this assumption to modify their internal knowledge. In the transition space model, there is no component corresponding to the notion of a routine.

An important precedent in experimental research regarding human perception of events is that of Heider and Simmel [1944]. These researchers showed animated movies to subjects and asked for accounts of the activity. Given a sequence of activity involving an interaction of geometric shapes such as triangles and circles, many subjects were found to offer explanations in which the shapes symbolically represented animate entities capable of human-like motivations and actions.

Concerning the perception of physical events and causality, an important body of research has been reported by Michotte [1946]. Michotte presented his subjects with either (1) a disk rotating behind a slot, such that stripes painted on the disk yielded an impression of two objects moving and colliding with one another, or (2) a screen projection of two objects moving and colliding, these produced by a pair of still-image projectors that could be panned across the screen. Given this stimulus, subjects were asked whether or not they experienced a "causal impression" concerning the interaction of the two viewed objects. Michotte found that such a causal impression was produced in several circumstances, most notably that of "entraining" (one object approaches a second object, contacts it, and both continue in the direction of the first object) and "launching" (one object approaches a second object, contacts it, and stops as the second object continues in the direction of the original motion). From these experiments, Michotte drew two conclusions. First, in opposition to Hume, Michotte claimed that in cases such as described above, causality is directly perceived and not the result of intermediate analysis. Second, in opposition to Piaget, Michotte claimed that phenomenal causality—as experienced in the above cases—is distinct from the notion of activity, whereby a human exerts force on an object and moves it.

In Michotte's experiments, a direct perception of causality appears primarily in those cases involving motion on the part of the two objects; however, Michotte expresses an intuition that, given sufficiently improved experimental apparatus, similar causal impressions will be found for sequences of qualitative changes: for example, change of color from a chemical reaction, striking of a bell, or the breaking of a plate when it falls to the ground. In all cases of supposed causality to be tested, Michotte views this phenomenon as an association between changes.

It should be noted that several other conditions are required for the causal impression tested by Michotte. In particular, there must not be too great a delay between the first motion and the second, and the second object must lie in the path of the first object. As regards the causal reconstruction task described here, these temporal and spatial considerations are of reduced importance. When presented with a *verbal description* of an activity—rather than a visual presentation—the recipient has no information regarding temporal and spatial contiguity of events and thus cannot bring these factors into an analysis of whether a causal activity has occurred. Rather, the recipient must rely on remembered causal sequences (these having previously met the necessary requirements for consideration as "causal"), assembling these into a plausible model of the described activity. Matching in transition space may thus be viewed as the *reuse* of part of the knowledge already present concerning causal situations (in particular, knowledge concerning simultaneity and sequencing of *changes* in the temporal unfolding of these causal situations) as a means of determining how overlaps between such situations might associate events referenced in a causal description.

Research related to that of Michotte includes experimental studies by Leslie and Keeble [1987], indicating that at 27 weeks old, infants can recognize the causal nature of the "launching" scenario, and analyses by Shultz [1982], Bullock *et al.* [1982] and others concerning the nature of rules used to determine whether observed sequences of activity are causal. White [1988] argues that causal processing originates in children with the direct perception of causal situations such as "launching," with regularities from these situations later abstracted for use as rules in determining the causal nature of observed activities (e.g., temporal priority, and temporal and spatial contiguity).

Separate from the above research concerning perception of causal situations, experimental studies by Newtson *et al.* [1976] [1977] have targeted the perception of observed actions. For these studies, subjects were shown movies of actions such as a hand grasping a cup, and were provided with a button to press whenever, in their judgment, one meaningful action ended and another began. These studies indicate that perceived actions are delimited by "breakpoints"—or time points at which distinctive changes occur relative to previous activity. Additionally, subjects could detect short deletions from the film more accurately if these occurred during breakpoints.

Mental Models

Mental models research attempts to uncover the mechanisms by which humans reason in particular domains. Much of this research has focused on commonsense reasoning about the physical world. A good collection of articles on mental models research appears in Gentner and Stevens [1983]. Of interest regarding the causal reconstruction task are two sorts of results from this research: (1) documentation of cases where humans successfully employ analogy to reason about abstract domains in terms of simpler or more accessible domains (e.g., reasoning about electricity as if it were flowing water or a moving crowd [Gentner and Gentner, 1983]), and (2) documentation of cases where human reasoning fails due to a reliance on faulty models (e.g., taking force as responsible for motion rather than acceleration [diSessa, 1983] [McCloskey, 1983] [Clement, 1983]). Both types of results suggest components of supplementary knowledge useful for the comprehension of causal descriptions— the latter being useful if we wish to compensate for faulty explanations offered by the writers of particular causal descriptions. In the other direction, it may also be possible for work in causal reconstruction to contribute to mental models research, as the process of getting a program to understand written causal descriptions inherently involves the articulation of a range of underlying knowledge. In principle, this process could be applied in a broad fashion to help determine which physical domains and which events in those domains are fundamental, and which may be considered derivative.

A somewhat different formulation of the notion of mental models appears in [Johnson-Laird, 1983]. This work relates human-like reasoning to the construction of models in a model-theoretic logic formulation. According to Johnson-Laird, human attempts at deductive reasoning rely on a three-stage process: (1) construction of one or more models fitting the constraints of a described situation, (2) a drawing of novel conclusions by looking for commonalities among the constructed models, and (3) an attempt to disprove such conclusions by constructing alternate models of the described situation.

Finally, research by Tversky and Kahneman [Kahneman et al., 1982] appeals to many of the same concerns as mental models research. This work outlines several heuristics employed by humans in simple reasoning tasks. The Representativeness Heuristic is used by humans to determine if an object belongs to a class: if the object's properties are similar to those of a stereotypical member of the class, the object is considered to belong to that class. The Availability Heuristic is used by humans to estimate whether a proposition is true by relying on data most readily available in their own knowledge. Other research by the authors has illustrated that humans tend to ignore prior probabilities in many cases, and that in calculating quantities they often form an initial approximate answer, then adjust it as necessary to form a final answer. Of these results, the presence of the Availability Heuristic is perhaps most relevant to the task of causal reconstruction, as by this heuristic, a program with a limited preset knowledge base of events, rules of inference and rules of restatement may draw conclusions by generalizing over the possible reconstructions given its limited repertoire of knowledge.

9.3   Research in Linguistics and Philosophy

In reviewing related literature in linguistics and philosophy, we limit the discussion to work directly relevant to the causal reconstruction task and the approach described here. A much larger body of work relates to important linguistic issues regarding the structure of unrestricted natural language and important philosophical issues regarding the nature of causality, the physical world, and human perception. A summary of current syntactic theory in the generative grammar tradition appears in [van Riemsdijk and Williams, 1986]. Also relevant is [Leech and Svartvik, 1975], an interesting summarization of English grammar from the standpoint of communication. In this source, for example, one may find grouped together a range of syntactic constructions and vocabulary permitting a speaker to express spatial relationships, temporal relationships, causality, comparisons, exceptions, and other conceptual classifications of communicated thought. A brief summary of philosophical literature related to artificial intelligence appears in [Gardner, 1985].

Two interesting analyses concerning the semantic content of language are [Jackendoff, 1983] and [Talmy, 1988]. Jackendoff proposes a semantic representation consisting of a few major ontological categories (e.g., thing, place, direction, action, event, manner and amount) and a few major types of events (e.g., go, be and stay), these specialized as necessary to accommodate the circumstances of particular semantic fields (e.g., spatial, temporal, possessive, identificational, circumstantial and existential). Distinctions are drawn between the major ontological categories on the basis of usage patterns in language. Talmy proposes a "cognitive semantics" involving several central semantic categories (number, aspect, mood, evidentiality, and force dynamics). Regarding the analysis of descriptions of activity, the category of force dynamics is of particular interest. Force dynamics concerns the interaction of entities with respect to force. This includes static patterns, as for instance, when one entity prevents motion on the part of another; appearance and disappearance of forces between entities; and situations involving a shift in the balance of force between two entities, as when one agent overpowers another. By analogy, a broad range of phenomena may be viewed in terms of simple situations involving force dynamics: mechanical interactions, enabling and prevention, social influence, wanting and refraining, modal operators such as "can" and "must," and so forth. Similar to the mental models research discussed above, the theories of Jackendoff and Talmy are pertinent to the question of how a program might acquire new causal knowledge through the analogical extension of a preset, core knowledge base of causal situations.

Also related to the causal reconstruction problem are research efforts in lexical semantics (e.g., as summarized in [Levin, 1985]) and in discourse analysis (e.g., see [Brown and Yule, 1983]). Research in lexical semantics attempts to classify words—often focusing on verbs—on the basis of usage patterns in language. One important criterion used in the classification of verbs is their ability to accept arguments filling various thematic roles (agent, patient, instrument, and so forth). The transition space representation would seem to mesh well with such an analysis. In particular, thematic roles may have much in common with particular arrangements of changes within event traces: the agent is often the object that changes first, the patient changes later, and an instrument will typically be changed in a less significant or permanent manner than the patient. The other mentioned research area, discourse analysis, also has some elements in common with the research described here. Typically, discourse analysis involves the identification and characterization of regularities in the structure of texts, both spoken and written:

for example, the existence and character of references to external objects, the advancement of presuppositions, implications advanced by a text, shifts in discourse topic, and so forth. Concerning the relationship of individual assertions to other assertions in a text, such an analysis may speak of "cohesion"—whereby the interpretation of one element depends on the interpretation of another (e.g., anaphoric references)—and "coherence"—whereby two elements describe a common situation. These notions are somewhat different from the integration of events into causal chains and overlapping accounts of activity as pursued here; however, it may be the case that by working out in detail the sorts of inter-event relationships examined in this book, an analysis of cohesion and coherence issues is thereby simplified.

Grice's maxims of conversation [Grice, 1975] were discussed in chapters 1 and 2. Such rules form the basis by which we may evaluate a program's performance regarding the causal reconstruction task. Other uses for Grice's maxims exist as well. In particular, if no acceptable reconstruction exists for a given causal description, then the comprehender must assume either: (1) that the writer of the description is being uncooperative in failing to adhere to the maxims, or (2) that for the particular description in question, two or more of the maxims are in conflict, such that a compromise has been forced. In the latter case, it may be still possible for a comprehender to produce a reasonable reconstruction, this on the basis of having formed an initial reconstruction of the described scenario and subsequently having examined alternate forms of verbal description for that reconstruction, concluding that the supplied description violates Grice's maxims to a lesser degree than do the alternative descriptions.

The final research effort to be examined is that presented in [Lakoff and Johnson, 1980] and elaborated in [Johnson, 1987]. This work advances a view that metaphorical language appears not only for stylistic reasons, but for reasons of underlying *comprehension* of circumstances in certain domains in terms of circumstances in other domains. As illustrations, the authors present a number of extended analogies permitting not only redescription of one activity in terms of another, but as well, reasoning about one activity in terms of another. Examples of these analogies are: an-argument-is-war, time-is-a-limited-resource, the-mind-is-a-container, ideas-are-objects, love-is-a-journey and theories-are-buildings. In [Johnson, 1987], a philosophical stance is advanced in which a broad range of meaning is grounded in analogies arising from basic functions and experiences of the human body. In combination with the work of Jackendoff and Talmy, this theory would seem to suggest that a suitable source of core events supporting causal reconstruction in a range of domains might be a combination of bodily-kinesthetic and simple mechanical interactions.

10 Conclusions

This chapter summarizes the central contributions of the research and discusses a range of extensions to the work. The final section, 10.3, returns to the six application areas introduced in chapter 1, reexamining each in light of possible contributions offered by the approach presented in this book.

10.1 Contributions of the Research

There are three main contributions of this work. The first is a characterization of the causal reconstruction problem, including a set of criteria for evaluating performance of a program at the task and a sample program interface for testing out particular approaches. Second is the transition space representation and its accompanying machinery for associating events and answering questions about causal descriptions. As highlighted in previous parts of the book, key aspects of the transition space representation are its focus on information about *changes* as a basis for determining how the events in a causal description might fit together, and its grounding in simple statements articulated in everyday language. The third component is the PATHFINDER program, including a specific set of association heuristics for use in causal reconstruction, and a range of simple examples processed by the program.

The Causal Reconstruction Problem

Causal reconstruction is related to causal modeling in that both tasks involve acquisition of knowledge needed for causal reasoning. In order to demonstrate successful completion of the task, a program must use its acquired knowledge to engage in causal reasoning to the extent that it may answer questions directed to it. In this manner, the causal reconstruction problem involves a combination of language comprehension, language generation and reasoning skills. Key components of the characterization of causal reconstruction presented here are:

A general problem framework. This framework portrays the task of understanding written causal descriptions as one of reading a piece of text, forming an internal model, and demonstrating comprehension by answering questions posed at two levels: (1) the *object level*, concerning properties, relationships and other attributes

of participating objects, and how these quantities change in the
time course of the described activity, and (2) the *event level*, concerning interrelationships between pairs of events referenced in the
description or introduced via questions posed to the system.

Criteria for assessing success at the task.   These criteria are derived from Grice's maxims of conversation and follow from the stip-
ulation that a comprehender's model of a described situation must
also be describable using the supplied input description. As such,
assessing comprehension of causal descriptions is still grounded in
intuition—as would seem to be inescapable given that only humans
possess the ability to judge the contents of causal descriptions—
yet this assessment relies on measures that are much more specific
than the general assessment "Has the comprehender understood
the description?"

A sample program interface.   Implementation of the PATHFINDER
program has resulted in the specification of a simplified English
syntax for entering causal descriptions and supplementary information, a set of simplified discourse conventions for conveying information of different types (event definitions, rules of inference,
precedent events, etc.), and a set of four question types for prob-
ing a comprehender's model. While these simplifications bypass a
number of more difficult issues regarding general natural language
comprehension, they also provide a convenient framework for examination of the causal reconstruction task in a focused sense,
concentrating on particular aspects of language relevant to the
communication of causal knowledge.

The Transition Space Representation

The transition space representation draws its origins from a desire to capture "what happens" during physical events in a cognitively-motivated
way, such that detailed relationships may be worked out between events
referenced in causal descriptions. Major distinguishing features of the
representation are:

An emphasis on representation in terms of changes.   This emphasis is motivated by human perception and intuitive character-

ization of causal situations. In particular, the heuristic of partial matching over change-oriented descriptions of events has been found to be quite useful in causal reconstruction for the set of examples run on PATHFINDER. This utility has been illustrated in a range of physical domains, including solid objects, liquids, heat and fire, light, electric currents, radio signals and more.

Characterization of intuitive and abstract quantities. Given its grounding in simple natural language statements, the representation covers not only scientifically-motivated quantities, but also a broad range of other phenomena describable in terms of objects and changing attributes, including conceptualizations such as dents, scratches, collections, portions, events, paths, boundaries, systems, and conceptual attributes such as being a part of something, being engaged in an event, being in possession of an object or in control of an object, and so forth.

Support for abstraction and analogy. Transition space explicitly distinguishes between accounts of events at different levels of abstraction and in terms of different underlying metaphors. Through the use of simple transformations applied to event representations, clusters of alternate representations are formed, which in the course of matching serve to bridge discontinuities in a causal description as introduced by the writer's use of analogy or abstraction.

A simple link to language. Event representations can easily be converted to simple, stylized verbal accounts of activity and vice-versa. This grounds the representation in such a way as to obviate reliance on a specialist in knowledge representation for an assessment of the content of particular knowledge structures. As well, the link to language provides an efficient mechanism by which new event definitions may be generated for use in processing.

The PATHFINDER Program

The third contribution is the PATHFINDER program. In addition to the above-mentioned contribution of providing a specific simplified English syntax, a set of discourse conventions and a set of question types for causal reconstruction, PATHFINDER offers the following:

A demonstration of the approach. From the examples processed by the program, a general measure of support is offered for the strategy of performing causal reconstruction by looking for partial matches among transition space representations of events. As well, the examples themselves range over various physical domains and types of associations between events, offering evidence of breadth of applicability for the approach.

Heuristics for ranking partial matches. In the course of implementation and testing on the described examples, several additional heuristics were identified concerning the ranking of partial matches. These concern: proximity to description events, narrative ordering of event references, current status of the association structure, and types of associations. As well, on the basis of the examples run, an initial set of relative scoring weights for these heuristics has been developed.

Refinement of the association process. Prior to implementation, it was felt that transformations of event traces might be required only *after* the identification of partial matches, serving to strengthen particularly promising partial associations between events. However, in the course of running PATHFINDER on a range of examples, it was found that partial matches between events at different levels of abstraction or involving different analogically-related sets of attributes often become apparent only if suitable exploratory transformations to the original event traces have been performed *before* the matching step. In this manner, implementation of the approach has resulted in an important refinement of the approach.

As noted in the preceding chapters, several simplifications of the general problem of causal reconstruction were required in order that the problem could be addressed in a focused manner. Among these are a restriction to textual input of limited syntactic variety, an assumed absence of relevant background knowledge on the part of the program, and a particular selection of question types to be handled. Additionally, the transition space representation does not capture three important types of knowledge related to the comprehension of causal descriptions: (1)

spatial relationships of a non-propositional nature, such as might be best
described in a diagram or picture, (2) rules for the *classification* of objects from specifications of their various attributes, and (3) measures of
likelihood for alternative causal sequences.

10.2 Extending the Approach

The approach embodied in PATHFINDER may be extended in several
ways, even within the framework of the simplifications outlined above.
The following list outlines several such extensions.

Inference. In PATHFINDER, inference is used only with respect to
individual event traces (plus relevant background information), or
between pairs of matched event traces for the detection of inconsistencies only. Inference is not used to add new assertions on the
basis of assertions appearing in two or more event traces, nor is it
used to detect inconsistencies among three or more event traces.
Such a capability could be provided as follows: as clusters of event
traces are associated together, a preliminary composite trace could
be formed which would concurrently be extended through the application of inference. Individual event traces used in forming the
composite trace could then be extended to include relevant assertions generated by the inference process. In general, this approach
would, at the expense of additional processing time, be expected
to produce stronger matches in certain cases, and in others, detect
conflicts not currently detected in PATHFINDER.

Multiple paths of association. The association structure as generated by PATHFINDER contains only a single path of association
between any two event traces (that is, taking event traces as individual points in a graph, the association structure is a tree).
This prevents PATHFINDER from performing causal reconstruction on descriptions involving multiple paths of association between events. Examples of such situations are:

- Descriptions involving two or more associated events which,
  in combination, are summarized by another event. A good
  example is that of continuous or repetitive events: if a wheel

revolves once, then revolves again, and it is separately specified as "spinning," this spinning might be taken as a summarization of both revolutions. A separate example concerns the
"recording" of the image for the camera description discussed
in chapter 8: this event could be construed as summarizing
the entire sequence of activity beginning with light entering
the camera, rather than only the critical interval at which an
image appears on the film.

- Descriptions involving forks in the causal path that rejoin at
  a later point. An example is the activity of hammering a
  nail into a piece of wood. Here, the nail separately pushes
  sideways on several clusters of wood fibers, these spring back
  to push on the nail, and the pressure from opposing clusters
  constitutes a gripping event. A second example is the vibration of a loudspeaker, as discussed briefly in chapter 3: the
  diaphragm pushes on the surrounding air, which moves away
  from the diaphragm independently of the diaphragm's initial
  recoiling from increased tension. Then, there is a joining of
  causal paths whereby the recoiling diaphragm exerts tension
  on the surrounding air and pulls it back.

To process descriptions involving multiple paths of association between events, records must be kept regarding the matching of individual *assertions* between event traces, rather than simply the
matching of event traces as wholes. Only in this way can unmatched assertions be used to trigger the search for auxiliary paths
of association between events.

Backtracking, beam search and interactive association. In its
current form, PATHFINDER cannot undo associations once they
are made. The program is thus overly dependent upon its set of
heuristics for proper selection of partial matches for elaboration.
Three ways to lessen this dependence are: (1) to permit backtracking, such that the appearance of inconsistencies or an absence of
partial matches later in the association process may lead to the
undoing of initial associations, (2) to pursue the association process by means of a beam search, concurrently exploring several
alternative, partially-completed association structures, or (3) to

allow the program to ask questions of the user whenever several closely-ranked, alternative partial matches present themselves for elaboration.

Selective application of exploratory transformations. Exploratory transformations are currently applied in a rather blind fashion in PATHFINDER. It is possible that appropriate heuristics might be developed to selectively transform the representations of events only where there is an indication of a potential match following the transformation. However, as observed above, it would seem that in many cases, partial matches do not become apparent until after appropriate exploratory transformations of event traces have been performed. A compromise solution might be to first determine a suitable common level of abstraction and metaphorical specification for all events, then apply only those transformations that take events closer to this common "arena" in transition space. Included in this approach would most likely be a utilization of metric information regarding sizes of objects and durations of temporal intervals—this being expressible in transition space through the use of reference standards, but not yet exploited—to determine when and in which direction to apply object composition and interval composition transformations to event traces.

Continuing to broader extensions of the approach outlined in this book, the following areas of exploration merit further investigation:

Natural language input. As noted above, PATHFINDER currently does not address a number of issues in generalized natural language processing and could thus benefit from the incorporation of additional techniques for handling such phenomena as syntactic ambiguity, lexical and semantic ambiguity, reference, tense and aspect, metonymy, ellipsis, and focus. It is possible, however, that the transition space representation may in turn be able to provide assistance in addressing some of these issues. For example, regarding reference resolution, it is conceivable that one important constraint governing the association of antecedents with pronouns might be whether or not the particular event occurrences implied by such associations fit together with other events in the sense explored here.

Other types of input. The previous chapter mentioned the possibility of combined causal reconstruction/causal modeling carried out by a program accepting a written description of an activity while exposed to a demonstration of the same activity. A related extension concerns the processing of written descriptions coupled with diagrams. For both tasks, it may be the case that a more elaborate treatment of *spatial* aspects of physical behavior is required—that is, beyond the propositional treatment currently employed in PATHFINDER (see, for example, [Faltings, 1990], [Narayanan and Chandrasekaran, 1991], [Caine, 1993]). An enhanced spatial representation could also help in processing descriptions containing many events involving translational motion, as the heuristic of partial matching may fail to distinguish among many possible overlaps among the events unless suitable background statements are added to designate spatial regions in which the events occur. Separately, it may also be useful to explore causal reconstruction involving a combination of text and equations as input, as when a written description provides intuitive background knowledge surrounding the use of a highly-technical model of a physical process.

Incremental causal reconstruction. It may be worthwhile to explore incremental reconstruction of causal scenarios, such that an initial attempt is made to associate the first two events referenced in a description, then incorporate the next referenced event, and so forth. This would appear to be more in line with human comprehension of causal descriptions. This approach was not taken in the construction of PATHFINDER because it requires the development of yet another set of heuristics, these regarding decisions of when to proceed with the best current match for the sentences read so far, versus when to forgo a match in hopes of obtaining a better match once more sentences are read.

Disjunctions of behaviors. Many descriptions of the sort appearing in encyclopedias simultaneously specify several variants of a target behavior through the use of conditional statements, hypothetical situations, or enumeration of alternate behaviors. To handle such descriptions, a mechanism for representing and reasoning about disjunctions of behaviors is required. As part of this, a facility for reasoning about relative *likelihoods* of alternatives would presumably be required. Also related to disjunctive behaviors are repetitive events and feedback cycles. While transformations of the event-object reification variety can be constructed to abstract sequences of repeated activities into simple declarations of repetition of particular events, the ability to handle disjunctions of behaviors could support reasoning about specific numbers of iterations (if small) for these types of events.

Accumulated supporting knowledge. Also mentioned in chapter 9 was the possible incorporation of a preset knowledge base of core events, background statements, transformations and so forth, supporting causal reconstruction in a range of domains. One way to construct such a knowledge base is to perform causal reconstruction in a *cumulative* manner, maintaining supplementary knowledge between processing sessions and perhaps weeding out knowledge used only sparingly in the future. As suggested in chapter 9, a suitable approach might be to start with causal situations involving bodily-kinesthetic events or simple mechanical events, then progress to other, less perceptually vivid domains (e.g., radio signals, electricity, biological processes) by relying heavily on analogies to the original set of events. Some of the examples explored on PATHFINDER provide initial support for this hypothesis. As a further extension of this idea, it may even be possible to employ such a core knowledge base in the service of understanding physically-metaphorical descriptions in abstract domains such as political science, law, and management science.

10.3   New Horizons

Returning to the broader context, there are a number of projected applications requiring the sort of capabilities embodied in the causal reconstruction task. Chapter 1 listed six such applications, and these six are described in greater detail here. In the order presented, the applications would seem to require an increasing range of capabilities regarding language comprehension, language generation, and reasoning. Three of the applications suggest alternatives at two levels of sophistication: a lower-level version dealing directly with event traces or event definitions, and a higher-level version dealing with causal descriptions.

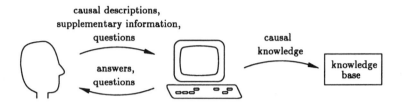

Figure 10.1
Knowledge acquisition facilities.

Knowledge Acquisition Facilities

The first application—illustrated in Figure 10.1—uses causal reconstruction as a means of acquiring knowledge for subsequent use in causal reasoning. Here, a human having sufficient expertise in the target domain
enters causal descriptions augmented with supplementary information,
as with PATHFINDER. Additionally, the program is designed to ask
questions if it is unable to reconstruct particular described activities.
When the human expert has finished entering a description and answering questions posed by the system, he or she may test for comprehension
by posing questions to the system, again as with PATHFINDER. Following this, knowledge structures such as event traces, background assertions, association structure fragments and transformations may then be
transferred to a target knowledge base for subsequent use in reasoning
tasks.

Constructed in this way, the knowledge acquisition facility has several advantages. First, the comprehension process allows the program
to use knowledge it already possesses, and this in turn allows the human
to streamline the input descriptions, omitting event references, background statements, individual participants and so forth where it may be
expected that the acquisition system will succeed in filling in these missing components. At the same time, the comprehension process provides
an immediate check for the presence of assumed background knowledge
on the part of the program, for if the program fails in its reconstruction
task, the human will be forced to supply missing pieces in the form of
additional supplementary information.

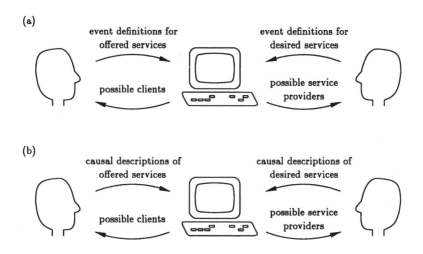

Figure 10.2
Intelligent service directories: (a) involving matching between event definitions, (b) involving causal reconstruction.

Intelligent Service Directories

Figure 10.2 illustrates two versions of the second application, intelligent service directories. In this application, companies, government entities and individuals who provide various services are placed in contact with others requiring those services. For instance, companies may specify an availability or need for transportation services, manufacturing services, inspection services, repair services, information services and so forth. Government entities may advertise services they provide to companies and individuals, or service contracts to be awarded to others. Individuals may specify personal skills as contractors, consultants or job applicants, as well as other services required by those individuals. The potential success of such an application rests on the fact that services are ultimately events or sequences of events and can thus be represented in transition space or described via causal descriptions. Matching in transition space provides a means by which service providers and consumers may be placed in contact with one another.

In Figure 10.2 (a), a simpler system is illustrated in which providers and consumers submit specifications of services in the form of event definitions as entered to PATHFINDER. In this scenario, the service directory does not perform full-fledged causal reconstruction; rather, it simply matches provided services to requested services and provides lists of the matches to both the providers and consumers. One advantage of using transition space is that, given a standardized set of attributes and reference standards, an extremely broad spectrum of services may be specified while maintaining the ability to identify matches between these services. Thus, it is not necessary to explicitly anticipate possible matches by providing huge numbers of indexing links for particular services. A second advantage is that by decomposing services into underlying transitions, partial matches can be identified, whereby a service provider can supply part, but not all of a requested service.

A more complex version of the application appears in Figure 10.2 (b). In this configuration, services are specified by entering causal descriptions, and matching occurs both at the level of complete descriptions and portions of those descriptions. This requires that the service directory not only possess an ability to perform causal reconstruction with a preset knowledge base, but that it also possess a mechanism for reasoning about humans plans and actions underlying the sequence of events making up particular services. (The simpler application in Figure 10.2 (a) can escape this requirement by identifying matches directly between individual events *performed* in the course of various plans.) Allowing services to be specified via causal descriptions takes some of the burden off human users and also allows services to be matched to missing components in descriptions—this in a manner analogous to the use of precedent events in PATHFINDER's understanding of causal descriptions.

Intelligent Technical Manuals

The third application concerns the development of intelligent, on-line user manuals for physical systems such as mechanical or electronic artifacts. This application is illustrated in Figure 10.3. Such systems combine causal reconstruction with technology for intelligent tutoring systems and technology for reasoning about the physical world. Specifically, causal reconstruction contributes in two capacities: (1) as a means of preparing the programs via written descriptions possibly accompanied by diagrams, and (2) as a means of enabling the programs to understand user descriptions of ongoing events and tentative causal explanations of

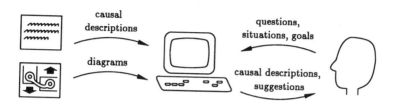

Figure 10.3
Intelligent technical manuals.

artifact behavior. The user may ask questions, describe situations and specify tasks to be performed using the modeled system. The system responds with explanations of causal phenomena and suggestions for action.

Some expected benefits of using transition space in the construction of intelligent technical manuals include an ability to comprehend descriptions employing abstraction and analogy—both during the initial preparation phase and later during program operation—and a corresponding ability to produce descriptions at different levels of abstraction or employing novel analogies in an attempt to foster user comprehension. Regarding the production of causal descriptions, causal reconstruction as outlined in this book can be of use in internally "auditioning" candidate explanations before presenting them to the user.

Technical Design Documentation Systems

The fourth application concerns the construction of technical documentation systems supporting teams of engineers engaged in the design of physical artifacts. In this scenario, a single software interface coordinates many aspects of the rich exchange of causal information occurring in design contexts by organizing and routing specifications of desired physical behavior for the designed system and its modules, characterizations of previously-designed systems and their modules, explanations of faults in designed systems, explanations of desirable and undesirable interactions among modules in a system, and so forth. As with intelligent service directories, technical design documentation systems could

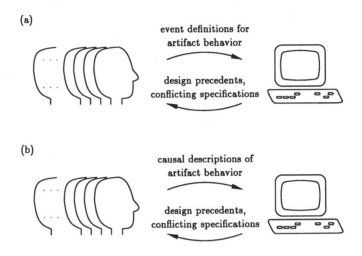

Figure 10.4
Technical design documentation systems: (a) accepting event definitions as
specifications of artifact behavior, (b) accepting causal descriptions of artifact
behavior.

be constructed at two levels of sophistication: a lower level involving
reasoning and communication in terms of transition space representations or event definitions, and a higher level involving reasoning and
communication in terms of full causal descriptions. These two versions
of the application are illustrated in Figure 10.4.

In the simpler version depicted in Figure 10.4 (a), human designers
submit specifications of artifact behavior in the form of event definitions
as input to PATHFINDER. Each specification is labeled according to
a range of distinguishing categories: desired behavior for the artifact,
predicted behavior according to an engineering model of the artifact,
observed behavior for a prototype version of the artifact, faulty behavior envisioned for part of the artifact, and so forth. Additionally,
behavioral specifications could be time-stamped to distinguish between
past, present and future versions of a design. Finally, alternate view-
points could be flagged, such as exist when two design teams focus on
different sides of an interface between two modules. Given all of these
behavioral specifications, the program could use matching in transition

space both to detect inconsistencies—as when an observed behavior deviates from a predicted behavior or a predicted behavior deviates from a desired behavior—and additionally identify new associations between behaviors—as when a design precedent is found for a desired behavior, or when a predicted behavior is found to lead conceivably to a faulty behavior.[1]

The more complex version of the application, depicted in Figure 10.4 (b), accepts causal descriptions rather than event definitions as input. Such a system could target all of the tasks targeted by the simpler version, plus tasks such as summarization and elaboration of descriptions for the benefit of particular recipients, question answering, and support for hybrid man-machine design environments—whereby other programs perform particular subtasks in the design process and communicate with human designers via causal descriptions and questions.

Speculative Causal Reasoning Systems

Figure 10.5 illustrates the fifth application: speculative causal reasoning systems. These systems perform "what-if" reasoning about actions affecting complex systems such as transportation networks, corporations and manufacturing facilities. Supporting the operation of these systems is a combination of (1) causal reasoning based on knowledge of the sort acquired via causal reconstruction, and (2) rationale management techniques used to capture the internal structure of arguments (e.g., see [Lee, 1992]). Information from databases is used as background knowledge on objects, individuals and other components within the system to be modeled, and an accompanying knowledge base supplies causal knowledge concerning important types of events that might occur for those components. The knowledge base may conceivably include contributions offered by a large number of individuals exposed to different segments of the complex system being modeled (e.g., managers at different production sites for a company). The user may examine previous actions taken with respect to particular sets of goals and may interactively explore possible consequences and side-effects for these and other actions, given the current status of the modeled system.

---

[1]Ruecker [1992] is currently investigating selected aspects of such a design documentation system—in particular, the retrieval of design precedents using transition space as one component in the representation of designed artifacts.

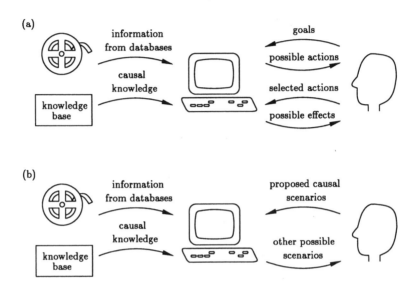

Figure 10.5
Speculative causal reasoning systems: (a) with interaction based on an exchange of
event references, (b) with interaction based on an exchange of causal descriptions.

In the simpler version of this application—illustrated in Figure 10.5
(a)—the user and program interact via an exchange of event references
augmented where necessary with event definitions. Given a specification of goals—target events desired by the user—rationale management
techniques are employed to identify actions previously claimed to attain
those goals. Next, possible effects of actions are identified by enumer-
ating partial chaining matches between transition space representations
for those actions and various domain events. Additional facilities may be
included, allowing the user to commit to a particular action and enabling
the system to track the consequences of chosen actions.

In the more complex version of the application—illustrated in Figure
10.5 (b)—the user and program interact via an exchange of causal descriptions. This provides the user with greater flexibility in omitting information meant to be filled in by the reasoning system. In this scenario,
the user proposes causal sequences of actions leading to desired effects,

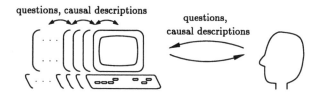

Figure 10.6
Collaborative diagnosis/prediction systems.

and the system responds with alternate sequences involving different actions or concerning possible side-effects of user-suggested actions.

Collaborative Diagnosis/Prediction Systems

The final application—collaborative diagnosis/prediction systems—combines work in cooperative problem solving with advanced capabilities for causal reasoning and the comprehension and generation of causal descriptions. This application is illustrated in Figure 10.6. Such systems incorporate much of the work leading toward development of the preceding applications, producing an environment in which several reasoning systems work as a team in solving difficult prediction, diagnosis and planning problems. Each reasoning system may have its own internal representations, reasoning algorithms and areas of expertise, and the systems may be maintained at different sites and independently updated, yet communication among these differing systems and with human users is facilitated in part by an exchange of written causal descriptions and questions. Critical to the success of this exchange is the capability of each participant to supply causal explanations in a variety of forms—summarized, elaborated, paraphrased in terms of an analogy, and so forth—to meet the comprehension capabilities of requesting parties.

Using causal descriptions and questions as a means of communication between reasoning programs has several advantages. First, it facilitates the translation of knowledge structures between diverse internal representations by mapping these structures to an intermediate, common representation linked to human language. Second, it permits humans to monitor the communications between programs, such that they may

contribute to the discussion when appropriate and identify faulty chains
of reasoning when recognized by them. Finally, it provides an archival
record of the interactive reasoning process, supporting future inquiries
into the contributions of individual programs participating in the reasoning task.

Other Applications

The above descriptions only begin to explore the range of uses for combined causal reasoning and communication skills on the part of programs. Many other applications will require this same combination
of skills, because causal reasoning and communication reinforce one
another in particularly important ways. Without the ability to reason,
it is difficult for language comprehension programs to demonstrate the
effectiveness of their processing. Likewise, without the ability to communicate, it is difficult for causal reasoning programs to benefit from
human experience and expertise or to pass along the results of their
reasoning to humans. Ultimately, it is the synergistic interaction of
many reasoning individuals that permits particular individuals to rise
above the level of competence they would otherwise achieve in isolation.
Admitting programs into this synergy enhances both their competence
and ours.

A PATHFINDER Implementation

Summarized below are: (1) the heuristic evaluation function used to score partial matches during PATHFINDER's association process, and (2) major program components and their functionality.

The Heuristic Evaluation Function

New event traces are added to the association structure when: (1) PATHFINDER processes description events and precedent events in the input description, (2) inference and exploratory transformations are applied to event traces presently in the association structure, and (3) intermediate event traces are produced as a result of elaboration of a partial match. As characterized in chapters 4 and 5, inference, reduction and equivalence associations in the association structure determine which traces are considered "active" for matching. (Inactive traces would not generate any distinctly different matches from those generated for active traces.) New active traces are then matched with all existing active traces not belonging to the same cluster of traces in the association structure.

Partial matches enumerated by the program are labeled as either partial chaining matches or partial restatement matches, using the rule specified in chapter 4:

> A partial chaining match between two event traces is a single-transition partial match involving at least one definite change (APPEAR, DISAPPEAR, CHANGE, INCREASE or DECREASE) and situated such that exactly one of the traces is begun by the matching transition and continues beyond that transition.

All other partial matches are labeled as partial restatement matches. Partial restatement matches may involve more than a single matching transition, in which case the matching transitions need not occur in direct sequence within the two event traces (although this is usually the case). For partial chaining matches, a record is made of assertions appearing in the consequent trace that are covered by assertions in the antecedent trace. For partial restatement matches, a record is made of assertions appearing in the trace previously existing in the association structure that are covered by assertions in the trace newly added to the association structure.

Given a partial match determined in this manner, PATHFINDER first forms a raw score for the partial match, as follows:

((10 ×   [the number of definite changes (APPEAR, DISAP-
              PEAR, CHANGE, INCREASE and DECREASE)
              covered in the match]) +
(3 ×   [the number of other dynamic assertions (NOT-AP-
              PEAR, etc.) covered in the match]) +
(1 ×   [the number of static assertions (PRESENT, etc.)
              covered in the match]))
÷
    [the number of temporal intervals involved in the match]

This raw score is then reduced in response to applicable penalties from the following list (e.g., for two 10% penalties and one 30% penalty, the raw score is multiplied by $(0.9) \times (0.9) \times (0.7)$).

Regarding proximity to description events:

10% penalty   [if the first trace has been formed by exploratory
                  transformation and does not lie along a path of
                  association between two description or
                  precedent events]
10% penalty   [if the second trace has been formed by
                  exploratory transformation and does not lie
                  along a path of association between two
                  description or precedent events]
30% penalty   [if the first trace depicts a precedent event]
30% penalty   [if the second trace depicts a precedent event]

Regarding narrative ordering of event references:

10% penalty   [if the match is not a partial chaining match
                  between successively-referenced events in the
                  description]
10% penalty   [if the match is a partial chaining match from one
                  referenced event to the immediately preceding
                  event]

Regarding the current status of the association structure:

10% penalty	[if the match involves a hypothesized object]
30% penalty	[if the match equates two hypothesized objects]
30% penalty	[if the match provides a redundant causal antecedent for an event]
30% penalty	[if the match provides a redundant causal consequent for an event]
100% penalty	[if the match involves two events already connected by a path of association]

Regarding types of associations:

10% penalty	[if the match is a partial restatement match rather than a partial chaining match]
30% penalty	[if the match does not complete a path of association fulfilling an explicitly-entered connecting statement]
100% penalty	[if the match completes a path of association that conflicts with an explicitly-entered connecting statement]

Once a partial match has been selected for elaboration (and removed from the agenda), there are three additional conditions that may result in a cessation of processing for that partial match. These are:

Equivalences between description objects. If the match directly or indirectly draws an equivalence between two distinct objects mentioned in the input text, processing of the match is terminated, and a single reduced match omitting the offending object binding pair is inserted into the agenda.

Logical inconsistency. After elaboration of the match, a composite trace is formed by merging both original traces plus all intermediate traces produced in the elaboration process. If inference applied to this composite trace results in detection of a logical inconsistency, processing of the match is terminated, and a set of reduced matches is inserted into the agenda, each formed by removing one of the binding pairs in the mapping for the original match.

Violated connecting statements. If, following elaboration, the produced sequence of associations connects two events in such a way
as to conflict with an explicitly-entered connecting statement, processing of the match is terminated.

The first and second tests are made *after* selection of a partial match,
because they may involve computationally-expensive generation of new,
reduced partial matches. The third test follows up on tests concerning
connecting statements made during the initial heuristic scoring of partial
matches. In some cases, it is not easy to tell in advance whether a partial
match will elaborate to include particular types of associations.

Major Program Components

Basic Operations on Event Traces

Contents of event traces. Utilities are provided for expanding the
assertions within an event trace to equivalent assertions involving the primitive predicates EQUAL, GREATER, NOT-EQUAL
and NOT-GREATER; condensing event traces from this expanded
form to redescribe activity in terms of the defined predicates AP-
PEAR, CHANGE, PRESENT, MATCH, and so forth; and enu-
merating lists of time points, objects, reference standards, attributes, variables and time intervals involved in an event trace.

Matching. The matching routine takes as arguments an event trace
serving as a pattern (this trace possibly containing variables for
time points, objects, tuples or attributes), a list of other event
traces to which this trace is to be matched, a specification of
whether partial chaining or partial restatement matches are desired, and additional flags governing such factors as whether assertions from the pattern must cover assertions from traces in the
list or vice-versa, whether partial or complete coverage is required,
and any initial bindings for variables in the pattern trace. In enu-
merating partial matches between two event traces, the matcher
first determines all correspondences between pairs of assertions in
the two traces, then combines these corresponding pairs into larger

matched sets based on compatibility of required variable bindings for these matches. The matcher returns a list of all partial matches found between the pattern trace and all members of the list of event traces.

Mapping and reduction. Utilities exist for copying event traces while mapping quantities to new quantities (time points, objects, reference standards or attributes); for copying traces while removing assertions involving certain specified quantities; and for copying traces while retaining only assertions involved in a partial match or paralleling these assertions at other time points in a trace.

Parsing and Encoding the Input

Parsing the input. Due to the simple nature of the grammar employed by PATHFINDER, a recursive-descent parser was found to be adequate. Additional information in the grammar specification enables this parser to prompt the operator in a useful manner regarding new entries for the lexicon—for example, asking the operator if an attribute occurs at the beginning of a sequence of unprocessed tokens. An initial lexicon contains three reference standards ("the background," "physical object" and "event"); about 100 attributes; a few dozen verb groups supporting the construction of event definitions, rules of inference and rules of restatement; and about 50 prepositions.

Encoding the input. Once the input sentences and questions are parsed, a number of additional operations are performed. These include: instantiation of the parse records with specific objects, reference standards and attributes known to the system; assignment of consecutive statement numbers to statements, and cross-indexing of the parse records where they refer to other statements; assignment of time points to event references (also considering temporal qualifiers such as "First," "Next," and so forth); and translation of the processed parse records to event traces, background statements, rules of inference and so forth, using built-in rules for verbs like "appears," "changes," etc., and using event definitions previously processed by the system for other verbs.

The association structure and other maintained quantities.
Once a segment of input text has been translated to an event trace,
background statement, rule of inference, etc., further routines enter
the quantity into the association structure or insert it into an appropriate list of such quantities known to the system (background
statements, connecting statements, rules of inference and rules of
restatement).

Inference and Exploratory Transformations

Inference. To perform inference on an event trace, PATHFINDER includes all relevant background and connecting statements and proceeds with the application of built-in and example-specific inference rules in a forward chaining manner, as described in chapter
5. Also as described in chapter 5, PATHFINDER streamlines this
process by performing inference not on individual assertions, but
on equivalence classes of attribute–object–time-point triples. Certain built-in inference rules detect logical inconsistencies.

Exploratory transformations. Transformations are applied to event
traces in clusters, as described in chapter 6. These clusters may
be applied in either a forward direction—from their first scenarios
to their second scenarios—or in a reverse direction.

Association

Processing new traces in the association structure. Whenever
new traces are entered into the association structure, inference and
exploratory transformations are carried out if required, and the
matcher is called to enumerate partial matches between the new
traces (if active) and active traces in other clusters. These new
partial matches are added to the agenda, which contains entries
for partial matches previously enumerated.

Choosing a partial match to elaborate. Once the partial matches
for new traces in the association structure have been generated,
the agenda entries are individually analyzed with respect to individual factors contributing to the heuristic scoring function. Some
of these factors must be recalculated at each iteration of the association process (e.g., those concerning current status of the as-

sociation structure), while others require only a single calculation upon first entry of a partial match into the agenda. Following this calculation, the total score for each partial match is computed, and the agenda is sorted in decreasing order by score. The first element is then the partial match to be elaborated during the current iteration of the association cycle.

Elaborating the chosen partial match. To elaborate a partial match, a routine is called to determine an exact intersection of primitive-level assertions for the two traces in question. Using this information, the partial match is expanded to include a possible reduction transformation, a possible chaining association (for partial chaining matches), a possible reduction transformation in the reverse direction, and a possible equivalence transformation (or a substitution transformation if one of the original traces depicted a precedent event).

Question Answering

Questions of type 1. Each type of question is processed by a specialized routine. For questions of type 1, a composite trace is formed, combining the event traces in the association structure. To form simplified English accounts for dynamic assertions, a special routine draws upon wording appearing in the question and in relevant parse records generated from the original entry of input text.

Questions of type 2. Questions of type 2 require a routine that performs a depth-first search through the association structure for a path connecting the two specified events. Two other routines express selected event traces in simplified English (by referring to the question and retained parse records) and express sequences of inter-event associations in simplified English (by the association prioritization scheme as outlined in chapter 1 and elsewhere).

Questions of types 3 and 4. These questions involve further invocation of the association mechanism, followed by answering as for questions of type 2. For questions of type 3, a new connecting statement is included, specifying the desired causal association. This connecting statement has the effect of excluding the processing of partial matches not elaborating to a causal association. For questions of type 4, after the association process has completed, an additional check is made to see if the assertions of the new event are covered by assertions in a composite trace of the entire activity, as described in chapter 8.

Program Operation and File Interface

Menu interface. Top-level operation of PATHFINDER is governed by a system of pull-down menus, these coupled with a mechanism for moving back and forth between an input/output screen for PATH-FINDER (displaying input text and question answering), and a debugging screen for displaying and listing the contents of event traces, association structures and so forth. From the debugging screen, a wide range of operations may be executed on a range of data structures involved in PATHFINDER's operation.

Display. Specialized routines handle the display of event traces and association structures, producing diagrams approximating those depicted in this book.

File interface. Additional routines handle file storage and retrieval for event traces and association structures (so that the results of processing sessions may be retained for inspection at a later time) and the loading of input text files. Additionally, once a text file has been processed and the lexicon correspondingly expanded to include new entries for verbs, objects and so forth appearing in that file, the lexicon may be saved and reloaded for subsequent processing sessions involving that text file.

B PATHFINDER Test Examples

The following list contains input descriptions and commentary for 62
test examples run on PATHFINDER, including all of the examples appearing as illustrations in chapters 4, 5, 6 and 7, but excluding the
extended example described in chapter 8. The examples listed here explore different types of associations between events—this dimension being used to organize the list—as well as activities in a range of physical
domains.

For each example, the input description is provided, followed by a
brief commentary specifying the components of supplementary information included in the input file and subsequent processing by PATH-
FINDER.

1. Simple chaining

(a) The block moves. The block continues moving.

(Given definitions for moving and continuing to move, PATH-
FINDER chains the first event to the second.)

(b) The finger starts applying pressure to the block. The
finger pushes the block.

(Given definitions for the two events, the first event is chained to
the second.)

(c) The steam moves into contact with the metal plate. The
steam condenses on the metal plate.

(Discussed in section 1.3, with objects and time points renamed
for ease of exposition. Given definitions for the two events, the
first event is chained to the second.)

2. Restatement

(a) The hand grips the block. The block remains between
the first finger and the second finger.

(Given a definition for gripping, the second event is matched with
the first, equating "the first finger" and "the second finger" with
hypothesized fingers for the gripping event.)

(b) The ball rolls. The contact between the ball and the
floor does not disappear.

(Given a definition for rolling, the two events are related by a
simple restatement match.)

3. Chaining involving hypothesized objects

(a) The brick moves toward the block. The block is hit.

(The first event is chained to the second, matching "the brick"
with the hypothesized object hitting "the block.")

(b) The board is dented. The wrench is dropped.

(Discussed in section 4.2. The second event is chained to the first,
matching "the wrench" with the hypothesized object denting "the
board.")

(c) Object 1 slides. Object 2 is scratched. Object 3 is
struck.

(The first event is chained to the second, matching "object 1"
with the hypothesized object doing the scratching and "object 2"
with the surface upon which "object 1" slides. The striking and
scratching events are then taken as co-occurring—these associated
via a restatement match.)

4. Chaining involving a precedent event

(a) The trigger moves. The hammer is released.

(Discussed in section 4.3. Given a precedent event "Object 21
unlatches object 22." the program chains the moving event to the
precedent and the precedent to the releasing event, matching "the
trigger" with the hypothesized object releasing "the hammer.")

(b) The ball rolls toward the cage. The ball enters the
cage.

(Given a precedent event "Object 21 rolls into object 22." the
program chains the first event to the precedent and matches the
end of the precedent with the second event.)

5. Inference regarding predicates

(a) The burner becomes hotter than the portion of liquid.
The burner heats the portion of liquid.

(The definition for "heating" specifies two objects in contact and initially matching in temperature. The temperature of the first object increases, while that of the second remains steady. Then, the temperature of the second object increases to match that of the first. Inference at the level of (NOT-)EQUAL and (NOT-) GREATER concludes that after the initial increase in temperature for the burner, its temperature exceeds that of the portion of liquid. A partial chaining match is then elaborated from the first event to the second event.)

(b) Vehicle 1 decreases in speed to match vehicle 2.
Vehicle 2 increases in speed to match vehicle 1.

(Discussed in section 5.2. Symmetry of the EQUAL predicate strengthens a restatement match between the two events.)

6. Inference regarding individual attributes

(a) The rocket propels the jet of exhaust. The jet of exhaust moves away from the rocket.

(Discussed in section 5.2. Given rules of inference regarding the symmetric properties of "distance" and "contact," the second event is matched with the end of the first event.)

(b) The hand pushes the box up to the ceiling. The hand remains below the ceiling.

(Given a rule of inference regarding transitivity of "below," PATH-FINDER concludes from the first event that "the hand" remains below "the ceiling." The second event is then matched with the inference image of the first event.)

7. Inference between attributes

(a) The pressure between the steam and the wall increases.
The contact between the steam and the wall does not disappear.

(Given a rule that "pressure" implies "contact," inference on the first event produces an assertion matching the second event.)

(b) The elevation of the ball increases.   The ball moves.

(Discussed in section 5.2. Given rules of inference relating an increase or decrease in "elevation" to a change in "position," inference on the first event produces an assertion matching part of the second event.)

8.   Inference used to detect inconsistent matches

(a) The wheel rolls.   The rod is twisted.

(Given a rule of inference regarding symmetry of the attribute "restrained," an initial partial chaining match from the first event to the second event is discarded. This initial match falsely equates the hypothesized surface upon which "the wheel" rolls with the twisted end of "the rod." "The wheel" is in contact with both of these objects but is only restrained by the twisted end of "the rod." A subsequent chaining match omitting this binding succeeds.)

(b) The arrow is released.   The arrow strikes the target.

(Discussed in section 5.2. An initial chaining match equates the target with the hypothesized spring that propels the arrow—this because the arrow is not in contact with both objects. Inference discards this match because the distance between "the arrow" and the spring is increasing, yet the corresponding distance to "the target" is decreasing. A subsequent match omitting the offending binding succeeds.)

(c) Object 1 moves forward toward object 2.   Object 1 moves backward.

(Given a precedent "Object 31 bounces off object 32." plus a rule of inference that "the forward direction" does not match "the backward direction," a restatement match between the first and second events is found to yield a contradiction. PATHFINDER chains the first event to the precedent and the precedent to the second event.)

9. Descriptions incorporating background statements

(a) The ball is inside the basket. The basket descends to
the floor. The ball remains above the floor.

(Discussed in section 5.3. Given a rule stating that being inside
one object that is above another object implies being above the
other object, PATHFINDER extends the first event to include an
assertion that the ball remains above the floor. This assertion is
matched with the second event.)

(b) The support of the screw by the table is present. The
hand ungrasps the screw. The screw collides with the
wrench.

(Discussed in section 5.3. Given two precedents, "Object 21 drops
object 22." and "Object 31 lets roll object 32." plus a rule stating
that support of an object by another implies that the first object
is "supported," PATHFINDER chains from the first event to the
second precedent and from this precedent to the second event.
The first precedent cannot be used because it asserts that the
dropped object is not supported.)

(c) Object 2 is not compressible. Object 1 applies
pressure to object 2. The shape of object 2 changes.

(Given two precedents, "Object 21 compacts object 22." and
"Object 31 deforms object 32." the program chains from the first
event to the second precedent and matches the end of this precedent with the second event. The first precedent cannot be used
because it requires a compressible object and this conflicts with
the initially-supplied background statement concerning "object
2.")

(d) The portion of liquid is not combustible. The burner
heats the portion of liquid. The portion of liquid
ceases to exist.

(Given precedent events "Liquid 21 boils away." and "Liquid 31
combusts." the program chains from the first event to the first
precedent and matches part of this precedent with the second
event. The second precedent cannot be used because it requires
a combustible quantity.)

10. Listing of assumptions

(a) The hand ungrasps the screw. The screw collides with the wrench.

(Given a precedent event "Object 21 drops object 22." the program chains from the first event to the precedent and from the precedent to the second event. Assumptions facilitating chaining to the precedent include: "the screw" becoming not supported, no initial change in the position or elevation of "the screw," and no initial appearance of speed or heading for "the screw.")

(b) The steam rises. The steam contacts the metal plate.

(Discussed in section 5.4. Given a precedent "Object 21 rises into contact with object 22." the program chains from the first event to the precedent and from the precedent to the second event. Assumptions facilitating chaining to the precedent include "the steam" decreasing in distance to "the metal plate," not appearing in contact with "the metal plate," and remaining below "the metal plate.")

11. Exploratory equivalence transformations

(a) The iron bar comes into contact with the water. The iron bar rusts.

(Supplementary information includes a background statement asserting that "the water" is made of "water," a precedent event "Substance 21 oxidizes the iron in object 22." plus four rules of inference regarding symmetric properties for "contact" and "distance," two rules of inference stating that being made of "iron" and "water" are mutually exclusive, and a rule of restatement stating that being made of "rust" and "iron oxide" are equivalent. The program chains the first event to the precedent and matches the end of the precedent to the second event—this latter match facilitated by an exploratory transformation derived from the supplied rule of restatement.)

(b) The block collides with the stone. The block becomes in contact with the stone.

(Discussed in section 6.2. Given a rule of restatement specifying an equivalence between statements involving the attributes "contact" and "in contact," exploratory transformations applied to traces for the referenced events facilitate a restatement match.)

12. Substitution of object types

(a) The block starts to push from above on the water. The water starts to push from below on the block.

(Discussed in section 6.2. Supplementary information includes background statements specifying that "the block" is a "rigid object" and "the water" a "liquid"; a precedent event "Object 21 compresses spring 22."; rules of inference relating "above" and "below," specifying symmetry for "distance" and "contact," and stating that a liquid is not a flexible object; and a rule of restatement stating that a liquid may be viewed as a flexible object when subjected to pressure. The program chains the first event to a transformed image of the precedent and matches part of the transformed precedent with the second event, with the use of the precedent event facilitated by an exploratory transformation derived from the supplied rule of restatement.)

(b) The fire moves along the stream. The fire moves away from the stream.

(Supplementary information includes background statements asserting that "the fire" is a "fire" and "the stream" is a "liquid," a precedent event "Object 21 passes by object 22." a rule of inference stating that a fire is not a physical object, and a rule of restatement stating that a fire may be viewed as a physical object when it moves. The program chains the first event to a transformed image of the precedent event and matches part of the transformed precedent with the second event.)

13. Substitution regarding spatial orientation

(a) The ball rolls toward the cage. The ball enters the cage.

(Given a precedent "Object 21 lowers into object 22." plus a cluster of rules of restatement specifying an analogy between moving forward and moving downward, PATHFINDER chains the first event to a transformed image of the precedent and matches the end of the transformed precedent with the second event.)

(b) Object 1 starts to push on object 2. Object 1 starts
to move to the left.

(Discussed in section 6.2. Given a precedent "Object 31 pushes
forward off object 32." plus a cluster of rules of restatement specifying an analogy between moving leftward and moving forward,
the program chains the first event to a transformed image of the
precedent and matches part of the transformed precedent with
the second event.)

14. Other substitution of attributes

(a) The block starts to push on the stick. The stick
starts to bend.

(Given background statements concerning object types, plus a
precedent "Object 21 compresses spring 22." plus a rule of restatement specifying an analogy between bending and compression, the program chains the first event to a transformed image
of the precedent and matches part of the transformed precedent
to the second event.)

(b) The wheel rolls on the concrete. The wheel is pushed
by the axle. The wheel spins on the axle. The wheel
stops spinning on the axle.

(Given a precedent "Object 51 slides to a stop." plus a cluster of rules of restatement specifying an analogy between slowed
spinning on an axle and sliding on a surface, the program reconstructs the scenario as follows: the pushing event is taken as
ending in the rolling event, which coincides with the spinning on
the axle. The spinning event then chains to a transformed image
of the precedent—here, the wheel spinning to a stop on the axle.
Lastly, the wheel stopping its spinning on the axle is matched
with part of the transformed precedent.)

(c) The radio wave is transmitted into space. The strength
of the radio wave decreases.

(Discussed in section 6.2. Given a precedent "Liquid 11 spreads
thin over surface 12." plus two rules of restatement specifying an
analogy between a radio wave in space and a quantity of liquid
on a surface, the program chains the first event to a transformed
image of the precedent and matches part of the transformed precedent with the second event.)

15. Generalization

(a) The block starts to push on the sponge. The sponge is
compressed.

(Discussed in section 6.3. Given background statements specifying object types, plus a rule of restatement summarizing a sponge
as a flexible object, a transformed version of the first event is
chained to the second event.)

(b) The fire ignites the block. The block starts to burn.

(Given background statements concerning object types and com-
positions, plus a rule of restatement specifying that being made of
wood may be summarized as being made of flammable material,
PATHFINDER matches part of the first event with a transformed
image of the second event.)

16. Interval composition

(a) The wheel slows. The wheel stops.

(Discussed in section 6.3. Given a rule of restatement summarizing slowing followed by stopping as simply stopping, the first
event is chained to a transformed image of the second event.)

(b) The elevation of the block does not change. The
elevation of the block increases.

(Given a rule of restatement summarizing no change in elevation
followed by increase in elevation as simply an increase in elevation,
the first event is matched with the beginning of a transformed
image of the second event.)

17. Attribute composition

(a) The block combines with the pile of blocks. The pile
of blocks gets taller.

(Discussed in section 6.3. Given a rule of restatement summarizing an increase in height accompanied by no change in width or
depth as a simple increase in size, the program elaborates a partial restatement match between a transformed image of the first
event and the second event.)

(b) The water is poured into the solution. The
concentration of the solution decreases.

(Supplementary information includes a background statement
specifying that "the water" is a solvent; a rule of inference stating
that if a solvent becomes part of another liquid, the amount of
solvent in that other liquid increases; and a rule of restatement
summarizing an increase in the amount of solvent accompanied
by no change in the amount of solute in a liquid as simply a decrease in the concentration of the liquid. The program matches
the end of the first event with a transformed image of the second
event.)

18. Object composition

(a) The hub is a part of the wheel, and the hub is
restrained by the wheel. The wheel turns. The hub
turns.

(Discussed in section 6.3. Given a rule of restatement summarizing a restrained part of an object turning with the whole object
turning, PATHFINDER elaborates a partial restatement match
between the first event and a transformed image of the second
event.)

(b) The finger is a part of the hand. The finger
participates in an event. The hand participates in an
event.

(Given a rule of restatement summarizing activity involving a
part of an object engaging in an event with activity involving the
whole object engaging in an event, PATHFINDER elaborates a
partial restatement match between the first event and a transformed image of the second event.)

19. Attribute-object reification

(a) The fire raises the temperature of the wax. The wax
melts.

(Given a background statement specifying that "the temperature
of the wax" is a measurement of temperature for "the wax," plus
a cluster of rules of restatement summarizing changes in tempera-

ture for a quantity as changes in "elevation" for a second quantity representing that temperature, the program chains the first event to a transformed image of the second event.)

(b) The block enters the water. The water reduces the speed of the block.

(Discussed in section 6.3. Supplementary information includes a background statement specifying that "the speed of the block" is a measurement of speed for "the block," two precedent events "Object 21 comes into contact with liquid 22 by entering liquid 22." and "Object 31 is slowed by contact with object 32." and a cluster of rules of restatement summarizing changes in speed for a quantity as changes in "size" for a second quantity representing that speed. The entering event is matched with part of the first precedent event, which chains to second precedent event, which in turn associates with the end of a transformed image of the reducing event.)

20. Event-attribute reification

(a) The light strikes the floor. The floor remains illuminated.

(Discussed in section 6.3. Given background statements concerning object types and the fact that the attribute "illuminated" is an assertion of the event type "illumination," plus a rule of restatement summarizing light contacting an object as illumination of the object, a partial restatement match is elaborated between the first event and a transformed image of the second event.)

(b) The tank remains leaky. The weight of the tank decreases.

(Given a rule of restatement summarizing transfer of a portion of liquid to the outside of a container as leakiness of the container, a partial restatement match is elaborated between the second event and a transformed image of the first event.)

(c) The block becomes not moving. The ball becomes moving.

(Given a precedent "Object 1 hits object 2." plus a cluster of rules of restatement summarizing changes in position, speed and heading in terms of application of the attribute "moving" to an object, partial restatement matches are elaborated between the precedent event and transformed images of the first and second events.)

21. Event-object reification

(a) The cue ball transfers the motion to the eight ball. The eight ball rolls into the pocket.

(Discussed in section 6.3. Supplementary information includes two background statements specifying that "the motion" is an event and is an occurrence of the event type "motion," a precedent event "Object 21 starts and continues to move." plus a cluster of two rules of restatement specifying an equivalence between being "in possession of" an event and being "engaged in" an event, and a cluster of four rules of restatement summarizing changes in "position," "speed" and "heading" in terms of being engaged in a motion event. PATHFINDER chains a transformed image of the first event to the precedent event and chains an image of the precedent event to the second event.)

(b) The vacuum becomes engaged in the suction. The dirt enters the vacuum.

(Supplementary information includes two background statements stating that "the suction" is an event and is an occurrence of the event type "suction," a background statement specifying that "the dirt" is not a part of "the vacuum," a precedent event "Object 11 sucks up object 12." and a cluster of rules of restatement summarizing one object's decrease in pressure directed toward a second object in terms of the first object being engaged in a suction event. PATHFINDER chains a transformed image of the first event to the precedent and matches the end of the precedent with the second event.)

22. Temporal ordering statements

(a) The ball moves. The block is hit. The ball moving occurs after the hitting of the block.

(Given a precedent "Object 31 moves against object 32." plus two rules of inference regarding transitivity and anti-symmetry of "after," the program abandons an attempt to chain the first event to the second event—this due to interference with the supplied temporal ordering statement. The final reconstruction chains the second event to the precedent event and matches the end of the precedent with the first event.)

(b) The ball rises. The ball falls. The rising by the ball occurs after the falling by the ball.

(Discussed in section 7.2. Given two precedents "Object 31 is overcome by gravity." and "Object 41 bounces vertically off object 42." plus rules of inference regarding transitivity and anti-symmetry of "after," the program abandons a reconstruction of the scenario as involving the ball rising, being overcome by gravity and falling—this due to interference with the supplied temporal ordering statement. The final reconstruction matches the falling event with the end of the first precedent—being overcome by gravity—then chains to the second precedent—bouncing vertically—and matches the end of this precedent with the rising event.)

(c) The ball rises. The ball falls. The falling by the ball occurs after the rising by the ball.

(Discussed in section 7.2. A variant of example 22(b). Provided with a reversed temporal ordering statement, the program reconstructs the scenario by chaining the ball rising to the first precedent—being overcome by gravity—and matching the end of that precedent with the ball falling.)

(d) The ball rises. The ball falls.

(Discussed in section 7.2. A further variant of example 22(b). Provided with no temporal ordering statement, PATHFINDER reconstructs the activity in the same manner as for example 22(c), when a reversed temporal ordering statement is supplied.)

23. Specifications of causation

(a) The electric current travels from the first circuit junction to the second circuit junction. The electric current passes through the filament. The electric current traveling from the first circuit junction to the second circuit junction causes the electric current to pass through the filament.

(Discussed in section 7.3. Supplementary information includes background statements concerning object types, a rule of inference specifying that an electric current is not a physical object, and two rules of restatement specifying that an electric current may be viewed as a physical object when "at" or "inside" another physical object. PATHFINDER complies with the supplied connecting statement by chaining a transformed image of the first event to a transformed image of the second event.)

(b) The structure expands. The component moves. The structure expanding causes the component to move.

(Given two precedents "Object 21 expands against object 22." and "Object 31 pushes object 32." plus a rule of restatement summarizing a part of an object moving forward with respect to the object as the whole object expanding, PATHFINDER reconstructs the scenario as follows. The structure expanding is matched with the first precedent—expanding against an object. This precedent is then chained to the second precedent—pushing. Finally, the end of the second precedent is matched with the component moving. In this manner, PATHFINDER has fulfilled the supplied connecting statement.)

(c) The ball moves. The block is hit. The ball moving is caused by the hitting of the block.

(A variant of example 22(a). Here, a specification of causation has the same effect as the temporal specification in 22(a).)

(d) The ball rises. The ball falls. The rising by the ball is caused by the falling by the ball.

(A variant of example 22(b). The specification of causation here has the same effect as the temporal specification in 22(b).)

24. Specifications of analogy

(a) The steel table is hot. The copper bar rubs against the steel table. The copper bar becomes hot.

(Supplementary information includes two precedent events "Object 11 gets hot from contact with object 12." and "Object 21 gets hot from friction with object 22." plus two connecting statements specifying that "the copper bar" becoming hot parallels the first precedent and not the second. PATHFINDER complies by elaborating a partial restatement match between the first event and the first precedent and a partial restatement match from the end of the first precedent to the second event.)

(b) The electric current travels from the first circuit junction to the second circuit junction. The electric current passes through the filament. The electric current traveling from the first circuit junction to the second circuit junction is equivalent to the electric current passing through the filament.

(Discussed in section 7.3. A variant of example 23(a). Here, the specification of equivalence directs PATHFINDER to elaborate a partial restatement match between a transformed image of the second event and a transformed image of the first event.)

25. Specifications of abstraction

(a) The structure expands. The component moves. The structure expanding summarizes the component moving.

(A variant of example 23(b). Specification of the expanding event as summarizing the moving event results in an alternate reconstruction in which the second event is matched directly with a transformed image of the first event. For this match, "the component" is mapped to a hypothesized part of "the structure" moving as part of the expansion activity.)

(b) The nail deflects the hammer toward the block of wood. The block of wood deflects the hammer toward the box. The heading of the hammer changes. The changing by the heading of the hammer is a part of the nail deflecting the hammer toward the block of wood.

(Given a definition for deflecting, PATHFINDER matches the third event with a part of the first event, rather than with a part of the second event.)

(c) The device pushes away from the wall. The device continues to move away from the wall. The pressure between the device and the wall does not appear. The not appearing by the pressure between the device and the wall is implied by the device continuing to move away from the wall.

(Given a rule of inference specifying that absence of contact implies absence of pressure, PATHFINDER reconstructs the scenario by chaining the first event to the second event and elaborating a partial restatement match between the third event and the second event—this as opposed to elaboration of an alternative partial restatement match between the third event and the first event.)

Association structure. A set of event traces, plus zero or more complete associations linking various pairs of those traces. Also, informally, a graphical diagram of the sort used in this book to characterize particular association structures.

Association type. The type of a (complete) association. In PATHFINDER, associations representing complete matches are assigned an association type of either "chaining" or "equivalence," and associations representing the application of transformations are assigned an association type corresponding to the type of transformation employed ("reduction," "inference," or one of the exploratory transformations).

Attribute composition transformation. A non-information-preserving exploratory transformation involving the reexpression of activity involving a set of related attributes (e.g., "height," "width," and "depth") with activity involving a single, encompassing attribute (e.g., "size").

Attribute-object reification transformation. A non-information-preserving exploratory transformation in which activity involving a particular attribute (e.g., "speed") is replaced with activity involving a newly-created object representing the attribute applied to its arguments (e.g., a new object "the-speed-of-object-32").

Attribute. A property, relationship or function of one or more objects, such as can be described using one of the simplified English templates grounding the transition space representation. Attributes may be perceptual (e.g., "length") or conceptual (e.g., being a part of something).

"the-background." A reference standard serving as a fixed frame of reference for motion.

Background statement. A statement describing an attribute value or relationship between attribute values that is maintained for the duration of the activity specified by a causal description. For example: "The hub is a part of the wheel." Background statements constitute one of three varieties of statements appearing in the stylized causal descriptions supplied to PATHFINDER. Such statements may also appear within the supplementary information provided to the program.

Causal description. A body of text composed by a human for the purpose of conveying knowledge of the causal workings of a particular physical system to another human or to a computer program. As specialized for PATHFINDER: an ordered set of statements, each of which may be an event reference, a background statement, or a connecting statement.

Causal reconstruction. The task of reading a causal description, forming an internal model of the described activity, and demonstrating comprehension through question answering. In the context of PATHFINDER, special restrictions apply to the exact forms of causal descriptions and questions permitted.

Change characterization. A specification of a change's type. In transition space, ten partially-overlapping change characterizations are used, corresponding to the predicates APPEAR, NOT-APPEAR, DISAPPEAR, NOT-DISAPPEAR, CHANGE, NOT-CHANGE, INCREASE, NOT-INCREASE, DECREASE and NOT-DECREASE.

Complete association. (Or, simply: "association.") The representational specification of either: (1) a complete match existing between two event traces, or (2) a relationship whereby a transformation applied to one event trace produces another event trace.

Complete chaining match. Between two event traces: a single-transition complete match involving at least one definite change (APPEAR, DISAPPEAR, CHANGE, INCREASE or DECREASE) and situated such that exactly one of the traces is begun by the matching transition and continues beyond that transition. A complete chaining match is formed through elaboration of a partial chaining match and indicates a presumed causal association between the two matching events.

Complete match. An identical correspondence between one or more transitions in one event trace and an equivalent number of transitions in another event trace. Paired transitions must match in all details, containing assertions with identical predicates and arguments. A further distinction is made between complete chaining matches and complete restatement matches.

Complete restatement match. A complete match that does not meet the specifications of a complete chaining match. Complete restatement matches are only implicitly represented in association structures—as sequences of reduction and equivalence associations formed by elaboration of partial restatement matches. Such sequences of associations indicate a presumed overlap in the activity described by two separate events.

Composite trace. An event trace representing the sum total of the activity specified in a causal description and formed by merging the sets of assertions for relevant event traces in the association structure. Some amount of mapping of object and time point labels may be required during the combination process due to the presence of equivalence associations in the association structure.

Connecting statement. A statement explicitly declaring the presence of a causal, temporal, or other kind of relationship between two events referenced in a causal description. For example: "The structure expanding causes the component to move." Connecting statements constitute one of three varieties of statements appearing in the stylized causal descriptions supplied to PATHFINDER. Such statements also appear within certain types of supplementary information provided to the program.

Elaboration. The process of replacing a partial association with a sequence of complete associations. Partial chaining and restatement associations can always be elaborated into sequences of complete associations involving the association types "chaining," "equivalence" (or "substitution") and "reduction."

Equivalence transformation. An information-preserving exploratory transformation in which one or more time points, objects, reference standards or attributes are mapped to synonym quantities, yielding an alternate description of the same event.

Event definition. A stylized, written account of changes and momentary attribute values in the temporal unfolding of a particular type of event. Event definitions appear in the supplementary information accompanying causal descriptions supplied to PATHFINDER.

Event level. The portion of knowledge with regard to physical activity that has to do with properties, relationships and other attributes of particular events. The event level may be contrasted with the object level, concerning knowledge about particular objects participating in events.

Event reference. A statement declaring the occurrence of a particular event. For example, "The screw collides with the wrench." Event references constitute one of three varieties of statements appearing in the stylized causal descriptions supplied to PATHFINDER. Such statements also appear within certain types of supplementary information provided to the program.

Event trace. (Or, simply: "trace.") A transition space representation of a physical event, equating to a directed, acyclic graph of transitions, each of which specifies a temporally-coordinated combination of changes occurring during the unfolding of the event. Also, informally, a graphical diagram of the sort used in this book to characterize particular event traces.

Event-attribute reification transformation. A non-information-preserving exploratory transformation replacing part of an event trace (e.g., changes involved in light striking a surface) with assertions involving a newly-introduced attribute applied to one of the participating objects (e.g., "illuminated" applied to the surface).

Event-object reification transformation. A non-information-preserving exploratory transformation replacing part of an event trace (e.g., changes involved in a collision) with assertions involving a newly-created object representing the replaced activity (e.g., a new object representing the collision, with other objects "engaged-in" the collision object).

Exploratory transformation. A transformation applied in a conditional manner to an event trace prior to matching. Exploratory transformations typically generate alternate accounts of activity at different levels of abstraction or in terms of different underlying metaphors, so that subsequent matching may bridge discontinuities introduced by the writer's own use of abstraction and analogy within a description.

Generalization transformation. A non-information-preserving exploratory transformation involving the replacement of a reference standard (e.g., an object type such as "container") with a new, more general reference standard (e.g., "physical-object").

Inference transformation. A non-information-preserving transformation in which the set of assertions comprising an event trace is extended through deductive inference according to a combination of built-in and externally-supplied rules of inference.

Information-preserving transformation. A transformation from event traces to event traces which belongs to an inverse pair of such transformations.

Interchange transformation. An information-preserving exploratory transformation involving selective mapping of time points, objects, reference standards or attributes to new quantities only in particular contexts within an event trace (e.g., exchanging time points only within temporal ordering assertions, yielding a retrograde version of an event trace). Interchange transformations have not been explored in PATHFINDER.

Interval composition transformation. A non-information-preserving exploratory transformation involving a merging of two adjacent time intervals to produce a single, composite interval, with changes specified according to the composition of the changes in the original two intervals.

Non-information-preserving transformation. A transformation from event traces to event traces which does not belong to an inverse pair of such transformations.

"null." A reference standard depicting the "false" or "absent" state for all attributes.

Object composition transformation. A non-information-preserving exploratory transformation involving reexpression of activity originally involving the parts of an object as activity involving the whole object.

Object level. The portion of knowledge with regard to physical activity that has to do with properties, relationships and other attributes of objects participating in events. The object level may be contrasted with the event level, concerning knowledge about properties, relationships and other attributes of the events themselves.

Object. Anything having properties, relationships and other attributes, such as may be described using one of the simplified English templates grounding the transition space representation. Also, anything that may participate in an event. Objects may be perceptual (e.g., a physical object) or conceptual (e.g., a collection of objects).

Partial association. The representational specification of a partial match existing between two event traces. A partial association may be converted into a chain of complete associations through the process of elaboration.

Partial chaining match. Between two event traces: a single-transition partial match involving at least one definite change (APPEAR, DISAPPEAR, CHANGE, INCREASE or DECREASE) and situated such that exactly one of the traces is begun by the matching transition and continues beyond that transition. A partial chaining match may be taken as a clue to a possible causal association between two specified events.

Partial match. A condition whereby some subset of the assertions in one or more transitions of one event trace matches a subset of the assertions in an equivalent number of transitions of a second event trace, also allowing for a possible mapping of time points and objects between the two traces. Partial matches are are subdivided into partial chaining matches and partial restatement matches

Partial restatement match. A partial match that does not meet the specifications of a partial chaining match. A partial restatement match may be taken as a clue to a possible overlap in the activity specified in two events.

Precedent event. An event relevant to the comprehension of a particular causal description, yet not referenced explicitly in that description. Precedent events are made available to PATHFINDER through event references and corresponding event definitions included in the supplementary information accompanying a causal description.

Predicate. As in mathematical logic. For the transition space representation, four primitive predicates (EQUAL, NOT-EQUAL, GREATER and NOT-GREATER) are used to define sixteen non-primitive predicates (PRESENT, NOT-PRESENT, MATCH, NOT-MATCH, EXCEED, NOT-EXCEED, APPEAR, NOT-APPEAR, DISAPPEAR, NOT-DISAPPEAR, CHANGE, NOT-CHANGE, INCREASE, NOT-INCREASE, DECREASE and NOT-DECREASE).

Reduction transformation. A non-information-preserving transformation in which one or more assertions are removed from an event trace. Reduction transformations are employed in the course of elaborating partial associations.

Reference standard. A fixed point of reference for comparing attribute values. For example: specific object types, colors, substances, numbers and directions.

Rule of inference. A stylized, written account specifying a deductive inference permitted for the transition space representation. Rules of inference appear in the supplementary information provided to PATHFINDER and facilitate the application of inference transformations during causal reconstruction.

Rule of restatement. A stylized, written account specifying an acceptable reexpression of one physical activity in terms of another physical activity—possibly at a different level of abstraction or in terms of a different underlying metaphor. Rules of restatement appear in the supplementary information provided to PATHFINDER and generate exploratory transformations to be applied to event traces in the course of causal reconstruction.

Substitution transformation. An information-preserving exploratory transformation in which one or more time points, objects, reference standards or attributes are mapped to different, but parallel quantities, producing a description of an event distinct from the original event, yet parallel in the types of changes involved.

Supplementary information. Generic background knowledge supplied in written form to PATHFINDER and accompanying a causal description in order to compensate for the program's empty knowledge base. Five varieties of supplementary information are utilized: (1) additional background statements, (2) event definitions, (3) precedent events, (4) rules of inference, and (5) rules of restatement.

Time point. An instant in time, as designated by a symbol in the transition space representation.

Transition space. A conceptualized space having points corresponding to transitions, or temporally-coordinated combinations of changes in various attributes of various objects, with paths among these points corresponding to specifications of physical events at particular levels of abstraction or in terms of particular underlying metaphors.

Transition. A point in transition space, corresponding to a temporally-coordinated combination of changes in one or more attributes of one or more objects, typically within the focus of activity for a particular event. Representationally, a transition consists of one or more assertions at and between two time points.

Bibliography

Allen, J. F., "Maintaining Knowledge about Temporal Intervals," *Communications of the ACM* 26:11, 1983, 832–843.

Allen, J. F., "Towards a General Theory of Action and Time," *Artificial Intelligence* 23:2, 1984, 123–154.

Alterman, R., "A Dictionary Based on Concept Coherence," *Artificial Intelligence* 25:2, 1985, 153–186.

Amsterdam, J., "Temporal Reasoning and Narrative Conventions," *Proc. Second International Conference on Principles of Knowledge Representation and Reasoning,* 1991, 15–21.

Batali, J. D., *Automatic Acquisition and Use of Some of the Knowledge in Physics Texts,* Ph.D. Dissertation, Department of Electrical Engineering and Computer Science, Massachusetts Institute of Technology, 1991.

Borchardt, G. C., *A Computer Model for the Representation and Identification of Physical Events,* Master's Thesis, Department of Computer Science, University of Illinois, Report T–142, Coordinated Science Laboratory, University of Illinois, Urbana, IL, 1984.

Borchardt, G. C., "Event Calculus," *Proc. Ninth International Joint Conference on Artificial Intelligence,* 1985, 524–527.

Borchardt, G. C., "Incremental Inference: Getting Multiple Agents to Agree on What to Do Next," *Proc. AAAI Sixth National Conference on Artificial Intelligence,* 1987, 334–339.

Borchardt, G. C., "Understanding Causal Descriptions of Physical Systems," *Proc. AAAI Tenth National Conference on Artificial Intelligence,* 1992, 2–8.

Borchardt, G. C., "Causal Reconstruction," submitted for publication to *Artificial Intelligence.*

Brent, M. R., "A Simplified Theory of Tense Representations and Constraints on Their Composition," *Proc. 28th Annual Meeting of the Association for Computational Linguistics,* 1990, 119–126.

Brown, G. and Yule, G., *Discourse Analysis,* Cambridge University Press, 1983.

Bruce, V. and Green, P. R., *Visual Perception: Physiology, Psychology and Ecology,* Second Edition, Lawrence Erlbaum Associates, 1990.

Bullock, M., Gelman, R. and Baillargeon, R., "The Development of Causal Reasoning," in Friedman, W. J. (ed.), *The Developmental Psychology of Time,* Academic Press, 1982.

Bylander, T. and Chandrasekaran, B., "Understanding Behavior Using Consolidation," *Proc. Ninth International Joint Conference on Artificial Intelligence,* 1985, 450–454.

Caine, M. E., *The Design of Shape from Motion Constraints,* Ph.D. Dissertation, Department of Mechanical Engineering, Massachusetts Institute of Technology, Technical Report 1425, Artificial Intelligence Laboratory, Massachusetts Institute of Technology, 1993, to appear.

Carbonell, J. G., "Learning by Analogy: Formulating and Generalizing Plans from Past Experience," in Michalski, R. S., Carbonell, J. G. and Mitchell, T. M. (eds.), *Machine Learning: An Artificial Intelligence Approach,* Tioga Publishing Co., 1983.

Carbonell, J. G. and Minton, S., "Metaphor and Commonsense Reasoning," in Hobbs, J. R. and Moore, R. C. (eds.), *Formal Theories of the Commonsense World,* Ablex Publ. Co., 1985, 405–426.

Carey, S., *Conceptual Change in Childhood,* MIT Press, 1985.

Clement, J., "A Conceptual Model Discussed by Galileo and Used Intuitively by Physics Students," in Gentner, D. and Stevens, A. L. (eds.), *Mental Models,* Lawrence Erlbaum Associates, 1983, 325–340.

Collins, A. M. and Loftus, E. F., "A Spreading-Activation Theory of Semantic Processing," *Psychological Review* 82:6, 1975, 407–428.

Davis, R., "Diagnostic Reasoning Based on Structure and Behavior," *Artificial Intelligence* 24:1–3, 1984, 347–410.

Davis, R. and Hamscher, W., "Model-Based Reasoning: Troubleshooting," in Shrobe, H. E. (ed.), *Exploring Artificial Intelligence,* Morgan Kaufmann, 1988, 297–346.

DeJong, G. and Mooney, R., "Explanation-Based Learning: An Alternate View," *Machine Learning* 1:2, 1986, 145–176.

de Kleer, J. and Brown, J. S., "A Qualitative Physics Based on Confluences," *Artificial Intelligence* 24:1–3, 1984, 7–83.

de Kleer, J. and Brown, J. S., "Theories of Causal Ordering," *Artificial Intelligence* 29:1, 1986, 33–61.

diSessa, A. A., "Phenomenology and the Evolution of Intuition," in Gentner, D. and Stevens, A. L. (eds.), *Mental Models*, Lawrence Erlbaum Associates, 1983, 15–33.

Dorr, B., "Solving Thematic Divergences in Machine Translation," *Proc. 28th Annual Meeting of the Association for Computational Linguistics*, 1990, 127–134.

Doyle, R. J., *Hypothesizing Device Mechanisms: Opening Up the Black Box*, Ph.D. Dissertation, Department of Electrical Engineering and Computer Science, Massachusetts Institute of Technology, Technical Report 1047, Artificial Intelligence Laboratory, Massachusetts Institute of Technology, 1988.

Doyle, R. J., "Reasoning About Hidden Mechanisms," *Proc. Eleventh International Joint Conference on Artificial Intelligence*, 1989, 1343–1349.

Doyle, J. and Wellman, M. P., "Impediments to Universal Preference-Based Default Theories," MIT/LCS/TM–416, Laboratory for Computer Science, Massachusetts Institute of Technology, 1989.

Dyer, M. G., *In-Depth Understanding*, MIT Press, 1983.

Dyer, M. G, Flowers, M. and Hodges, J., "Naive Mechanics Comprehension and Invention in EDISON," *Proc. Tenth International Joint Conference on Artificial Intelligence*, 1987, 696–699.

Falkenhainer, B., Forbus, K. D. and Gentner, D., "The Structure-Mapping Engine," *Proc. AAAI Fifth National Conference on Artificial Intelligence*, 1986, 272–277.

Faltings, B., "Qualitative Kinematics in Mechanisms," *Artificial Intelligence* 44:1–2, 1990, 89–119.

Fikes, R. E. and Nilsson, N. J., "STRIPS: A New Approach to the Application of Theorem Proving to Problem Solving," *Artificial Intelligence* 2:3–4, 1971, 189–208.

Fillmore, C. J., "The Case for Case," in Bach, E. and Harms, R. (eds.), *Universals in Linguistic Theory*, Holt, Rinehart and Winston, 1968.

Forbus, K. D., "Qualitative Process Theory," *Artificial Intelligence* 24:1–3, 1984, 85–168.

Forbus, K. D., "Qualitative Physics: Past, Present and Future," in Shrobe, H. E. (ed.), *Exploring Artificial Intelligence*, Morgan Kaufmann, 1988, 239–296.

Gardner, H., *The Mind's New Science*, Basic Books, 1985.

Genesereth, M. R. and Nilsson, N. J., *Logical Foundations of Artificial Intelligence*, Morgan Kaufmann, 1987.

Gentner, D., "Structure-Mapping: A Theoretical Framework for Analogy," *Cognitive Science* 7:2, 1983, 155–170.

Gentner, D. and Forbus, K. D., "MAC/FAC: A Model of Similarity-Based Retrieval," *Proc. Thirteenth Annual Conference of The Cognitive Science Society*, 1991, 504–509.

Gentner, D. and Gentner, D. R., "Flowing Waters or Teeming Crowds: Mental Models of Electricity," in Gentner, D. and Stevens, A. L. (eds.), *Mental Models*, Lawrence Erlbaum Associates, 1983, 99–129.

Gentner, D. and Stevens, A. L. (eds.), *Mental Models*, Lawrence Erlbaum Associates, 1983.

Grice, H. P., "Logic and Conversation," in Cole, P. and Morgan, J. L. (eds.) *Syntax and Semantics, Volume 3: Speech Acts*, Academic Press, 1975, 41–58.

Grolier Inc., *The Encyclopedia Americana*, International Edition, 1989.

Grosz, B. J., "The Representation and Use of Focus in a System for Understanding Dialogs," *Proc. Fifth International Joint Conference on Artificial Intelligence*, 1977, 67–76.

Gruber, T. R., "Model-Based Explanation of Design Rationale," *Proc. AAAI Workshop on Explanation*, 1990.

Hammond, K. J., "CHEF: A Model of Case-Based Planning," *Proc. AAAI Fifth National Conference on Artificial Intelligence*, 1986, 267–271.

Hanks, S. and McDermott, D., "Default Reasoning, Nonmonotonic Logics, and the Frame Problem," *Proc. AAAI Fifth National Conference on Artificial Intelligence*, 1986, 328–333.

Hayes, P. J., "The Second Naive Physics Manifesto," in Hobbs, J. R. and Moore, R. C. (eds.), *Formal Theories of the Commonsense World*, Ablex Publ. Co., 1985a, 1–36.

Hayes, P. J., "Naive Physics I: Ontology for Liquids," in Hobbs, J. R. and Moore, R. C. (eds.), *Formal Theories of the Commonsense World*, Ablex Publ. Co., 1985b, 71–107.

Heider, F. and Simmel, M., "An Experimental Study of Apparent Behavior," *American Journal of Psychology* 57, 1944, 243–259.

Hendrix, G. G., Sacerdoti, E. D., Sagalowicz, D. and Slocum, J., "Developing a Natural Language Interface to Complex Data," *ACM Transactions on Database Systems* 3:2, 1978, 105–147.

Hobbs, J. R., Stickel, M., Martin, P. and Edwards, D., "Interpretation as Abduction," *Proc. 26th Annual Meeting of the Association for Computational Linguistics*, 1988, 95–103.

Holland, J. H., Holyoak, K. J., Nisbett, R. E. and Thagard, P. R., *Induction: Processes of Inference, Learning, and Discovery*, MIT Press, 1986.

Honeck, R. P. and Hoffman, R. R. (eds.), *Cognition and Figurative Language*, Lawrence Erlbaum Associates, 1980.

Iwasaki, Y. and Simon, H. A., "Causality in Device Behavior," *Artificial Intelligence* 29:1, 1986, 3–32.

Jackendoff, R., *Semantics and Cognition*, MIT Press, 1983.

Johnson, M., *The Body in the Mind*, University of Chicago Press, 1987.

Johnson-Laird, P. N., *Mental Models*, Harvard University Press, 1983.

Kahneman, D., Slovic, P., and Tversky, A. (eds.), *Judgment Under Uncertainty: Heuristics and Biases*, Cambridge University Press, 1982.

Katz, B., "Using English for Indexing and Retrieving," A.I. Memo 1096, Artificial Intelligence Laboratory, Massachusetts Institute of Technology, 1988.

Katz, B. and Levin, B., "Exploiting Lexical Regularities in Designing Natural Language Systems," A.I. Memo 1041, Artificial Intelligence Laboratory, Massachusetts Institute of Technology, 1988.

Kintsch, W., "The Role of Knowledge in Discourse Comprehension: A Construction-Integration Model," *Psychological Review* 95:2, 1988, 163–182.

Kolodner, J. L., "Maintaining Organization in a Dynamic Long-Term Memory," *Cognitive Science* 7:4, 1983, 243–280.

Kolodner, J. L., Simpson, R. L. and Sycara-Cyranski, K., "A Process Model of Case-Based Reasoning in Problem Solving," *Proc. Ninth International Joint Conference on Artificial Intelligence,* 1985, 284–290.

Kuipers, B., "Qualitative Simulation," *Artificial Intelligence* 29:3, 1986, 289–338.

Lakoff, G. and Johnson, M., *Metaphors We Live By,* University of Chicago Press, 1980.

Larkin, J. H. and Simon, H. A., "Why a Diagram is (Sometimes) Worth Ten Thousand Words," *Cognitive Science* 11:1, 1987, 65–100.

Lee, J., *A Decision Rationale Management System: Capturing, Reusing, and Managing the Reasons for Decisions,* Ph.D. Dissertation, Department of Electrical Engineering and Computer Science, Massachusetts Institute of Technology, 1992.

Leech, G. and Svartvik, J., *A Communicative Grammar of English,* Longman, 1975.

Lehnert, W. G., "Knowledge-based Natural Language Understanding," in Shrobe, H. E. (ed.), *Exploring Artificial Intelligence,* Morgan Kaufmann, 1988, 83–131.

Lehnert, W. G. and Loiselle, C. L., "An Introduction to Plot Units," in Waltz, D. (ed.), *Semantic Structures: Advances in Natural Language Processing,* Lawrence Erlbaum Associates, 1989, 125–165.

Lenat, D. B., "Automated Theory Formation in Mathematics," *Proc. Fifth International Joint Conference on Artificial Intelligence,* 1977, 833–842.

Lenat, D., Prakash, M. and Shepherd, M., "CYC: Using Common Sense Knowledge to Overcome Brittleness and Knowledge Acquisition Bottlenecks," *AI Magazine* 6:4, 1986, 65–85.

Lenat, D. B. and Feigenbaum, E. A., "On the Thresholds of Knowledge," *Proc. Tenth International Joint Conference on Artificial Intelligence,* 1987, 1173–1182.

Leslie, A. M. and Keeble, S., "Do Six-Month-Old Infants Perceive Causality?" *Cognition* 25, 1987, 265–288.

Levin, B. (ed.), *Lexical Semantics in Review,* Lexicon Project Working Paper 1, Center for Cognitive Science, Massachusetts Institute of Technology, 1985.

Macaulay, D., *The Way Things Work,* Houghton Mifflin, 1988.

McCloskey, M., "Naive Theories of Motion," in Gentner, D. and Stevens, A. L. (eds.), *Mental Models,* Lawrence Erlbaum Associates, 1983, 299–324.

McDermott, D., "A Temporal Logic for Reasoning about Processes and Plans," *Cognitive Science* 6:2, 1982, 101–155.

McDermott, D. V., *A Critique of Pure Reason,* Technical Report, YALEU/CSD/RR #480, Yale University, 1986.

Michotte, A., *The Perception of Causality,* Translated by T. and E. Miles from French edition, 1946, Methuen, London, 1963.

Miller, G. A. and Johnson-Laird, P. N., *Language and Perception,* Harvard University Press, 1976.

Minsky, M., *The Society of Mind,* Simon and Schuster, 1986.

Mitchell, T. M., Keller, R. M. and Kedar-Cabelli, S. T., "Explanation-Based Generalization: A Unifying View," *Machine Learning* 1:1, 1986, 47–80.

Morgenstern, L. and Stein, L. A., "Why Things Go Wrong: a Formal Theory of Causal Reasoning," *Proc. AAAI Seventh National Conference on Artificial Intelligence,* 1988, 518–523.

Narayanan, N. H. and Chandrasekaran, B., "Reasoning Visually about Spatial Interactions," *Proc. Twelfth International Joint Conference on Artificial Intelligence,* 1991, 360–365.

Nayak, P. P., Joskowicz, L. and Addanki, S., "Automated Model Selection Using Context-Dependent Behaviors," *Proc. AAAI Tenth National Conference on Artificial Intelligence,* 1992, 710–716.

Newtson, D. and Engquist, G., "The Perceptual Organization of Ongoing Behavior," *Journal of Experimental Social Psychology* 12, 1976, 436–450.

Newtson, D., Engquist, G. and Bois, J., "The Objective Basis of Behavior Units," *Journal of Personality and Social Psychology* 35:12, 1977, 847–862.

Norvig, P., "Marker Passing as a Weak Method for Text Inferencing," *Cognitive Science* 13:4, 1989, 569–620.

Novak, G. S., "Representations of Knowledge in a Program for Solving Physics Problems," *Proc. Fifth International Joint Conference on Artificial Intelligence,* 1977, 286–291.

Patil, R. S., Szolovits, P. and Schwartz, W. B., "Causal Understanding of Patient Illness in Medical Diagnosis," *Proc. Seventh International Joint Conference on Artificial Intelligence,* 1981, 893–899.

Patil, R. S., "Artificial Intelligence Techniques for Diagnostic Reasoning in Medicine," in Shrobe, H. E. (ed.), *Exploring Artificial Intelligence,* Morgan Kaufmann, 1988, 347–379.

Pearl, J. and Verma, T. S., "A Theory of Inferred Causation," *Proc. Second International Conference on Principles of Knowledge Representation and Reasoning,* 1991, 441–452.

Piaget, J. and Inhelder, B., *The Psychology of the Child,* Basic Books, 1969.

Pollack, M. E. and Pereira, F. C. N., "An Integrated Framework for Semantic and Pragmatic Interpretation," *Proc. 26th Annual Meeting of the Association for Computational Linguistics,* 1988, 75–86.

Pople, H. E., "On the Mechanization of Abductive Logic," *Proc. Third International Joint Conference on Artificial Intelligence,* 1973, 147–152.

Quillian, M. R., "The Teachable Language Comprehender: A Simulation Program and Theory of Language," *Communications of the ACM* 12:8, 1969, 459–476.

Rao, S., *Knowledge Repair,* Master's Thesis, Department of Electrical Engineering and Computer Science, Massachusetts Institute of Technology, 1991.

Rieger, C., "An Organization of Knowledge for Problem Solving and Language Comprehension," *Artificial Intelligence* 7:2, 1976, 89–127.

Reiter, R., "Nonmonotonic Reasoning," in Shrobe, H. E. (ed.), *Exploring Artificial Intelligence,* Morgan Kaufmann, 1988, 439–481.

Ruecker, L., *mSIBYL: A Design Documentation and Management System*, Master's Thesis, Department of Electrical Engineering and Computer Science and Department of Mechanical Engineering, Massachusetts Institute of Technology, 1992.

Russell, S. J., "A Quantitative Analysis of Analogy by Similarity," *Proc. AAAI Fifth National Conference on Artificial Intelligence*, 1986, 284–288.

Schank, R. C. and Riesbeck, C. K., *Inside Computer Understanding*, Lawrence Erlbaum Associates, 1981.

Schmolze, J. G., "Physics for Robots," *Proc. AAAI Fifth National Conference on Artificial Intelligence*, 1986, 44–50.

Schubert, L. K. and Hwang, C. H., "An Episodic Knowledge Representation for Narrative Texts," *Proc. First International Conference on Principles of Knowledge Representation and Reasoning*, 1989, 444–458.

Sembugamoorthy, V. and Chandrasekaran, B., "Functional Representation of Devices and Compilation of Diagnostic Problem-Solving Systems," in Kolodner, J. and Riesbeck, C. (eds.), *Experience, Memory, and Reasoning*, Lawrence Erlbaum Associates, 1986, 47–73.

Shoham, Y., "Chronological Ignorance: Time, Nonmonotonicity, Necessity and Causal Theories," *Proc. AAAI Fifth National Conference on Artificial Intelligence*, 1986, 389–393.

Shoham, Y. and Goyal, N., "Temporal Reasoning in Artificial Intelligence," in Shrobe, H. E. (ed.), *Exploring Artificial Intelligence*, Morgan Kaufmann, 1988, 419–438.

Shultz, T. R., "Rules of Causal Attribution," *Monographs of the Society for Research in Child Development* 47:1, No. 194, 1982.

Siskind, J. M., "Acquiring Core Meanings of Words, Represented as Jackendoff-Style Conceptual Structures, from Correlated Streams of Linguistic and Non-Linguistic Input," *Proc. 28th Annual Meeting of the Association for Computational Linguistics*, 1990, 143–156.

Siskind, J. M., *Naive Physics, Event Perception, Lexical Semantics, and Language Acquisition*, Ph.D. Dissertation, Department of Electrical Engineering and Computer Science, Massachusetts Institute of Technology, 1992.

Stanfill, C. and Waltz, D., "Toward Memory-Based Reasoning," *Communications of the ACM* 29:12, 1986, 1213–1228.

Szolovits, P. and Pauker, S. G., "Categorical and Probabilistic Reasoning in Medical Diagnosis," *Artificial Intelligence* 11, 1978, 115–144.

Talmy, L., "Force Dynamics in Language and Cognition," *Cognitive Science* 12:1, 1988, 49–100.

van Riemsdijk, H. and Williams, E., *Introduction to the Theory of Grammar*, MIT Press, 1986.

Vere, S. and Bickmore, T., "A Basic Agent," *Computational Intelligence* 6:1, 1990, 41–60.

Vilain, M. B., "A System for Reasoning about Time," *Proc. AAAI Second National Conference on Artificial Intelligence*, 1982, 197–201.

Vilain, M. and Kautz, H., "Constraint Propagation Algorithms for Temporal Reasoning," *Proc. AAAI Fifth National Conference on Artificial Intelligence*, 1986, 377–382.

Waltz, D. L., "On the Interdependence of Language and Perception," *Proc. Theoretical Issues in Natural Language Processing-2*, Association for Computing Machinery, 1978, 149–156.

Waltz, D. L., "Event Shape Diagrams," *Proc. AAAI Second National Conference on Artificial Intelligence*, 1982, 84–87.

Waltz, D. L. and Pollack, J. B., "Massively Parallel Parsing: A Strongly Interactive Model of Natural Language Interpretation," *Cognitive Science* 9:1, 1985, 51–74.

Webber, B. L., "Event Reference," *Proc. Theoretical Issues in Natural Language Processing-3*, Association for Computational Linguistics, 1987, 158–163.

Weld, D. S., "Comparative Analysis," *Artificial Intelligence* 36:3, 1988, 333–373.

Weld, D. S., "Exaggeration," *Artificial Intelligence* 43:3, 1990, 311–368.

White, P. A., "Causal Processing: Origins and Development," *Psychological Bulletin* 104:1, 1988, 36–52.

Wilensky, R., Arens, Y., and Chin, D., "Talking to UNIX in English: An Overview of UC," *Communications of the ACM* 27:6, 1984, 574–593.

Wilks, Y., "What Sort of Taxonomy of Causation Do We Need for Language Understanding?," *Cognitive Science* 1:3, 1977, 235–264.

Winston, P. H., "Learning New Principles from Precedents and Exercises," *Artificial Intelligence* 19:3, 1982, 321–350.

Winston, P. H. and Rao, S., "Repairing Learned Knowledge Using Experience," in Winston, P. H. and Shellard, S. A. (eds.), *Artificial Intelligence at MIT: Expanding Frontiers,* MIT Press, 1990.

Wiser, M. and Carey, S., "When Heat and Temperature Were One," in Gentner, D. and Stevens, A. L. (eds.), *Mental Models,* Lawrence Erlbaum Associates, 1983, 267–297.

Woolf, B., "Intelligent Tutoring Systems: A Survey," in Shrobe, H. E. (ed.), *Exploring Artificial Intelligence,* Morgan Kaufmann, 1988, 297–346.

Index

A

Abstraction, 18, 131, 235, 273–274
"Active" traces, 86, 103, 251
Allen, J. F., 216
Alterman, R., 223
Analogy, 19, 131, 218, 235, 272–273
APPEAR, 11–12, 55–56, 69, 252
Artificial intelligence in medicine, 216
Association; *see* Complete association
Association structure, 16, 24, 72, 131, 134, 173, 251, 253, 256
Association type, 20, 32
Assumption, 106, 123–125, 264
Attribute, 10–11, 13, 18, 21, 43–44, 49, 52, 56, 65, 71, 100–101, 131
Attribute composition transformation, 21, 131, 151–153, 267–268
Attribute-object reification transformation, 21, 131, 154, 156–160, 268–269

B

Background statement, 18, 22, 41, 44, 104–105, 117–122, 263
Batali, J. D., 221
Bickmore, T., 221
Borchardt, G. C., 220
Brown, G., 229
Brown, J. S., 51, 213, 217
Bullock, M., 226
Bylander, T., 215

C

Caine, M. E., 240
Carbonell, J. G., 218
Case-based reasoning, 218
Causal description, 1, 22, 35–41
Causal modeling, 5, 217, 233
Causal reasoning, 5, 219, 233
Causal reconstruction, 1–2, 5–9, 22, 35–48, 233–234, 236
Causality, 50–51
Chandrasekaran, B., 215, 240
Change, 9–13, 50–51, 55–56, 63–65, 69, 234, 252
Change characterization, 11–12, 55–57
Clement, J., 227
Collaborative diagnosis/prediction systems, 4, 249
Collins, A. M., 223

Complete association, 16–17, 32; *see also* Complete chaining association, Equivalence association, etc.
Complete chaining association, 20, 32, 84, 104, 135
Complete chaining match, 16
Complete match, 15; *see also* Complete chaining match, Complete restatement match
Complete restatement match, 16
Composite trace, 29, 80–81
Composition association, 32, 132, 135
Conceptual dependency, 222
Connecting statement, 8–9, 21–22, 24–25, 41, 45, 169–182, 253–254, 270–274
Consolidation, 215
CYC project, the, 214–215

D

Davis, R., 214
de Kleer, J., 51, 213, 217
DECREASE, 11–12, 56, 69, 252
DeJong, G., 218
DISAPPEAR, 11–12, 55–56, 69, 252
Discourse analysis, 229
diSessa, A. A., 227
Doyle, J., 217
Doyle, R. J., 217
Dyer, M. G., 221–222

E

EDISON program, the, 221
Elaboration, 16–18, 23–24, 251, 253, 257
Encyclopedia Americana, The, 2, 185
Episodic logic, 221
EQUAL, 11, 18, 53–54
Equivalence association, 32, 84, 104, 132, 135
Equivalence transformation, 16, 20, 130, 136–137, 264–265
Event, 11–13, 21, 40, 51, 58–62, 66–67, 131, 251
Event calculus, 220
Event definition, 22, 41, 45
Event level, 37, 46, 234
Event reference, 7, 22, 40–41, 44
Event shape diagrams, 219–220
Event trace, 12–13, 16, 58–62, 66–67
Event-attribute reification transformation, 21, 131, 160–162, 269–270

Event-object reification transformation, 21, 131, 162–167, 270
EXCEED, 55
Explanation-based learning, 218
Exploratory transformation, 18–20, 22–24, 127–167, 173, 239, 251–252, 256; *see also* Substitution transformation, Interval composition transformation, etc.

F

Falkenhainer, B., 218
Faltings, B., 240
Feigenbaum, E. A., 215
Fikes, R. E., 82
Fillmore, C. J., 8
Forbus, K. D., 51, 213
Force dynamics, 229
Functional representation, 215

G

Gardner, H., 228
Generalization association, 32, 132, 135
Generalization transformation, 20, 131, 147–149, 267
Genesereth, M. R., 156
Gentner, D., 218, 227
Gentner, D. R., 227
Goyal, N., 216
GREATER, 11, 18, 53–54
Grice, H. P., 6, 9, 35, 38, 122, 230, 234
Grosz, B. J., 222
Gruber, T. R., 214

H

Hammond, K. J., 218
Hamscher, W., 214
Hanks, S., 216
Hayes, P. J., 214
Heider, F., 225
Hendrix, G. G., 44
Hobbs, J. R., 221
Hwang, C. H., 221
Hypothesized object, 24–25, 71–72, 134, 173, 253, 260

I

INCREASE, 11–12, 56, 69, 252
Inference, 18, 22, 24, 99–104, 106–117, 171, 237, 251, 253, 256, 261–262

Inference association, 32, 104, 135
Inference transformation, 20
Information-preserving transformation, 15–16, 19–20, 130–131, 136–146; *see also* Equivalence transformation, Substitution transformation, Interchange transformation
Intelligent service directories, 4, 243–244
Intelligent technical manuals, 4, 244–245
Intelligent tutoring systems, 221
Interchange transformation, 146
Interval composition transformation, 21, 131, 149–151, 267
Iwasaki, Y., 217

J

Jackendoff, R., 228–229, 231
Johnson, M., 230
Johnson-Laird, P. N., 10, 49–50, 224, 227

K

Kahneman, D., 227
Katz, B., 221
Kautz, H., 216
Keeble, S., 50, 226
Knowledge acquisition facilities, 4, 242
Kolodner, J. L., 218, 222
Kuipers, B., 51, 213

L

Lakoff, G., 230
Lee, J., 247
Leech, G., 228
Lehnert, W. G., 222
Lenat, D. B., 23, 214–215
Leslie, A. M., 50, 226
Levin, B., 221, 229
Loftus, E. F., 223
Loiselle, C. L., 222

M

Match; *see* Complete match, Partial match
MATCH, 54
McCloskey, M., 227
McDermott, D. V., 216
Memory-based reasoning, 218
Mental models, 227
Metaphor, 19, 230, 235

Michotte, A., 50, 225–226
Miller, G. A., 10, 49–50, 224
Mitchell, T. M., 218
Model-based reasoning, 214
Mooney, R., 218
Morgenstern, L., 217

N

Naive physics, 214
Narayanan, N. H., 240
Natural language semantics, 228–229
Natural language understanding, 219–224
Nayak, P. P., 214
Newtson, D., 50, 226
Nilsson, N. J., 82, 156
Non-information-preserving transformation, 15–16, 19–20, 130–131, 147–167; see also Inference transformation, Generalization transformation, etc.
Non-monotonic logic, 216
Norvig, P., 223
NOT-APPEAR, 11–12, 55–56
NOT-CHANGE, 11–12, 56
NOT-DECREASE, 11–12, 56
NOT-DISAPPEAR, 11–12, 55–56
NOT-EQUAL, 11, 18, 53–54
NOT-EXCEED, 55
NOT-GREATER, 11, 18, 53–54
NOT-INCREASE, 11–12, 56
NOT-MATCH, 55
NOT-PRESENT, 54
"null," 53–55, 105

O

Object, 11, 13, 21, 25, 43–44, 49, 52–53, 71, 131, 253
Object composition transformation, 19, 21, 131, 153–155, 268
Object level, 36–37, 46, 233

P

Partial association, 15
Partial chaining match, 15, 24, 69–70, 72, 134, 173, 251–253, 259–260
Partial match, 2, 9, 14–18, 23–25, 69–73, 251–252, 254; see also Partial chaining match, Partial restatement match
Partial restatement match, 15, 24, 69–70, 72, 134, 173, 251, 253, 259–260

PATHFINDER, 2, 22–32, 39–48, 69–73, 80–90, 99–106, 127–135, 169–173, 233, 235–236, 254–258
PATHFINDER agenda, 23–24, 256
PATHFINDER heuristics, 18, 21, 24–25, 71–72, 134, 236, 251–254
PATHFINDER input grammar, 41–43, 62–67, 234
Patil, R. S., 216
Pauker, S. G., 216
Pearl, J., 217
Perceptual psychology, 49–50, 224–226
Plot units, 222
Precedent event, 22, 24, 41, 72, 91–96, 134, 173, 251–252, 260
Predicate, 11, 53, 99–100; see also EQUAL, APPEAR, etc.
PRESENT, 54

Q

Qualitative physics, 51, 213
Question answering, 1–3, 6, 23, 25, 29, 31–32, 36–37, 46–48, 80–90, 135, 257
Quillian, M. R., 223

R

Reasoning about time, 216
Reduction association, 32, 84, 104, 135
Reduction transformation, 16, 20
Reference standard, 43–44, 53, 71
Reification association, 32, 132, 135
Rieger, C., 219
Riesbeck, C. K., 222
Ruecker, L., 247
Rule of inference, 22, 41, 45
Rule of restatement, 22, 41, 45, 128, 132

S

Schank, R. C., 222
Schubert, L. K., 221
Semantic grammar, 41
Sembugamoorthy, V., 215
Shoham, Y., 216–217
Shultz, T. R., 226
Simmel, M., 225
Simon, H. A., 217
Siskind, J. M., 220
Speculative causal reasoning systems, 4, 247–248
Spreading activation, 223–224

Stanfill, C., 218
START system, the, 221
Stein, L. A., 217
Stevens, A. L., 227
STRIPS assumption, 82
Substitution association, 32, 132, 135
Substitution transformation, 19–20, 92, 130, 138–146, 265–266
Supplementary information, 22, 33, 45; see also Event definition, Rule of inference, etc.
Svartvik, J., 228
Szolovits, P., 216

T

Talmy, L., 228–229, 231
Technical design documentation systems, 4, 245–247
"the-background," 13, 53
Time point, 11, 13, 21, 49, 53, 71, 131
Transformation, 15–20; see also Exploratory transformation, Information-preserving transformation, Non-information-preserving transformation
Transition, 2, 9–13, 16, 24, 51, 57–58, 61–62, 72, 134, 173
Transition space, 2, 9–21, 49–67, 233–235
Tuple, 11, 54
Tversky, A., 227

U

UC system, the, 221

V

van Riemsdijk, H., 8, 228
Vere, S., 221
Verma, T. S., 217
Vilain, M. B., 216

W

Waltz, D. L., 218–219
Wellman, M. P., 217
White, P. A., 50, 226
Wilensky, R., 221
Wilks, Y., 219
Williams, E., 8, 228
Winston, P. H., 218
Woolf, B., 221

Y

Yule, G., 229

Artificial Intelligence (selected titles)

Patrick Henry Winston, founding editor
J. Michael Brady, Daniel G. Bobrow, and Randall Davis, current editors

Artificial Intelligence: An MIT Perspective, Volumes I and II, edited by Patrick Henry Winston and Richard Henry Brown, 1979

NETL: A System for Representing and Using Real-World Knowledge, Scott Fahlman, 1979

The Interpretation of Visual Motion, Shimon Ullman, 1979

Turtle Geometry: The Computer as a Medium for Exploring Mathematics, Harold Abelson and Andrea di Sessa, 1981

Robot Manipulators: Mathematics, Programming, and Control, Richard P. Paul, 1981

Computational Models of Discourse, edited by Michael Brady and Robert C. Berwick, 1982

Robot Motion: Planning and Control, edited by Michael Brady, John M. Hollerbach, Timothy Johnson, Tomás Lozano-Pérez, and Matthew T. Mason, 1982

Robot Hands and the Mechanics of Manipulation, Matthew T. Mason and J. Kenneth Salisbury, Jr., 1985

The Acquisition of Syntactic Knowledge, Robert C. Berwick, 1985

The Connection Machine, W. Daniel Hillis, 1985

Legged Robots that Balance, Marc H. Raibert, 1986

ACTORS: A Model of Concurrent Computation in Distributed Systems, Gul A. Agha, 1986

Knowledge-Based Tutoring: The GUIDON Program, William Clancey, 1987

AI in the 1980s and Beyond: An MIT Survey, edited by W. Eric L. Grimson and Ramesh S. Patil, 1987

Visual Reconstruction, Andrew Blake and Andrew Zisserman, 1987

Reasoning about Change: Time and Causation from the Standpoint of Artificial Intelligence, Yoav Shoham, 1988

Model-Based Control of a Robot Manipulator, Chae H. An, Christopher G. Atkeson, and John M. Hollerbach, 1988

A Robot Ping-Pong Player: Experiment in Real-Time Intelligent Control, Russell L. Andersson, 1988

The Paralation Model: Architecture-Independent Parallel Programming, Gary Sabot, 1988

Automated Deduction in Nonclassical Logics: Efficient Matrix Proof Methods for Modal and Intuitionistic Logics, Lincoln Wallen, 1989

Shape from Shading, edited by Berthold K.P. Horn and Michael J. Brooks, 1989

Ontic: A Knowledge Representation System for Mathematics, David A. McAllester, 1989

Solid Shape, Jan J. Koenderink, 1990

Theories of Comparative Analysis, Daniel S. Weld, 1990

Artificial Intelligence at MIT: Expanding Frontiers, edited by Patrick Henry Winston and Sarah Alexandra Shellard, 1990

Vector Models for Data-Parallel Computing, Guy E. Blelloch, 1990

Experiments in the Machine Interpretation of Visual Motion, David W. Murray and Bernard F. Buxton, 1990

Object Recognition by Computer: The Role of Geometric Constraints, W. Eric L. Grimson, 1990

Representing and Reasoning with Probabilistic Knowledge: A Logical Approach to Probabilities, Fahiem Bacchus, 1990

3D Model Recognition from Stereoscopic Cues, edited by John E.W. Mayhew and John P. Frisby, 1991

Artificial Vision for Mobile Robots: Stereo Vision and Multisensory Perception, Nicholas Ayache, 1991

Truth and Modality for Knowledge Representation, Raymond Turner, 1991

Made-Up Minds: A Constructivist Approach to Artificial Intelligence, Gary L. Drescher, 1991

Vision, Instruction, and Action, David Chapman, 1991

Do the Right Thing: Studies in Limited Rationality, Stuart Russell and Eric Wefald, 1991

KAM: A System for Intelligently Guiding Numerical Experimentation by Computer, Kenneth Man-Kam Yip, 1991

Solving Geometric Constraint Systems: A Case Study in Kinematics, Glenn A. Kramer, 1992

Geometric Invariants in Computer Vision, edited by Joseph Mundy and Andrew Zisserman, 1992

HANDEY: A Robot Task Planner, Tomás Lozano-Pérez, Joseph L. Jones, Emmanuel Mazer, and Patrick A. O'Donnell, 1992

Active Vision, edited by Andrew Blake and Alan Yuille, 1992

Recent Advances in Qualitative Physics, edited by Boi Faltings and Peter Struss, 1992

Machine Translation: A View from the Lexicon, Bonnie Jean Dorr, 1993

The Language Complexity Game, Eric Sven Ristad, 1993

The Soar Papers: Research on Integrated Intelligence, edited by Paul S. Rosenbloom, John E. Laird, and Allen Newell, 1993

Three-Dimensional Computer Vision: A Geometric Viewpoint, Olivier Faugeras, 1993

Contemplating Minds: A Forum for Artificial Intelligence, edited by William J. Clancey, Stephen W. Smoliar, and Mark J. Stefik, 1994

Thinking between the Lines: Computers and the Comprehension of Causal Descriptions, Gary C. Borchardt, 1994